In the Eye of the Great Depression

■

In the Eye of the
Great Depression

New Deal Reporters and the Agony
of the American People

John F. Bauman

■

Thomas H. Coode

NORTHERN ILLINOIS UNIVERSITY PRESS

DeKalb 1988

© 1988 by Northern Illinois University Press
Published by the Northern Illinois University Press, DeKalb, Illinois   60115

Design by Julia Fauci

Library of Congress Cataloging-in-Publication Data

Bauman, John F., 1938–
    In the eye of the Great Depression.

    Bibliography: p.
    Includes index.
    1. New Deal, 1933–1939. 2. United States—Economic
conditions—1933–1945. 3. Depressions—1929–   —
United States. 4. United States—Social conditions—
1918–1945. 5. Reporters and reporting—United States—
History—20th century. I. Coode, Thomas H., 1931–
II. Title.
E806.B36 1988   973.917   88–5151

ISBN 0–87580–541–8 (pbk.)
5 4 3 2

For Cindy and Scott; and for Marty, Mary John,
Kelly, Saundy, Leigh Ellen, and Stevie

Contents

Acknowledgments

■ Like the authors of any scholarly work, the authors of this book owe an enormous debt to a countless number of people. Unfortunately, it is possible to recognize only a select few here. As in so many other endeavors, we are beholden especially to several mentors over the course of our academic and professional careers: the late J. Joseph Huthmacher and the late Warren G. Susman of Rutgers University; Robert E. Corlew of Middle Tennessee State University; Horace Montgomery of the University of Georgia; and Willard Gatewood of the University of Arkansas.

In the several years since this volume was conceived, the authors have become increasingly indebted to a considerable number of other generous friends and colleagues for their support in helping to bring the project to fruition. First of all, we are indebted to those scholars whose works in history and the social sciences have contributed both directly and tangentially to this book. They are recognized in the volume's note section as well as in the essay on the Sources. Others whose advice and encouragement proved useful in the development of this book include Michael Weber and John Bodnar. William Trimble and Edward Muller read earlier versions of the manuscript and improved it considerably.

The authors, as always, owe a debt to California University of Pennsylvania, where both teach. The staff of the school's Manderino Library graciously offered useful and helpful assistance; California University's Irene O'Brien Fund covered some typing and other costs; and the university's Faculty Research Committee and Council of Deans provided to the authors preferred class schedules and other amenities.

Professionals at other libraries and archives also shared with us their time and expertise. The staff of the Franklin D. Roosevelt Library, especially Mark Renovitch, offered advice and made materials available to us. At the National Archives, Robert Kvasnecki provided crucial assistance in our search among the Records of the Federal Emergency Relief Administration, not only in helping ferret out the scanty biographical information about the reporters available there but also in uncovering evidence of Harry Hopkins's other statistical and social data-gathering ventures.

At the Library of Congress, Frederick W. Bauman was, as usual, very helpful in locating biographical data on the reporters. Staff members of the Library of Congress Photographic Archives graciously helped the authors discover photographs of Depression America. Frank Kurtik, archivist at the University of Pittsburgh's Archives of Industrial Society, provided photos of the Great Depression in Pittsburgh, and the staff of the University of Pittsburgh's Hillman Library also aided the authors in the book's preparation.

The authors are grateful also to Ann DeVito, whose careful editing purged the manuscript of many early errors, and to Mary Elizabeth Martin Coode for her usual typing and editorial expertise.

We are also indebted to the staff of the Northern Illinois University Press. It was the press's director, Mary Livingston Lincoln, who offered the words of encouragement that provided the final momentum to complete the book. Barbara Berg and Susan Bean kindly and professionally sheparded the manuscript into production.

Finally, both authors must acknowledge the long and ongoing debt each owe their families. Their wives, Barbara and Liz, have always shown both an interest in and a devotion to their scholarly and other interests, as have their wonderful children to whom this book is affectionately dedicated.

In the Eye of the Great Depression

■

The Dimensions of the Depression and the Quest for Data

■ In the fall of 1933 the recently appointed director of the Federal Emergency Relief Administration (FERA), Harry Hopkins, launched a grass-roots inquiry into the condition and mood of depression-wracked America. From Washington, D.C., Hopkins dispatched a corps of sixteen reporters who were charged with investigating the enormity of the country's welfare problem and the effectiveness of the nation's local relief structure. His chief investigator was Lorena Hickok, a veteran journalist and confidante of Eleanor Roosevelt. Hopkins instructed Hickok "to go out around the country and look this thing over. I don't want statistics from you. I don't want the social-worker angle. I just want your own reactions, as an ordinary citizen. Go talk with preachers and teachers, businessmen, workers, farmers. Go talk with the unemployed, those who are on relief and those who aren't; and when you talk with them don't ever forget that but for the grace of God, you, I, and any of our friends might be in their shoes. Tell me what you see and hear. All of it. Don't ever pull your punches." [1]

Hickok and her colleagues traveled the length and breadth of America. Their reports to Hopkins comprise an extraordinarily rich and graphic portrait of the nation during the Great Depression. In fact, Arthur Schlesinger Jr. has quoted President Franklin Delano Roosevelt that Hopkins's epistolary venture produced "the best history of the Depression." [2]

According to Warren Susman in his *Culture as History*, during the 1920s Americans had revelled in their role of advancing modern civilization. That is, they self-consciously viewed themselves as participants in the growth and communication of knowledge which they saw as the sum of human technology, science, institutional development, and material achievement.

However, by the 1930s, reeling from the Great Depression, Americans now saw civilization as the enemy. In their search for meaning in the disastrous economic collapse and the social ravages accompanying it, writers, artists, and social scientists turned to the study of culture, looking among the people themselves for common patterns of belief, values, ways of doing things, and lifestyles. In contrast to materially oriented civilization, culture, they believed, imparted meaning, quality, and a normative foundation to society and collectively made up the American way of life.

Significantly, Hopkins's reporting project can be seen as part of this quest of American writers, artists, scholars, and social scientists to define every aspect of American life; to, in Susman's words, "document in art, reportage, social science, and history the life and values of the American people."

This quest produced both a new romanticization of bygone ways of life such as Margaret Mitchell's *Gone With the Wind* (1936) and social novels such as John Steinbeck's classic *The Grapes of Wrath* (1939) and the creative exposition of the plight of Southern sharecropper families found in James Agee and Walker Evans's classic, *Let Us Now Praise Famous Men* (1941). The quest also generated a voluminous outpouring of social science literature, including the reporting commissioned in 1933 and 1934 by Harry Hopkins.[3]

In this search for America's cultural identity, writers and social scientists neither rejected the past in radical fashion nor repudiated technology. Rather, the analysis of culture was both nonacrimonious and nonideological. Believing that human adaptive capacity lagged behind the pace of technological change, social scientists stressed the importance of personal adjustment to culture as it existed. Despite a generation of progressive emphasis on environmentalism, Americans still viewed success as primarily a matter of individual adjustment. Likewise, failure remained a personal matter, attributable mainly to the kind of lack of commitment most visibly seen in the lives of marginal men, people such as tramps, vagabonds, stranded miners, and other hapless people who scratched for existence in the backwash of urban-industrial society. While social scientists and other students of American culture in the 1930s seemed frightened by the size of this stranded population, they were appalled that so many of the sturdy working- and middle-class families seemed equally unable to cope with the awful calamity of the Great Depression. The writings of Hopkins's reporters, which form the basis of this book, mirrored these views.

Hopkins's reporters witnessed the agony and despair of the Great Depression captured so poignantly in James T. Farrell's trilogy, *Studs Lonigan* (1932–1935), and in Jack Conroy's biting *The Disinherited* (1933). Behind the horror of the nation's faceless mass misery, loomed equally horrifying facts. During the year 1932, net income plummeted from $90 to $42 billion. Four months before the New Deal began, *Business Week* found over 15,000,000 unemployed, or about 31 percent of those normally occupied. The magazine revealed 17 percent jobless in agriculture, 45 percent unemployed in the extractive industries, 46 percent in manufacturing, 10 percent in public service, over 10 percent in the professions, and 35 percent out of work in the domestic and personal services.[4]

Operations in America's key industries sputtered to near halt. Seventy percent of the nation's coal miners were idle, and the industry journal *Iron Age* reported in 1932 that steel plants were operating at only 12 percent of capacity. United States Steel's 1929 payroll of 225,000 full-time workers fell to almost zero in early 1933. For the thousands who retained their jobs, starvation wages often prevailed. Garment workers toiled for abysmal pay. Employees in Baltimore clothing firms averaged eight dollars for a forty-hour week. *Scribner's* reported in March 1933 that throughout the East, females in the garment trades earned less than five dollars a week. Some women garment workers in Massachusetts labored for five or six cents an hour. The highest paid employees earned only seven dollars for a forty-eight-hour week. Half the women employed in Pennsylvania earned fewer than seven dollars a week; 20 percent earned under five.[5]

The nation's farmers were virtually bankrupt. Farm prices declined 61 percent from 1929 to 1933, while total farm income plunged from $13 billion to $5.5 billion. One observer wrote that "it [was] almost impossible to describe the distress that [existed] among farmers." Wheat prices fell to the lowest level of the century, while the tax burden on wheat farmers had doubled since World War I.

In the Great Plains, bread lines snaked past grain elevators bulging with wheat. Wheat priced too low to move was piled high along railroad tracks. Montana wheat, which had been $100.00 a bushel in 1920, sold for only $19.23 in 1932. Thousands of farmers jammed the relief rolls in the Dakotas, Nebraska, and Oklahoma. Once rich agricultural states like Iowa groaned under the weight of mortgage debt. Sixty-five percent of the state's 214,000 farmers were precariously overmortgaged. In 1932, 60 percent of the North Dakota's farms were dispossessed by mortgage and tax sales. On one April day in 1932, a fourth of rural Mississippi was auctioned on the block. Farm foreclosures in America were so numerous that Metropolitan Life Insurance Company organized a special farm department to handle them.[6]

In urban America, city after city faced bankruptcy. The relief burden was overwhelming, the tax base too narrow, and both individual and corporate losses due to bank closings were ruinous. In New York City a future New Dealer, Rexford Tugwell, pondered whether modern times had ever witnessed so much distress just from sheer hunger and cold. City public health nurses found thousands of children famished. True, most of the apple vendors had disappeared from the city street corners by late 1932; hapless and dispirited, they crowded the bread lines and soup kitchens instead.[7]

In the South, where rural poverty had always been widespread, the Great Depression merely made matters worse. By Roosevelt's inauguration in 1933 the South had one-third of the nation's population, yet only one-fifth of its wealth, 20 percent of its wages; 27 percent of the country's property value, but only 14 percent of its bank deposits. With much of the nation's mineral wealth and hydroelectric potential untouched, the rural South had more farms than any other region, but the average acreage per farm was the smallest of any section.

Long mired in economic doldrums, southern farmers suffered further losses with the depression. In 1929, cotton returned $1.25 billion; three years later it was $374,000,000. In two years the drop was 62 percent. In 1932, forced farm sales throughout the country were 46 per thousand; North Carolina counted 68.2 per thousand; and in Mississippi, foreclosures hit an unbelievable 99.0 per thousand. By early 1933, sixty thousand farmers had lost their land. Farm cash income in Louisiana fell from $170,000,000 in 1929 to $59,000,000 in 1932, a decline of 65 percent.[8]

With rural poverty so pervasive, thousands of southerners fled to nearby cities looking for work. However, for the South's unemployed, rural as well as urban, there were no alternative occupations, only inadequate relief. Even the old category known as "Negro jobs" virtually ceased to exist as southern whites now flocked to these positions. Nor did the depression in the South spare the fortunate who had jobs, for wages steadily declined. By 1932, industrial labor in the South earned sixteen cents an hour less than the national average. Per capita income in Louisiana in 1933 was only $222 a year, less than half of what it had been four years earlier.[9]

Outside the South, in industrial states like Pennsylvania, the value of industrial products plummeted from over $8 million in 1929 to under $3 million in 1932. Wages dropped to less than half in the same years. The state's Department of Welfare estimated that one-third of the Commonwealth's people were entirely without income. At U.S. Steel's huge Homestead plant near Pittsburgh, only 424 workers were employed full-time in March 1932 as opposed to the average payroll of 5,235 three years earlier. Meanwhile, in the small mill town of Donora, only 277 people out of the town's 14,000 population had jobs in 1932.

It was no better in the Middle West where in 1933 some Ohio counties had over 70 percent of their population on the welfare rolls. In that year, almost 700,000 Ohioans were unemployed—about 37 percent of the state's normal working force.

Visitors to West Virginia and Kentucky coal counties described appalling conditions. One European visitor to Kentucky wrote: "Of all the desolate, god-forsaken spots I have ever known, American mining camps are certainly the worst. . . . Such abject poverty must be seen to be believed." Kentucky and West Virginia mining families burned furniture to keep warm, ate dandelions and blueberries, and, often evicted from their rented hovels, spent winters shivering in grimy tents.[10]

Even the awesome splendor of the Rocky Mountains failed to disperse the pall of depression. In Colorado, per capita income by 1933 had fallen by one-third, and one-sixth of the state's working force was idle. Employment in Montana's mining and smelting industries declined by 60 percent from 1929 to 1933. Failures in New Mexico copper and coal mines drove down the assessed value of mineral production from a high of $37,000,000 in the mid-1920s to about $20,000,000 in 1932. Moreover, the value of New Mexico's agricultural crops stood at $9.5 million in 1932, down from $40 million several years earlier.

Elsewhere, California's once bountiful fruit harvests wasted on the vine while many of the state's city dwellers starved. Bank failures scarred the sunshine-drenched landscape of the Sacramento Valley; formerly powerful motion picture companies declared bankruptcy or fell into receivership. Some of San Francisco's fanciest restaurants closed, and in Los Angeles people whose gas and electricity had been turned off cooked over back-yard wood fires.[11]

By March 4, 1933, the day Franklin Delano Roosevelt assumed the presidency, the nation's economy approached a standstill. Perhaps a third of the working force was unemployed, countless others worked for near starvation wages, and in many auto, rubber, steel, textile, and mining areas whole towns were virtually jobless. Corporate dividends were only a fraction of their 1929 values, and every day financial institutions foreclosed on hundreds of home mortgages; many other home owners desperately held onto their property, making 1929 payments in a 1933 economy. The suicide rate rose 25 percent in four years; more people left the United States than entered it, and at least a million migrants roamed the land, either on foot or stowed away on the undercarriages of freight trains. Thirty-eight states had closed their banks; nine million savings accounts had been lost; both the New York Stock Exchange and the Chicago Board of Trade locked their doors indefinitely.[12]

Not since the Depression of 1892 had America confronted economic conditions dire enough to wrench the fabric of American culture and force the nation to reexamine cherished values and traditional institutions. In the 1890s, mass poverty and the fears of labor anarchism helped transform philanthropy into scientific casework and caused some welfare reformers to challenge laissez-faire capitalism by demanding social legislation regulating tenement housing, child labor, and factory conditions. However, despite the severity of the Depression of 1892 and of the depths of the subsequent recessions of 1907, 1914, and 1921, it was voluntary charity rather than government that provided the first line of defense against large-scale social insecurity.

Therefore, the Roosevelt administration's decision in 1933 to launch the Federal Emergency Relief Administration (FERA) stands as a landmark in American social welfare history. The decision, which climaxed a decade of intense modernization and professionalization in the area of social welfare, inaugurated the intervention of the federal government into the world of public assistance. Fearing that the fabric of American culture was threatened by mass joblessness and the other social structural dislocations caused by technological change, progressive-minded, middle-class New Dealers deemed federal action crucial to preserve the "American Way of Life."

Economic collapse on the grand scale of the Great Depression exposed weaknesses in the nation's moral fiber as well as the more serious abscesses vitiating the culture. Depression, for example, laid bare the gnawing poverty and rampant poor health indigenous to the nation's many mining camps, textile villages, and scattered tenant farms. Federal intervention, it was hoped, would impose scientific standards of relief and, through the accumulation of knowledge and federally sponsored social engineering, restructure society and abolish such cultural malformations as the mining camp.

Plainly, in Hopkins's eyes, bold, experimental federal relief programs required close monitoring to gauge their positive or negative effect on the jobless. Was federal relief destructive of American values, or would works programs better strengthen the American value structure? How did politics undermine the government's objective to reinforce American culture? These were a few of the many questions that troubled Hopkins and his aides as the Federal Emergency Relief Administration determined to use federal policy to shore up the nation's moral fiber.

The American welfare system that emerged by 1935 reflected the outcome of a clash of ideas about joblessness, poverty, and relief that swirled around private and state welfare agencies and through the corridors of the Washington bureaucracy during the dolorous months of 1933 and 1934. This ideological ferment over the role of welfare in America formed the essential backdrop for Hopkins's broad inquiry into the extent of poverty and the effect of joblessness and relief on American families.[13]

During the 1920s, social workers had advanced into the foreground among those groups such as businessmen, urban planners, lawyers, and physicians seeking to fashion higher standards of efficiency in their professions. Throughout America, voluntary welfare organizations, family societies, children's aid societies, settlement houses, and other charity associations, organized at both the community and state level, championed the efficient coordination and delivery of services administered by professionals adhering to the tenets of scientific casework.

According to the private social agency, casework relieved the emotional stress or psychological trauma that impaired a client's ability to function effectively in modern society. Social workers, especially those trained at schools that integrated the psychology of Sigmund Freud with the friendly-visitor principles of Mary Richmond, eschewed material relief (charity) as abhorrent to sound casework practice. In this view, material relief, whether in the form of cash, clothing, or food, encouraged dependency and, therefore, impeded the necessary social and psychological rehabilitation of the client.[14]

Social workers identified material relief or the pejorative "dole" with public welfare. Across America in the early 1930s, public relief still remained mostly in the hands of ancient county and local poor boards, which often traced their origins to the seventeenth, eighteenth, or early nineteenth century and moreover, in cities like Philadelphia and Boston, were generally creatures of courthouse or ward politics. Poor boards, or overseers of the poor, retained powerful lobbies in state capitals. Everywhere, poor relief was mean or inadequate. In Wyoming, two poor boards and a public welfare commission dispensed only three forms of relief: aid to asylums, to children, and to prisoners. Beyond that, Wyoming levied a meager one-half-mill tax to support old age and mothers' pensions. Even in New York, where a welfare reform bill in 1929 abolished the poor boards, the state afforded needy families merely four dollars a week for food and one-half ton of coal a month. When in 1931 New York's Governor Franklin D. Roosevelt established the Temporary Emergency Relief Administration (TERA) and promulgated minimum standards of direct relief, deficient state appropriations limited TERA's role to mainly persuading localities to raise welfare standards.[15]

Cast in the mold of seventeenth-century Elizabethan poor relief, which distinguished sharply between the hard-working deserving poor and the presumably slothful undeserving, public relief in America had historically operated to discourage supplicants. The least fortunate expiated their poverty in county workhouses or poor farms. Social workers charged incompetent public welfare officials with political favoritism and applying "rules-of-thumb" standards of eligibility rather than scientifically investigating cases of poverty. Public welfare officials tended to be unfeeling, professionals argued, and often ignored the psychology of the applicants, which "pauperized the honest and industrious unemployed."[16]

Despite their disdain for the dole, social workers were cowed by the enormity of the Great Depression. Indeed, social workers implored the government to shoulder the massive burden of direct relief. By 1931, voluntary agencies across the nation tottered under the weight of rising caseloads. A study of thirty-two private family welfare agencies in Pennsylvania showed that between 1929 and 1932 professional staffs increased 23 percent while caseloads rose 131 percent. Alarmed by the trend, in 1930 President Herbert Hoover, buoyed by a deep-seated faith in the resiliency of voluntarism, created the President's Emergency Committee on Employment (PECE)—which became, after 1931, the President's Organization on Unemployment Relief (POUR). Other than urging business to rehire workers, PECE and POUR essentially provided national direction, moral support, and boosterism for giant fund-raising activities to undergird voluntary relief. But it was all for nought. As the depression worsened, private benevolence among both the rich and not-so-rich declined; and, more seriously, voluntary-agency endowment income plummeted in concert with the national economy.[17]

Exhausted and faced with depleted resources, social professionals who in the 1920s had prided themselves on having moved beyond amelioration to curing the cause of dependency, solemnly repressed their penchant for clinical approaches and discarded psychiatry for the grueling human salvage task. By 1932, agency after agency cut their budgets for "service" in order to extend coverage for material relief.

At the La Follette-Costigan Committee hearings on Federal Cooperation in Unemployment Relief in 1932, prominent social workers such as J. Prentice Murphy, Linton Swift, William Hodson, and Karl de Schweinitz conceded that voluntarism had collapsed. Emergency relief was too little and too late; relief workers described the poor scrounging for bits of decaying fruit and vegetables on city piers. Finally, the passionate and eloquent director of the Philadelphia Jewish Welfare Federation, Jacob Billikopf, reminded the committee of the prophet Isaiah's admonition that "when a man is hungry he is likely to fret himself, and in cursing his king and his God his heart is likely to be filled with revolt and rebellion."[18]

Hours of horror-ridden testimony by social workers, mayors, and civic leaders, backed by intense lobbying efforts, produced on May 12, 1933, the Federal Emergency Relief Administration with $5 million in direct or matching grants to be channeled by FERA through states and localities. Although FERA dispensed relief through state emergency relief bureaus, it nevertheless exercised considerable central authority over local relief standards, demanded accurate data reporting on joblessness, reemployment, and relief expenditures, and oversaw numerous relief experiments, mostly in the area of self-help.

Social workers enthusiastically involved themselves in fashioning the new public welfare edifice. Professional altruists envisioned a "system under which men and women of sympathy and training could administer public welfare according to the best preaching of scientific social work." Relief should be coordinated centrally, directed by nonpolitical professionals, and permanently funded by government appropriations. As former chief of the New York Temporary Relief Administration, Federal Emergency Relief Administrator Harry Hopkins presented impeccable social work credentials; naturally Hopkins surrounded himself with fellow professionals such as Jacob Baker, Aubrey Williams, and Joanna Colcord.[19]

FERA had the full support of charity organizations, settlement houses, and other urban reformers identified with professional altruism in the 1920s. Dazzled by FERA's potential as an instrument for achieving higher professional standards of social service, practitioners in the nation's 5,000 local emergency relief bureaus shaped relief after the professional image. In Philadelphia, professionals from the Family Society, Union Benevolent Association, and Jewish Welfare Society not only staffed the County Relief Board but also worked jointly or cooperatively on individual cases in order to shield "sensitive middle-class" clients from the stigma of public relief.

Accordingly, FERA's goals and standards reflected social work ideals. FERA field workers fought for adequate relief in cash rather than in humiliating food, clothing, and coal orders; FERA demanded thorough case investigations and relief tailored to the particular needs of individual families. Finally, for those capable of useful employment, FERA prescribed work instead of direct relief.

Under Hopkins and his core of professional social workers, FERA projected a psychosocial view of relief founded upon numerous studies of the human tragedy of unemployment. Social workers probed the mental state of jobless families whose savings vanished, whose homes were lost, and who dwelled on the precipice of despair. Students of the jobless counted the depression's toll in broken homes, evictions, overcrowded housing, impaired health, and the rising incidence of nervous disorders such as neurasthenia and psychoasthenia. How long, they asked, could the "respectable" or "deserving" poor maintain their moral and ethical principles; at what point does a man's faith in humanity and himself dissolve and "does he become downhearted and brooding and dangerous?"[20]

Clearly, as William Bremer has observed, FERA looked beyond the manifest purposes of relief to its latent function of preserving the present and future social order. Rumors that the long-term jobless viewed flour as "manna from heaven" reinforced social workers' belief that cash was the most effective form of direct relief since it "conserved and restored the unemployed's normal activity of a producing and consuming citizen."[21]

Although FERA opposed food orders and clothing doles, it supported experiments in self-help as psychologically rehabilitating. Thrift gardens, cooperative enterprises, and model farming communities received almost

ecstatic support from FERA. However, work programs occupied the foreground in FERA's war on poverty. In advocating work programs, social
workers carefully avoided linking work with relief. Relief work conjured
up too vivid images of the nineteenth-century workhouse with its stone
pile and wood yard. They campaigned, instead, for a "real-jobs" program,
not "work for relief." Work should be suited to the skills and aptitude of
the applicant and be rewarded by "prevailing wages."

The Civil Works Administration (CWA), Harry Hopkins's first large-
scale emergency employment program, passed all the professional tests.
Created in November 1933 to alleviate the rising tide of joblessness
through the harsh winter of 1933–1934, by the time it was terminated on
April 3, 1934, CWA had employed 4,260,000 people at prevailing wage
rates. Moreover, CWA accepted all applicants; workers were not forced to
pass a means test proving eligibility for relief. While social workers praised
CWA, conservative businessmen villified it as an extravaganza of "boon-
doggling." Locating jobs for over 4 million people necessarily involved
employing a fair number of workers at leaf-raking tasks, park manicuring,
or even research on the history of the safety pin. In the spring of 1934,
Hopkins and Roosevelt called the emergency over and ended CWA. But
for Hopkins and FERA social workers, the CWA experience confirmed
that work and not direct relief was the "American Way." The American
worker has "a right to a job," declared Homer Folks of the New York
Charities Aid Society. Bemoaning "wasted manpower," Corrington Gill,
later assistant administrator of the Works Progress Administration (WPA),
joined Hopkins in extolling work as an "antidote for joblessness, which focused a person's productive energies and mental talents and self-respect."
However, to Hopkins's chagrin, the objective of "real work" collided with
the American reverence for private enterprise. Capitalism proscribed government competition in the marketplace no matter how noble the objective; nor would the private sector tolerate wage rates for public work com-
petitive with rates paid by industry lest it lure the jobless into dependency.
As a result, perceptive observers asked whether linking wages paid for
works projects to a relief budget produced "real jobs" freed from the
stigma of charity.

Although a social worker himself, Hopkins abjured what he believed to
be the "nosy sentimentality" of social work and advocated in its place
practical humanitarianism. Pledged to bureaucratic efficiency, he contended that government relief stood the ground between radical revolution and the preservation of the American Way of Life. A liberal and practical idealist, Hopkins neither trusted business's enlightened self-interest
nor saw any limits to the politician's lust for power. Yet, despite his cynicism, Hopkins aspired to erect a politically chaste relief structure built
around a works program, ironically the most politically volatile form of
assistance.[22]

Hopkins's dispatch of Lorena Hickok and the other reporters to chronicle the condition of the jobless and assess the moral effect of relief reflected his voracious appetite for data. Indeed, his obsession with facts and statistics confirmed his allegiance to scientific efficiency. Accordingly, FERA's regional offices systematically supplied information on the number of jobless, reemployment, relief costs, new cases, the size of relief families, and the sex- and age-composition of client families. However, the material cited in this book is based mainly upon Hopkins's attempt to broaden his data base to include the affective realm of client psychological and social well-being. It is in this sense that Hopkins's quest for knowledge can be interpreted as a facet in America's more fundamental odyssey in search of its culture.

The nature of Hopkins's quest—the fact that he sought "soft" information—palpably shaped the descriptions of both joblessness and relief that his reporters submitted. It contributed, furthermore, to the uniqueness of the documents. As a professional altruist, Hopkins clearly structured FERA to be a centralized headquarters for receiving and processing the reams of hard data on poverty and relief which flowed from district and state offices across the country. But it will be evident in the following chapters that Hopkins's interests far transcended the bureaucratic fascination for hard facts. In making reporting assignments to Hickok and the others, he deliberately invited information about the human dimensions of the Great Depression. It is this untrammeled subjectivism that makes the reports most valuable. Not only did the reporters' mission carry them to mill towns, fishing villages, farming villages, coal patches, small cities and metropolises, wherever unemployment and poverty scarred the social landscape; but also, once there, the reporters invited the victims of the depression to unburden themselves about the enormity of their crisis.

Originally intended to help Hopkins assess the effectiveness of federal relief efforts and help determine the future of American social welfare, the reports ultimately amounted to—in cameo form—an exercise in national catharsis. Beleaguered relief officials, frustrated social workers, petty politicians and bureaucrats, conservative businessmen, beaten farmers, the desperate and hostile unemployed all shared with the reporters their anxieties about the adequacy as well as the believed abuses of relief and the grim prospects for a better future.

This assessment hardly exhausts the full range of the reports' contents. For although the reporters were instructed to chronicle what they saw and heard honestly, once sculpted into report form, this land they described reflected also their own personal images of America. Indeed, the fears and concerns expressed in these accounts mirrored much of the reporters' middle-class anxieties about the possibilities for American culture in a postindustrial civilization. At this juncture the reporters broached the world of social engineering, for if federal relief policy could strengthen the moral fiber of mainstream working- and middle-class families, might it not also help purge the culture of those persons cast permanently adrift in the tides of technological change? Disturbed by their encounter with sizeable populations of homeless men, with squalid settlements of unemployed miners, and pockets of apparently moronic families, several of Hopkins's reporters flirted seriously with eugenic theory and ruminated about the genetic damage caused by generations of syphilitic inbreeding. Here, it can be argued, the reporters mirrored the dark side of the New Deal, one rarely glimpsed in standard histories of the period. Contrary to the widely held view that New Dealers were unqualified champions of the "forgotten man," Hopkins's corps of writers betrayed a strain of intolerance for the so-called underdog, especially for the disinherited segment of the population, those presumably beyond the pale of middle-class norms and values.

Prone to innovation, New Dealers envisioned social engineering as a tool to shape American culture. Stranded populations could be resettled, backwater populations relocated in modern electrified towns; syphilis could be studied and controlled; moronics might be sterilized. However, social scientists during the 1930s perceived the task of culture-building to be enormous. In fact, much of the gloom clouding Great Depression writing concerned the belief that American culture harbored a vast pool of marginal people whose lives belied much of the American Dream.

The people whose forebodings about the enormity of America's marginal population produced speculation about social engineering were themselves social scientists. In contrast, Hopkins deliberately selected reporters whose ideas about poverty and relief were, he believed, untinged by the views of social work professionalism. Apparently he succeeded. Almost all of the reporters he chose were either young, ambitious writers in the springtime of their careers or established journalist/writers probably anxious for work in a job market where pickings were slim. Of course, Hopkins's star reporter, Lorena Hickok, had landed her job as much because of her friendship with the Roosevelts as for her sheer merit as a highly accomplished newspaperwoman.

None of the reporters—with the possible exception of Pierce Williams, whose main experience lay in medical welfare—possessed any appreciable familiarity with the world of poverty and relief. For example, prior to enlisting with Hopkins, Wayne Parrish's interest inclined toward aeronautical engineering; and in 1934, on the eve of the depression, poverty seemed but a vague abstraction to Lincoln Colcord, the sage of coastal Searsport, Maine, whose musings primarily concerned American's fleeting maritime heritage. Then, too, at the moment she packed for her journey through the wretched textile towns of New England and the Carolinas, Martha Gellhorn, a.k.a. the Marquess de Juvenel, had just published her first novel, not about poverty, but about rich coeds at a posh eastern women's college.

Writers by trade in 1934, little tutored in either the sociology of poverty or the science of welfare, yet all employed by the head administrator of FERA, it is clear that Hopkins's reporters afforded a fresh perspective on the Great Depression in America. True, these reporters were middle class and imparted their own progressive attitudes, but their rhetoric was free of bureaucratic or scientific jargon and was not yellowed by the harsh and doctrinaire verbiage of conservative or left-wing politics. Its significance rested essentially in its brutal honesty. Although tinctured generously by the writers' ethnocentrism and middle-class orientation, nevertheless, the reports constitute a frank, unembroidered discussion of life in Great Depression America. To use the parlance of the 1960s and 1970s, the reporters "told it like it was."

Therefore, Hopkins's quest for information produced the grist for an extraordinary social history of America as it struggled to survive the battering of the Great Depression. As stated earlier, the reporters participated in America's quest for cultural identity. The task entailed no less than a redefinition of the American Way of Life. The concerns of the reporters as outlined by Hopkins were highly germane to this "search for culture." Hickok and her journalistic colleagues focused often on the plight of America's middle class; they anguished over the tragedy of unemployment, pondered the meaning of the Unemployed Councils and other manifestations of radicalism; and bemoaned the sordidness of the nation's marginal peoples, its stranded miners, hoboes, and superannuated men.

The reports capture the foreboding expressed by social scientists about the burden of the permanent jobless, the homeless, and the stranded. Nevertheless, there are moments when the pall is shattered, and the reporters vent their hope that an enlightened government will restore a sense of community based on face-to-face relationships and help refurbish the American Dream.

All the succeeding chapters draw heavily upon the substance and the language of the reports. Chapter Two examines the background and careers of Hopkins's reporters and probes into those factors that might have shaped their observations about America. In addition, the chapter provides a better-defined context for the reports, inquiring more deeply into the origins of Hopkins's 1934 survey of the jobless, and it speculates on the historical significance of the massive body of reporting.

Chapter Three examines the American city in the years 1933 and 1934. The reporters are followed on their tour of closed urban factories and into the crowded halls of welfare offices. The chapter probes into the militancy of the city jobless and describes the effect of the depression on evolving American attitudes toward race and ethnicity.

Above all, Hopkins's reporters attempted to dissect the psyche of the American worker and his family. Chapter Four digests their evaluation of the American worker, his mood, his hopes, his dreams, and his proclivity or lack of same for radical political activity. Not only did the reporters delve into the worker's outlook and social and physical condition, but they also sought out the opinion of social workers and businessmen concerning the state of the American working-class family. What they found provides a keen and unique perspective on the nature of work, family roles, and family adaptation on the eve of major labor and social legislation.

Chapter Five follows the reporters into America's mining villages and mill towns. The FERA reports reveal the observers' belief in the strandedness of small-town industrial populations and afford a fascinating commentary on the role of the depression and federal relief policy in abetting the process of modernization in the 1930s.

The next three chapters examine the poverty of rural America. Chapter Six focuses on America's farming communities, especially the upper midwestern and northwestern farm belts, where a combination of drought, wind, and bitter cold pummeled farmers as relentlessly as the catastrophe of the rock-bottom prices paid for their crops. The reporters found gnawing poverty in the South, and Chapter Seven focuses on the southern problems of farm tenancy and escalating relief rolls as well as on New Deal rehabilitation projects such as the Tennessee Valley Authority. Chapter Eight describes what Hickok and other reporters found in their tour of the West, where they explored the poverty of sugar beet workers, the misery of transient camps, and the tragedy of once prosperous but now indigent cattle farmers.

Finally, the last chapter provides a general overview of the substance of the FERA reports and fits them into the context of our existing knowledge about the Great Depression and the unfolding New Deal.

Several related themes permeate the many pages of the FERA reports. One general theme concerns the role of the depression and relief in shaping American cultures. A second concerns the trend toward social alienation and massive disenchantment. A third theme involves the existence of a permanently unemployed people—people who because of age, lack of salable skills, or psychological impairment hovered permanently outside the pale of the American Dream. All of these themes that haunted the pages of the FERA reporting are linked. They are twentieth-century jeremiads welling up from a society caught in the throes of rampant modernization. It is the aim of this book, in probing the character and prolific expression of a group of ardent depression journalists, to attach broader significance to these themes, cast them into the larger context of twentieth-century change, and thereby assign fresh meaning to the agony of the Great Depression.

2

The Reporters and the Reports

■ Harry Hopkins's decision to enlist seasoned newspaper reporters, novelists, and journalists to explore the human side of the depression reflected the empathetic strain in the administrator's conduct of the Federal Emergency Relief Administration (FERA). It also reflected his concern about the social chasm separating his extensively bureaucratized welfare administration from its client population. Hopkins, of course, belonged to—some might say, led—the army of professional social workers which, in the depths of the Great Depression, seized the reins of private charity and public relief from the faltering grip of existing voluntary agencies and bankrupt poor boards and determined to restructure the American system of philanthropy into an efficient, bureaucratic system of public welfare. According to Hopkins, FERA became the master architect commissioned to transform voluntarism into public welfare. And, true to the modern bureaucratic tradition, FERA assigned a high priority to careful data gathering and record keeping. As the head of FERA, Hopkins pilloried the old state-run public poor-relief system, which had ignored the importance of data gathering.[1]

Data flowed into FERA's Washington, D.C., offices from cities and countryside. In Oregon, Colorado, Utah, North Dakota, and Illinois, among other states, FERA appointed Rural Research supervisors who worked closely with state relief administrators to collect and analyze data on rural poverty. For instance, twenty field statisticians gathered raw facts and figures from field supervisors in the several thousand rural townships of Illinois.

Beneath much of this data gathering lay Hopkins's determination to build an efficient, cost-effective federal relief bureaucracy on a foundation of modern social work principles. In Oregon, for example, FERA's regional social worker was a graduate of the University of California with a background in medical social work. In turn, boasted a 1934 FERA field report, "she judged everyone on the basis of their [sic] credentials in social work." Hopkins cringed at the thought that the local overseer of the poor might be the local barber who carelessly filed the name of supplicants in his pocket, discussed their peculiar needs with his tonsorial clients, and often "kept the records in pencil on the wall." [2]

Hopkins promptly established a centralized Division of Research and Statistics and Finance in FERA's Washington, D.C., headquarters and empowered it to gather statistics and conduct the research programs necessary to develop administration policies. Every month, reports from state and regional offices streamed into FERA's Washington headquarters. Thus, in addition to servicing the physical needs of the jobless, trained caseworkers and relief administrators transmitted to Washington the data for constructing an enormous demographic portrait of poverty in America. [3]

However, despite his penchant for facts and more facts about poverty and relief in America, Hopkins detected an element missing from his panorama of data. Recognizing the shortcomings of purely statistical information, he sought an interpretative key to afford insight into the heaps of data accumulating at FERA. In an attempt to translate the reams of hard facts into a throbbing figure of human pain and emotion, he requested subjective or "soft," data illuminating the agony of unemployment and the feeling of hopelessness among millions of formerly productive and happy people. Hopkins was not alone in this concern. As the mountain of statistical data accumulated in FERA's Research and Statistical Division it begged for interpretation. Thus, confronting a mound of hard data on relief cases in Portland, Oregon, an assistant director in the research division urged that these stacks of reports, this mass of quantifiable but inert, faceless evidence of despair, must be animated "with a more general knowledge of certain background material concerning the industrial and relief situation in each city." He pleaded for studies of family compositions, personal occupational histories, biographies of transient families, single persons, and others receiving relief.

Administrator Hopkins, for one, looked for an understanding of the crumpled pride, the sting of superannuation, and the anger of a poor family faced by the brazen intrusiveness of welfare investigators and frustrated by the impersonality of a mammoth welfare bureaucracy. Like Rexford Tugwell and other New Dealers, Hopkins believed that America was encountering a new societal phenomenon—mass unemployment created by the overproduction and underconsumption patterns of a mature industrial economy. He feared that an easy solution to such an enormous problem did not exist, and that meanwhile, the combination of long-term joblessness and unscientifically administered relief was eroding the moral fiber—including the work ethic—of America. [4]

Therefore, Hopkins's inquiry into the socioeconomic ramifications of the Great Depression extended far beyond the methodical accumulation of hard facts. His ultimate goal was to penetrate into the tragedy of joblessness, to understand the real prospects for the revival of the nation's manufacturing economy, to learn the effects of unemployment and relief on family life, and to assay the potential of work relief as a more American solution to the scourge of economic insecurity. But, more immediately, Hopkins was motivated by the urgent need to evaluate the impact of the Civil Works Administration (CWA), the temporary work relief program undertaken to help the jobless survive the harsh winter of 1933–1934, as well as by the requirement to assemble a body of information that could be used in erecting a permanent federal welfare structure to replace the existing emergency administration of relief.

In fact, between October 1933 and December 1934, Hopkins launched four separate investigations. He took his first step in this quest for soft information in July 1933 when he hired Lorena Hickok as FERA's chief investigator and dispatched her to depression-wracked states such as Pennsylvania. In Hopkins's own words, Hickok was "to look the [relief] situation over. . . . Miss Hickok is not acting as a field representative," explained Hopkins to Pennsylvania's chief administrator, Eric Biddle,

> but, she is, on my behalf, going to observe not only the status of relief work in the United States but its effect on people and try to get a picture of how the ordinary citizen feels about relief; whether in his judgment it is adequate or inadequate, and so forth. She is going to explore those avenues which would not normally be approached by our field representatives. She expects, for instance, to interview ministers, labor leaders, manufacturers, and visit the families themselves. She is particularly anxious, as am I, that her visit not be considered in any way an investigation of your relief machinery, nor will she advise you or your local units how the work should be done.

Hopkins concluded by asking Biddle to give Hickok "the type of cooperation that she will need."[5]

Second, in the spring and again the autumn of 1934, Hopkins directed each of his state Emergency Relief administrators to submit to him their "impressions of the jobless." Tell me, he requested, "just what shape are the clients in, physically and mentally, I mean morale? What are their prospects for reemployment? Will the relief load go up? What does the general public think the government ought to do about this unemployment business?" Forthwith, Hopkins collected this information into a sizeable volume entitled the "State of the Nation Reports."[6]

Next, to explore the relationship between modern technology, intensive industrialism, and the nation's unemployment crisis, as well as to look at the impact of the National Recovery Administration on industrial employment, Hopkins employed as FERA's chief field representative the economist Pierce Williams. Between 1934 and 1936, Williams prepared voluminous reports on the "Conditions and Prospects of Employment. . . ." in industries such as steel, lumber, bituminous coal, anthracite coal, cotton textiles, and automobiles.[7]

Finally, in the fall of 1934, with Edwin Witte's Committee on Economic Security meeting regularly and the outline of a permanent national welfare structure beginning to appear, Hopkins ordered his fourth investigation. This time he sought information on the mental and physical condition of the nation's unemployed. Hopkins wanted this study to be thorough and objective—"not the social-worker angle"—and focused on America's industrial centers. Apparently the full concept for this investigation evolved in the fall of 1933; with only a little nudging of the imagination, it is possible to reconstruct the scenario. In October of that year, Lorena Hickok and Bruce McClure, an ex-magazine editor who was Secretary of the Civil Works Administration and soon to be a FERA reporter himself, conferred frequently with Hopkins in his Washington office. Presumably, many of these conversations centered on Hopkins's need for more in-depth information on the plight of the jobless. During her first year as Hopkins's chief investigator, Hickok had periodically received from her Associated Press acquaintances fairly lengthy epistles concerning the jobless, relief, and politics in cities such as Los Angeles and Salt Lake City. These AP people, Hickok assured Hopkins, are "all New Deal supporters and write out of friendship for the Administration." Therefore, while speculative, it is probable that at one of these October meetings, Hopkins, Hickok, and McClure decided that, like Hickok, such writer-journalists were ideally suited for a crash two-month exploration of social conditions in America. Furthermore, it can also be safely hypothesized that the three conferees brainstormed, made a few phone calls, and produced a list of writers and journalists with pro-New Deal credentials who were free to devote two months of their lives to work as reporters for FERA. Hickok contacted the people, appraised them of the assignment, and awarded them "emergency appointments" with FERA.[8]

Although the reporters wrote their narratives for Hopkins—the reports were all addressed "Dear Mr. Hopkins"—Hickok coordinated the reporting expeditions and was assisted by another of the reporters, Pierce Williams, who had oversight of the investigations in cities and towns dominated by heavy industrialism. All of the reporters had orders similar to those given to Lorena Hickok in July 1933. However, rather than having the entire nation as a "beat," as Hickok did, each of the other reporters was assigned a specific region or locale. Ernestine Ball and Martha Bruere were dispatched to upstate New York; Julian Claff examined Camden, New Jersey, Philadelphia, and Scranton, Pennsylvania; Lincoln Colcord and Louisa Wilson covered the automotive centers of Detroit and Grand Rapids, Michigan, and Cleveland and Akron, Ohio; Martha Gellhorn toured primarily the textile regions of New England and the Carolinas. David Maynard spent his two months in midwestern industrial towns such as Cleveland, Cincinnati, and Indianapolis, Robert Collyer Washburn traveled through Connecticut cities and Boston, Edward J. Webster reported from Kansas City, St. Louis, and several Texas cities, while Hazel Reavis, Henry Francis, and Bruce McClure helped Pierce Williams examine social and economic conditions in the heavy mining and industry centers of western Pennsylvania, West Virginia, Birmingham, Alabama, and Youngstown, Ohio. Thomas Steep studied the Chicago area, Milwaukee, and Gary, Indiana, while Wayne Parrish concentrated on just one city— New York.[9]

In addition to the sixteen reporters mentioned above, Hopkins from time to time sought information from FERA staff members such as Pierce Atwater, T. J. Edmunds, Clarence King, Benjamin Glassberg, J. C. Lindsey, Alan Johnstone, and Winthrop Lane. These people were largely engaged as field statisticians in FERA's rural research division collecting and analyzing data on rural poverty. Since the focus here is on the reporting from Hopkins's special social investigation of 1933–34, these staff people are not profiled in this study.

The July 1933 to December 1934 operation produced 107 reports. Altogether, this documentary output constitutes an enormous, almost fathomless, body of social data about the Great Depression and its effect on the American people. It is always difficult if not dangerous to speculate on the significance of the written word. Scholars have waged lengthy and bitter battles seeking to gauge the historical impact of particular written works, such as Frederick Jackson Turner's frontier address and Upton Sinclair's *The Jungle*, to mention two. Nevertheless, mindful of the caveat, it is profitable to consider the potential importance of this body of reporting. Certain facts about it are indisputable. The reports were commissioned as part of a major information-gathering project which led to the creation in 1935 of both the Social Security Act and the Works Progress Administration. Second, in addition to Hopkins, copies of the reports were distributed to key New Deal personnel, many of whom were involved in the reshaping of America's social welfare system; the distribution included Jacob Baker, Corrington Gil, and Aubrey Williams, all of FERA, and, most significantly, on occasion to the president himself.

Because of her close relationship with Eleanor Roosevelt, Lorena Hickok kept the president regularly posted about her itinerary, mainly through letters addressed to the president's office staff. "A little letter for the Boss (and how is he, by the way? Mrs. Roosevelt said he looks pretty tired?)," wrote Hickok to "Dear Miss Van Meter" from Tallahassee,

Florida, in January 1934. "It's lovely and warm down here," she added, "but damn the tourists! They are an awful nuisance on the roads."

Likewise, a year later on December 10, 1934, Hopkins forwarded to FDR a thick sheaf of "confidential reports," indexed by subject and "to some extent by city." Hopkins noted that these studies were not made by the regular members of his staff "but by skilled observers who are employed for this particular purpose." In his letter submitting the reports to the president, Hopkins told FDR's secretary, Marguerite (Missy) LeHand, that "the President was anxious to go over these. I would appreciate it very much if you could give them to him tonight." [10]

Later that month, Hopkins rushed to Roosevelt some reports on Birmingham, Alabama, and attached a note suggesting that the president "might like to look them over because they represent a cross-section of America." Another important federal bureaucrat who eyed a few of the reports, especially those which discussed at length the activities of radical jobless groups such as the Unemployed Councils, was J. Edgar Hoover, Director of the Federal Bureau of Investigation. [11]

At another level the reporters provided important ad hoc insights and advice on the effectiveness of relief, as well as on its efficiency, (i.e., nonpolitical operation). These insights helped Hopkins to fine-tune his national machinery. [12] For example, writing from Morgantown, West Virginia, reporter Henry Francis informed Hopkins about the effort of state bosses to politicize the federal relief apparatus. "Won't you step on these people, please and quickly?" implored Francis. "Unless you do, the value of years of work here may be lost." [13]

However, it appears that the real policy significance of the reports lies in their convergence with the process of rethinking and reordering the nation's entire social welfare structure. As chief relief administrator, an influential voice in American social work, and Roosevelt's chief spokesman for social welfare legislation, Hopkins closely followed the deliberations of Edwin Witte's Committee on Economic Security. Moreover, through FERA officials Aubrey Williams and Josephine Brown, who served on advisory committees helping to draft the social security legislation, Hopkins played a major role in shaping the final bills. Hopkins unquestionably influenced the decision whereby public assistance became the principal responsibility of the states, and the federal government assumed responsibility for categorical grants, Aid to Dependent Children, Aid to the Blind, and Old Age Assistance. At Hopkins's urging and under his direction, the New Deal created a giant temporary program, the Works Progress Administration, which was intended to provide jobs for all employable persons on relief. [14]

Since it can be argued with some degree of confidence that Hopkins's convictions about the federal role in relief giving and the importance of work relief were at least strengthened by the information channeled to him by his roving reporters, it is necessary to examine the backgrounds of these people more carefully. Alas, extensive biographical data exists only for Hickok, Gellhorn, and Colcord.

Most significant, all of these writers and reporters recruited by Hopkins shared a common legacy. Brought up and educated in the years just before and after World War I, these middle-class Americans had social consciences and social philosophies molded by what historian Clyde Griffen has called the "progressive ethos." [15]

Progressivism defies any simple definition. Essentially, it was a broadly based reform movement that arose in the late nineteenth century in response to industrialism. Progressives encompassed intellectuals, businessmen, professionals such as doctors, lawyers, and engineers, farmers, labor leaders, blue as well as white collar workers, upper as well as lower and middle class Americans. The breadth of the progressive reform agenda stretched as far and wide as the realm of membership, from crusades to purify American politics, vanquish the corporate trusts, achieve world peace, and abolish child labor, to campaigns for more beautiful and efficient cities, and against the epidemic of pellegra and hookworm in the rural South. [16]

What united the diverse ranks comprising this army of reform, and coalesced a multitude of causes into a movement, was an idealized vision or ethos in which, according to Griffen, a piecemeal approach to reform was juxtaposed with a religious or at least quasi-religious faith in democracy. So powerful was this progressive ethos, argued Griffen, that between 1907 and 1915 a large part of the American population came to believe that they were marching together in a social movement. [17]

In particular, the ethos enraptured a generation of educated middle-class youth which came of age on the eve of World War I. It was an optimistic ethos. On the one hand, it espoused the essential soundness of American culture; on the other hand, it trumpeted the need for, if not the inevitability of, positive social change in order that America might confront problems stemming from a half-century of uncontrolled industrialism and urbanism.

Much of progressive optimism flowed from a deep-seated faith in environmentalism and the belief that human progress depended on controlled environmental change. Good housing, tree-shaded parks, playgrounds, modern sanitation, zoning ordinances, public health regulations, and the control or abolition of liquor and prostitution, for example, would positively alter human behavior and transform bad citizens into good citizens. According to the most ardent progressives, even such inherited defects as moronism could be assuaged through eugenics. [18]

Progressives believed that an informed and self-reliant public would yield the reins of society to experts, that is, to social engineers. But, undoubtedly, grave danger lurked in the recesses of the socially engineered society, a danger to which most progressives seemed oblivious. Educated middle-class reformers, who nurtured heady feelings about the possibilities of environmental change, frequently harbored ambivalent feelings about the subjects of their reformism, the tenement dweller, the Eastern European immigrant, the victim of disease, and the southern black. Too easily, such ambivalent feelings degenerated into disdain, and the social engineer metamorphosed into oppressor.

This danger notwithstanding, progressives exuded a boundless faith that in the hands of experts, modern science, efficiency, and bureaucratic organization offered the promise of a new, more humane world freed of squalid slums, sweatshops, and marginally productive farms. Therefore, they gladly and confidently entrusted to social engineers the task of building this modern, more culturally harmonious society. On the other hand, progressives felt too ambivalently about government, with its history of bossism and corruption, to bestow upon a public agency the power of social control. Consequently, during the heyday of progressivism, 1907–1915, progressive expertise resided not so much in government agencies as it did in voluntary organizations such as civic clubs, housing associations, tuberculosis societies, and settlement houses. These private agencies sought to advance what progressives dubbed "the public interest." Staffed with experts and priding themselves on bureaucratic efficiency, organizations such as the settlement house and the bureau of municipal research strove to temper social conflict and moderate the confusion obscuring the interest of society and the interest of the individual.[19]

During the 1920s the effusiveness and passion bulwarking progressivism faded, but the core philosophy—the belief in science, efficiency, bureaucracy, and social control—survived. And, with the onset of the Great Depression, not only did the desperate needs of society seemingly preempt the interests of the individual, but, likewise, the crisis of mass joblessness exposed the weakness of voluntarism in coping with societal disaster on a national scale. Now government, not voluntarism, seemed best equipped to articulate and service the needs of society.[20]

Harry Hopkins and his New Deal compatriots reflected progressivism's evolution during the Great Depression. Cloaked in scientific efficiency, staffed with trained social workers and other experts dedicated to discovering bureaucratic solutions to joblessness and the immediate needs of the unemployed, Hopkins's Federal Emergency Relief Administration, as well as his Civil Works Administration and Works Progress Administration bore the indelible markings of the progressive ethos. And, so did Hopkins's reporters. Indeed, the reporters must be understood in this context as writers and journalists who viewed America with a set of norms fashioned out of the progressive ethos, albeit honed, as will be explained, by their experiences during the 1920s and early 1930s.

In addition to this heritage of progressivism, Hopkins's reporters had another important common experience in their background: With but two exceptions, the reporters belonged to the world of newspaper journalism, writing, and publishing. The exceptions, Pierce Williams and David Maynard, had academic credentials. As for residential distribution, most of them seemed to have been recruited from the New York and Washington, D.C., metropolitan regions.[21]

Hopkins's leading social sleuth, Lorena Hickok, had earned her stripes as an investigative reporter. Born in East Troy, Wisconsin, on March 7, 1893, Hickok had a difficult childhood. Her mother died when she was thirteen, and her father, an itinerant butter-maker who drank heavily, treated her cruelly—on occasion brutally. At age sixteen Hickok left Wisconsin to live with her cousin in Battle Creek, Michigan. She finished high school there and entered Lawrence College in Appleton, Wisconsin. Twice she failed as a college student. Between misfortunes at Lawrence, she worked as a cub reporter for the Battle Creek *Evening News*. Later, turning away from college, she secured a job with the *Milwaukee Sentinel* where she established a reputation for being both ambitious and aggressive. Next, after a brief stay with the *New York Tribune*, she moved to Minneapolis, worked on the *Minneapolis Tribune*, and rose to become the paper's Sunday editor and its chief reporter, with her own by-line. Between 1925 and 1928, Hickok moved from Minneapolis to the *New York Mirror* and then to the Associated Press. As a reporter for the AP, she covered the Lindbergh baby kidnapping and in 1928 the Democratic National Convention, where she first met Eleanor Roosevelt. In her book *Ladies of the Press*, Ishbel Ross described Hickok in 1928 as "A big girl in a casual raincoat with a wide tailored hat, translucent blue eyes, and a mouth vivid with lipstick." During the next few years, Hickok and Eleanor Roosevelt developed such a close personal friendship that in 1933 Lorena left the AP convinced that her strong feelings for the Roosevelts prejudiced her ability to write objectively about national politics. When in 1933 Hopkins confided to Mrs. Roosevelt his plan to enlist an investigator to explore the social dimensions of the Great Depression, the latter, of course, strongly recommended Lorena Hickok.[22]

During her career as a reporter, Hickok had earned a reputation for being a tough, "hard-nosed" journalist, hustling for stories in a male-dominated profession. Legend has it that she smoked a pipe in the *Minneapolis Tribune* city room. True or not, for most of her life she chain-smoked Pall Mall cigarettes and in the mid 1930s constantly complained of a raspish smoker's cough. However, Eleanor Roosevelt found a soft heart beneath the calloused demeanor Hickok displayed before the world.[23]

After touring America in 1933–1934 as Hopkins's leading investigator, Hickok traversed the country again in 1935 and 1936, this time to investigate the impact of federal relief on the chances for a Democratic victory in the fall 1936 presidential election. Meanwhile, she roomed at the White House, and when not on assignment for Hopkins, accompanied Mrs. Roosevelt on numerous sightseeing expeditions, once to see raw unmitigated poverty in Puerto Rico, another time to enjoy the scenery and fresh air of Yosemite National Park and the Gaspe Peninsula. In November 1936, Hickok resigned from FERA and became a publicist for the New York World's Fair. During World War II she performed public relations and administrative assignments for the Democratic National Committee. After the war she assisted Eleanor Roosevelt in her writing, and, while free-lancing on her own, coauthored with Jane Gauley a book on Walter Reuther. Around 1955, having become partially blind, she moved to Hyde Park to be near Eleanor Roosevelt. She died there in 1968, six years after Mrs. Roosevelt's death.[24]

Lorena Hickok was not the only veteran lady of the press employed by Hopkins as a social investigator. To survey joblessness and relief in the automobile capitals of Detroit, Cleveland, and Akron, Ohio, Hopkins assigned another newspaperwoman, Louisa Wilson. In both background and appearance Wilson offered a sharp contrast to Hickok. The daughter of a missionary, Wilson was born in China at an inland missionary summer resort, and she received her early education in Shanghai at a private boarding school. When she was fifteen, she returned to America, where in time she was graduated from Wellesley College.

Fresh off the campus, a fair-complected, delicately built girl partial to girlish sweaters and flat sport shoes, Wilson appeared the antithesis of the hardened, thick-lipsticked Hickok as she begged and cajoled her first newspaper job at the New York *World*. However, like Hickok, she was ambitious and aggressive, and she deftly exploited her girlish appearance to wheedle an interview with the reputedly inaccessible Henry Ford. As a star reporter, Wilson's career took her to Washington where her beat included the Supreme Court. She was poised for a long, personally financed journalistic expedition back to her birthplace in China when Hopkins tapped her for two months of less enchanting work reporting on poverty among America's automobile workers.

Although she had earned her reputation as a newspaper woman by interviewing such celebrities as Henry Ford and John D. Rockefeller, on the reportorial circuit Wilson would defer to other reporters, allowing them to interview "key people in the industry, top public officials," the "big shots," while she pounded city sidewalks talking to social workers, unemployed engineers, the "small fry John Citizen," and the jobless automobile workers themselves.[25]

Hopkins enlisted three other women with newspaper backgrounds: Martha Gellhorn, Hazel Reavis, and Ernestine Ball. Because she established her reputation principally as an authoress, Martha Gellhorn's story comes later. In 1919, Reavis worked as a reporter for the Seattle Bureau of the Associated Press. There she met and married Smith Reavis, a distinguished AP correspondent whose 1927 interview with Aristide Briand is credited with laying the foundation for the Kellogg-Briand Peace Pact. After Hazel Reavis's tour as one of Hopkins's reporters, she worked for AP in New York. In 1940 she was appointed the publicity director of the Democratic National Committee.[26]

Like Reavis, Ernestine Ball carved her journalistic career in the West, in this case, San Francisco, where she worked for the *San Francisco Call and Post*. In 1926 she wrote a series of articles in the *Call and Post* entitled "Aimee in the Temple," which unveiled the life of the famous religious revivalist, Aimee Semple McPherson.[27]

Five of Hopkins's male reporters also had newspaper backgrounds. One of these, Thomas Steep, shared with Louisa Wilson a common interest in China. Born in 1880, Steep was in the throes of a mid-life career change when he acquired the Hopkins job in 1934. From 1900 to 1930, he had worked as a journalist, covering foreign assignments in Russia, Mexico, India, and China. In 1925, he used his knowledge of the social customs and traditions of China to write several articles followed by a book entitled *Chinese Fantastics*. With his reputation as an expert on Chinese culture, Steep worked for New York newspapers as their correspondent in Peking from 1926 to 1928. Later in the thirties he worked as a public relations representative, first for the New York Bureau of the Pan Pacific Press and finally for the Hawaiian Sugar Planters Association.[28]

None of Hopkins's journalists boasted a better education than Wayne Parrish; and few achieved his financial success. By 1953, long after his sojourn with Hopkins, Parrish had become the leading editor and publisher of aeronautical journals in the United States. However, when Hopkins recruited him in 1934, the future publisher was only a bright young reporter for the New York *Herald Tribune* who, a year later, would be fired for refusing a dull assignment.

Like Hickok, Parrish grew up in the Midwest, in Illinois, where his father was part owner of the Decatur *Herald*. After high school Parrish attended the University of Illinois where for two years he studied journalism. Then in 1923 he hitchhiked to New York City and enrolled at the Columbia University School of Journalism. After earning both bachelor's and master's degrees at Columbia, in 1930 Parrish was awarded the Pulitzer Traveling Scholarship which enabled him to travel third-class on a tour around the world. Therefore, during the worst years of the Great Depression in America, Parrish sipped wine in Parisian cafés, shopped in the Casbah of Spanish Morocco, and even gazed at the forbidding wastelands of the Arctic Coast. Upon his return he accepted a reporting job with the

Tribune. However, Parrish's real passion was for aeronautical technology. In 1933, he had written a little book entitled *An Outline of Technology.* After completing his assignment for Hopkins, he spent the years 1935–1937 editing the *National Aeronautical Magazine* before starting his own publication, *American Aviation.* By 1958, Parrish headed a multimillion-dollar Washington D.C.-based empire of aviation publications including *American Aviation Daily, Air Cargo, Airports,* and *Air Traffic News.*[29]

Julian Claff and Henry W. Francis also worked as journalists. Claff, who as a Hopkins reporter covered Philadelphia, Camden, and Scranton, was employed prior to 1933 as a Camden newspaperman. Usually out of work, Claff was supported by his wife, Ruby, who was Lorena Hickok's sister. Hickok, who often helped her sister financially, may have been responsible for Claff's tenure with the Hopkins group, if only to ease her own financial situation. In any case, Hickok later got Claff a job working on the federal census of 1940. Shortly afterward, Claff purchased the Beekman Place Bookstore in New York City. For the next twenty years he bought and sold books in his store, which provided a regular gathering place for such prominent writers as J. P. Marquand, John Steinback, and Clifford Odets.[30]

Francis wrote for the *New York Globe and Commercial Advertiser* during the 1920s. As a foreign correspondent for the paper, he reported on such topics as the plight of the German economy and France's demand for cable ships, neither of which suggests the important role he would play as the author for Hopkins of twelve brilliant essays on poverty in southwestern Pennsylvania and West Virginia.[31] Another Hopkins reporter, Lincoln Colcord, also had a newspaper background, but, as will be explained later, he gained most prominence as a publisher and essayist.

Bruce McClure, like Wayne Parrish, was born into a world of magazines and newspaper publishing, but he never served an apprenticeship as a working reporter. Nephew of the famous S. S. McClure, founder and publisher of *McClure's Magazine,* Bruce McClure was born in England and attended private schools in Switzerland. McClure was a teenager when he sailed home to America. Following military service in World War I, he worked during the 1920s as the editor of *Elks Magazine.* McClure was working for the magazine when Hopkins persuaded him to leave his editorial job and direct publicity for the Federal Emergency Relief Administration. Thus, McClure was one of the few reporters in 1934 assigned from within the ranks of FERA. In 1934, McClure served as secretary of the Civil Works Administration, and in the following year Hopkins selected him to head the professional service projects of the Works Progress Administration. His professional projects division administered the famous art, music, theater, and writers projects, which, while often controversial, deeply impressed the consciousness of America and added considerably to the nation's cultural heritage. Interestingly, in 1934 McClure was not commissioned to investigate the plight of jobless writers, actors, or actresses in the big cities such as New York or Philadelphia; instead, Hopkins sent him to depression-wracked western Pennsylvania where he described joblessness and relief among steelworkers and chemical employees.[32]

In all, Hopkins tapped three professional writers for his reporting assignments: Martha Gellhorn, Martha Bensley Bruere, and Robert Collyer Washburn. Only twenty-six years old in 1934, Martha Gellhorn ranked among the youngest of Hopkins's social surveyors. She had just published her first novel, *What Mad Pursuit*, when an invitation to have lunch and a chitchat with Hopkins landed her an engagement in October to report on poverty and relief in America's textile centers. She later incorporated the information she gathered that fall from the mill towns of New England and the South into her second book, *The Trouble I've Seen* (1936).[33]

Born in 1908 into an affluent St. Louis family, Martha Gellhorn graduated in 1928 from Bryn Mawr College. While on a post-graduate grand tour of Europe, she met her first husband, the Marquis Bertrand de Juvenel, a French journalist, and she was still technically the Marquess de Juvenel when Hopkins employed her to study the grinding labor conditions, miserable housing, and sordid poverty in New England and in North Carolina's Gastonia textile mills.

Gellhorn's first novel had received mixed reviews and in weighing her credentials Hopkins probably considered the young writer's exellent education and her brief experience as a journalist for an Albany, New York, newspaper. In fact, her novel hardly suggested any special insight or concern about poverty. It described three neurotic young women from an exclusive eastern woman's college (Bryn Mawr, we may safely assume) who steered their lives self-destructively into trouble. Not surprisingly, in her social sleuthing for Hopkins, Gellhorn leaned heavily on social-psychological explanations to interpret the morass of poverty entrapping industrial populations. Peculiarly, in her reports she frequently regarded poverty as symptomatic of a neurotic state characterized by incompetence and emotional lassitude. She dwelled on the chronic poverty which predestined its victims to perpetual indigency. However, in *The Troubles I've Seen*, based on her FERA experience, she cast the plight of the unemployed in a more sympathetic mold and grappled more with the trauma of families demeaned by the necessity of living on relief.[34]

Of all the reporters, Martha Gellhorn most evoked in her reports the pallor and gloom of the Great Depression. Yet, she found the work exhilarating and rewarding. For one thing, the job brought her within the orbit of the Hickok-Eleanor Roosevelt friendship. It was only after a few months of reporting that Gellhorn became so outraged by the wretched treatment of the unemployed and her belief that little was being done to assuage their suffering that she hastily rushed to Washington to submit her resignation. Hopkins urged her to see Eleanor Roosevelt first, and a luncheon was arranged with the first lady and the president. At that luncheon Eleanor Roosevelt stood up and exclaimed to her husband, who was preoccupied with conversation at the other end of the table, "Franklin, talk to that girl [Martha Gellhorn]; she says all the unemployed have pellegra and syphilis." According to Gellhorn, that silenced the table. She did not resign. She did get to speak with the president, and thus began a relationship with the Roosevelts that lasted the rest of their lives.

Intense and creative—much like Hickok and ER—in her own words Gellhorn was driven by a "sense of pressure and oncoming doom." In January 1935, exhausted and bedridden with the flu at a friend's house in Bryn Mawr, Gellhorn summoned enough energy to write Hickok that "probably one of the finest features of having returned to America and become a slave in the great forward movement of progress (known otherwise as the New Deal) is to have found you in the midst of it all. I consider you a definite addition to my life and am quite childishly delighted about the whole thing." Gellhorn, called "Marty" by some of her closest friends, ended the letter by promising to "come back to our happy family as soon as I get my legs back." [35]

That "happy family" included Eleanor Roosevelt. But the delight of her new-found friendship could not restrain Gellhorn from the whirl of traveling and writing that already characterized her life. Two years after her FERA assignment she alighted in Key West, Florida, where she wrote, disparagingly, "people live on relief cozily, steal coconuts off the municipal streets, amble out and catch a foul local fish called the grunt, gossip, maunder, sunburn, and wait for the lazy years to pass." Here Gellhorn resumed a dalliance with Ernest Hemingway which had begun during a vacation there in early 1934. "He's an odd bird," she wrote Mrs. Roosevelt, "very loveable and full of fire and a marvelous story teller." [36]

As she would reveal in several of her reports, Gellhorn's brooding sense of "oncoming doom" endowed her with a strong premonition of war, a premonition which had become stronger by 1937. Hitler was a "madman," she told ER, and if he "really sends two divisions to Spain my bet is that the war is nearer than even the pessimists thought. . . . If there is a war," Marty confided to ER, "then all the things most of us do won't matter any more. I have a feeling that one has to work all day and all night and live, too, and swim and get the sun in one's hair and laugh and love as many people as one can find around and do all this terribly fast, because time is getting shorter and shorter every day." [37]

War did come, and Gellhorn, once in the eye of the Great Depression, now found herself in the eye of a seething Europe. In 1938, Gellhorn was off to the fratricide and blitzkrieg of the Spanish Civil War. Amid the carnage of that terrible war, Gellhorn's romantic entanglement with Hemingway deepened, and it was to Gellhorn that Hemingway dedicated his novel *For Whom the Bell Tolls*. They were married in 1940, yet the union lasted only briefly, from 1940 to 1945. For most of the war years, Gellhorn traveled from one war theater to another writing stories mainly for *Collier's Magazine* and covering events in Finland, Czechoslovakia, Corsica, and along the Burma Road. Her short stories, which she compiled into *The Heart of Another* (1941), and a novel *The Wine of Astonishment* (1948) captured the pathos and agony of a world convulsed by war. *The Wine of Astonishment*, considered perhaps her best novel, described the loneliness and disillusionment of two young lovers engulfed in the horrors of the war. Here, as in *The Troubles I've Seen*, Gellhorn attempted to show how people often reacted to the social injustices which surrounded them. After World War II, Gellhorn lived and wrote in both Mexico and England and earned the reputation as a distinguished writer "of tested ability . . . with a journalistic gift for isolating pertinent . . . detail."[38]

Martha Bensley Bruere was the other woman author enlisted by Hopkins. Fifty-five years old in 1934, she was over twice Martha Gellhorn's age and one of Hopkins's most senior reporters. Like Gellhorn she was well-educated, with degrees from Vassar and the University of Chicago. Moreover, by the time Hopkins recruited her, Bruere had established herself as a writer whose ideas and interests flowed essentially in the mainstream of twentieth-century American progressivism. For example, her first book, *Increasing Home Efficiency*, written with her industrial-relations-specialist husband, bristled with progressive aphorisms about applying the organizational techniques of industry to the problems of home management. However, it was her book *Does Prohibition Work?* (1927) that really established her small niche in the pantheon of progressivism. The book was commissioned by the Conference of the National Federation of Settlements, which in 1926 had appointed a committee under Lilian Wald of the Henry Street Settlement to investigate the social effect of prohibition. Bruere, who had frequently contributed articles to *Survey Magazine*, used the social survey technique to research the issue of prohibition. *Does Prohibition Work?* was based on research data gathered by hundreds of social workers headquartered in settlements across the nation. Although it suggested that drunkenness had declined and community health improved, immigrants and the rich still had access to alcohol. This ambivalence notwithstanding, the book attracted considerable attention and ran in serial form in countless newspapers. Other works by Bruere including *Mildred Carver, U.S.A.* (1919), *Sparky for Short in Words and Pictures*, a children's book illustrated as well as written by Bruere, and *Laughing Their Way: Women's Humor in America* (1934), which she coauthored with Mary R.

Beard, wife of the well-known progressive historian Charles A. Beard, indicate the diversity of her interests and suggest, furthermore, the catholicism of Hopkins's standards for selecting literary talent. That Bruere joined the Forest Service of the U.S. Department of Agriculture in 1936, later writing *What Forests Give* (1940) and *Your Forests* (1945), attests to her lingering commitment to progressive values.[39]

Very little is known about Robert Collyer Washburn. A glance at his writings reveals a certain eclecticism and reaffirms the catholicism of Hopkins's selection process. With the exception of a self-published description of gift shops in Guilford, Connecticut, entitled *Gallery on the Green*, Washburn confined his professional writing to a four-year period, 1928–1931, during which he wrote *Sampson: Judge of Israel* (1928); *Prayer for Profit: Being the Colorful Story of Our Pilgrim Fathers* (1928), a popular history of Massachusetts; *The Jury of Death: Twelve Against the Underworld* (1930), a book published for the Crime Club, Inc; and finally, in 1931, *The Life of Lydia Pinkham*. Again, other than his qualification as a writer, none of his writings suggest that Washburn possessed any special background to examine poverty in America. In fact, like the other writers, his major attributes seemed to be a middle-class background, writing skill, and a total lack of technical expertise in the fields of sociology and philanthropy.[40]

Lincoln Colcord, or "Link" as his friends called him, was perhaps the most improbable candidate recruited by Hopkins and Hickok to examine poverty in Depression America. Like his progressive-minded sister, the prominent social worker and writer Joanna C. Colcord, Link was born at sea aboard his father's working coastal schooner, the *Charlotte A. Littlefield*, and throughout his life, he remained devoted to the sea and spent most of his time in his ancestoral home overlooking Penobscot Bay in Searsport, Maine.

After graduating from the University of Maine in his mid-twenties and working for several years as a civil engineer in the Maine woods, Colcord, whose tastes and values marked him as a survivor of Thoreau's New England, retired somewhat prematurely to the Searsport home, where he dabbled in horticulture, composed serious poetry, and wrote historical narratives about voyages on brigs and schooners.[41]

This romantic strain in Colcord ultimately lured him into the vortex of progressivism. In his *The New Radicalism in America*, historian Christopher Lasch portrays "the Sage of Searsport" as a passionate individual given to apocalyptic visions, prone to endow "private pursuits with public meaning," and disposed to regard politics as "a screen on which man's inner ambitions and secret fears were most vividly projected." He was only thirty-three when in 1916, at the urging of Colonel Edward House, then Woodrow Wilson's trusted confidant and adviser, Colcord moved to Washington to work as the capital correspondent for the Philadelphia *Public*

Ledger. House represented himself to Colcord and other journalists, such as Walter Lippmann, William Bullitt, and Bayard Swope, as the authentic voice of Wilsonian liberalism. House's visionary soarings appealed to Colcord's romanticism and his flair for the apocalyptic, and through House he came to see World War I not as a tragic blunder but as the great cataclysm inaugurating a new, more democratic age in which international justice and brotherhood prevailed. But when U.S. forces invaded revolutionary Russia in 1918, the landing at Murmansk shattered Colcord's faith in Wilsonian liberalism. Therefore, it was a badly disillusioned progressive who left Washington for New York in 1918 to take a job on the staff of Oswald Garrison Villard's *Nation*. Yet, Colcord's romanticism still seemed undimmed when he wrote to Bullitt in 1918 that the 'World is plunging onto revolution. . . . It will be a tragic but splendid time, lit by the lurid light of chaos."[42]

Yet, little of Colcord's progressive verve was reflected in his writing, either before or after his Wilsonian honeymoon. Certainly, it would not be emphasized in his depression reports to Hopkins in 1934. In fact, of all the reporters, Colcord urged the most caution in developing new policies. In his final report, he chided the administration for wavering between a socialistic and a capitalistic relief policy, and he emphasized time and again that the people he talked to—mostly businessmen—in Detroit, Cleveland, and Akron (where he was teamed with Louisa Wilson) "believe in the continuation of business for profit under capitalism and [are] not ready to support any drastic modification of this system."[43]

As a writer, Link's principal literary contribution would involve preserving the cultural heritage and tradition of what he viewed as a rapidly vanishing maritime civilization. His trilogy of sea stories, *Drifting Diamonds* (1912), *Game of Life and Death* (1914), and *Instrument of the Gods* (1922), represented his testimony not only to his enduring love for the sea but also to his belief in the superior values of the nation's seafaring people. He reaffirmed that faith in 1940 when with Samuel Eliot Morison he founded and helped edit the *American Neptune*, a magazine dedicated to publishing scholarly articles dealing with the nation's seafaring heritage.[44]

Although the evidence strongly argues that Hopkins sought as social observers skilled writers from outside the realm of social work and, therefore, without fixed points of view about poverty and relief, Pierce Williams was the exception. If not a social worker, Pierce Williams surely traveled in the social work milieu and bore the progressive mentality of the social work profession. Born in 1914, the Philadelphia native was an economist who specialized in studying the delivery of social welfare services. In 1930, as a member of the National Bureau of Economic Research, Williams published an analysis of corporate contributions to organized community welfare; two years later for the same institution, he undertook a thorough and sympathetic study of national health insurance and its applicability to American health care needs. In 1933, Hopkins employed Williams as the chief FERA field representative, and by the end of the decade, he counted Williams among FERA's ablest researchers. In 1934 the young economist/scholar joined Hickok, Wilson, Parrish, Colcord, and the others not only as one of the investigators but also as an administrator. In the case of McClure, Francis, and Reavis, Williams actually planned and mapped their itineraries throughout America's industrial centers.[45]

Hopkins also included a second economist, David M. Maynard, among his investigators. An academic and specialist in international economics from Claremont, California, Maynard belonged to the staff of the Economic Section of the League of Nations before joining Hopkins's group of reporters. Following his tour with Hopkins and World War II, Maynard worked in the Office of the U.S. Political Adviser in Tokyo. Later Maynard went to Athens, Greece, to assume the important post of Counsel in the Embassy for Economic Affairs.[46] Unfortunately, nothing is known of the career of Edward J. Webster, another one of Hopkins's reporters.

Although it is tempting to speak of Hopkins's entire assemblage of reporters as a team or corps, in fact they were hired singly. Wilson and Colcord worked as a team, Bruere assisted Ball in covering the smaller cities of upstate New York, and Francis worked with Williams in the coal- and steel-producing regions, but otherwise, the reporters traveled alone and reported independently. In fact, Gellhorn later recalled no interaction among the reporters.[47]

Some of the reporters—especially the women—encountered more problems than others with traveling. For instance, Hickok's assignment, which extended over three years and covered the entire country, forced her to learn how to drive. Prior to June 1934, Hickok had traveled by railroad, cab, trolley, subway, and rented car. On August 3, 1933, in Philadelphia, Hickok paid seven fares for trolley, cab, and subway transportation. In small cities and in rural townships, she often depended on relief administrators for her transportation. Finally, in June she convinced FERA that "the nature of her work required auto travel," and after that date she was reimbursed for travel in her own automobile.

But driving her own "wheezing Chevrolet" entailed its own problems. Often, as on July 25, 1936, in South Dakota, she drove three hundred miles "over loose gravel roads and in high wind. My eyes, ears, and mouth," she wrote, "are full of dust, also my hair!" Hickok described driving through a sea of grasshoppers which sounded like drums beating against the windshield. "They kept getting inside the car," she complained, and Hickok was as terrified of grasshoppers as she was of mice. "Quite some day!" she exclaimed. "It's been 108 here with that scorching dusty wind all day long." If it was not intense heat, dust, and a plague of grasshoppers, then it was a flat tire or a driving snow storm in a wintry North Dakota that added excitement and some dread to her automobile touring.[48]

On the other hand, Martha Gellhorn did not learn to drive an automobile. When she was not fortunate enough to be chauffered by a cooperative social worker, she endured two months of relative discomfort crisscrossing New England and North Carolina in a bus. After completing ten days of exploring conditions in Massachusetts textile towns, Lowell, Lynn, Oxford, Fall River, and Lawrence, she wrote her report and then clambered aboard a bus for a five-day spin through Rhode Island. The depression scenery passed before Gellhorn's eyes as a collage of unkept frame houses and paint-blistered hotels fronting a grimy main street in one industrial town after another. Full of youthful exuberance and ambition, Gellhorn strove to carry out her reporting assignment as vigorously and masterfully as possible. But despite her energy and ability she always doubted that she was doing any more than "scratching the surface." About to leave Massachusetts for Providence, Rhode Island, Gellhorn wrote Hopkins that "this is getting to be more of a bird's eye view [of depression conditions]. . . . A bird flying high and fast."[49]

And certainly there was a whirlwind quality to some of the investigations. Faithful to Hopkins's instructions, the reporters attempted to talk to anyone who might offer some insight into the conditions of local unemployment, the emotional fortitude of the jobless, and the impact of relief. For example, in New England textile towns Gellhorn interviewed relief administrators, social workers, mill owners, union leaders, physicians, and most important, the jobless themselves. Elsewhere, attempting to fathom the enormity of poverty and unemployment among midwestern stockyards and factory workers, Thomas Steep, in the tradition of many progressive forebears, found the famous settlement house Chicago Commons a perfect base for his social surveying operation. After all, the social survey was an outgrowth of the settlement house movement, apotheosized by the Hull House investigations of Jane Addams and the *Pittsburgh Survey* of Paul U. Kellogg. Lea Taylor, the director of the Chicago settlement, accompanied Steep during several trips through Chicago's working class neighborhoods and introduced him to many unemployed heads of Italian, Polish, and Greek households.[50]

In her report from Schenectady concerning the "reactions of employers, employees, and other citizens to the relief and unemployment situation," Martha Bruere carefully enumerated her sources:

> Four officials of the General Electric Company
> Two men still employed by the G.E.
> Eight former employees of the G.E.

The assistant manager of the American Locomotive Works
One employee of that plant
The acting Chief of Police
Two policemen
The Superintendent of Schools
Two teachers
The Commissioner of Health and his office assistants
Three doctors
One psychiatrist
One nurse
The presidents of the Junior League and Girl Scouts
Two members of the Board of Education
One banker
Two storekeepers
One lawyer
One labor leader . . . very "red"
Two businessmen
Several members of citizens committees
The head of the National Reemployment Service [51]

Lincoln Colcord and Louisa Wilson divided the task of investigating conditions in the automobile-manufacturing cities of Michigan and Ohio. While Colcord busied himself quizzing Detroit industrial tycoons, Wilson trudged door-to-door commiserating with jobless engineers and inquiring into the survival techniques of unemployed factory workers. In her canvass of the jobless "small fry," Wilson strove to balance her sample between families with breadwinners recently out of work and desperate households bereft of income for longer periods of two or three years. Wilson cast her intelligence net widely; she spoke on one occasion with the secretary of Detroit's Communist party and afterward spent hours talking with the wretched denizens of the city's 1,600-bed Fisher Lodge for Homeless Men.

The reporters interpreted their job literally as Hopkins instructed them. That is, they determined to relate exactly what they saw and heard. However, with objectivity less at stake, they strove to convey the honest emotion and the deep sentimentality of the poor and to fathom the anger and frustration which Hopkins believed gnawed at the moral fiber of the unemployed man and his family. Indeed, all the reporters hunted for evidence linking poverty and relief to a possible erosion of the quality of American norms, values, and beliefs—American culture, that is.

Thomas Steep, for one, grappled with the question of why the jobless he encountered in Chicago clung so tenaciously to their relief and seemed so afraid to take a job when one was offered. Other reporters pressed upon Hopkins an appreciation for the indignities endured by the jobless and the debasement felt by the unemployed man who after months of struggling to preserve his independence finally succumbs to relief. All of the reporters emphasized the deterioration of the human spirit which accompanied the precipitous descent from full employment to joblessness and then poverty.[52]

Since the reporting assignments required the reporters not only to explore but also to interpret joblessness and relief, impressions and feelings, the accounts were infused with subjective evidence. The writing naturally mirrored the reporters' shared genteel upper-middle-class origins and subscription to the progressive ethos. At least four biases imprinted their reports: a dualistic conception of the poor as either worthy or unworthy; a tendency to see inefficiency rampant in the delivery of welfare services (and a disposition to abhor that inefficiency); a conviction that professionalism must triumph over politically motivated dilettantism if the administration of relief was to become efficient and effective; and finally, with the exception of Colcord, a belief—shared by Hopkins—that only the provision of make-work would restore the self-respect and sanity of the worthy poor.

The reporters also displayed in their writing a deeply rooted ethnocentrism, which dictated their criteria for categorizing the poor as worthy or unworthy and which underscored the ambivalence with which the progressive-minded middle class viewed the victims of poverty and other less fortunate Americans. For example, blacks, Italians, Sicilians, and Mexican-Americans, established denizens of America's early-twentieth-century urban slums and, notoriously, the supplicants of social settlement or their philanthropic care, clearly rated as unworthy. Washburn branded the city of New Haven "a low-grade town" because of its Sicilian population. Among this ethnic group, Washburn denoted a premium placed on lying and concealing. These unworthy people, observed the progressive albeit intolerant Bruere, "contentedly accept[ed] relief and [were] usually unemployed; those others [the worthy] chaf[ed] under it, ready to revolt if they saw anything to be gained that way. . . ." Parrish felt the same way. The worthy jobless teetered on the edge of "mental deterioration," while "the lowest classes . . . are better off than ever before.[53] Speaking of the widespread concern he heard expressed about the creation of a permanent relief class, Colcord asserted that "the minority will use relief and already are using it as a permanent institution." Colcord feared that a too liberal relief program would only enlarge this permanent relief class.[54] Among the lower socio-economic strata who habituated the relief lines, Webster observed little of the emotional instability and despair experienced by so-called "high type people." "Nothing from nothing leaves nothing," mused Webster, "which of course is not without its own disquieting implication."[55]

Wherever they traveled, the reporters carefully scrutinized the administration of relief; their progressive bias made them especially sensitive to evidence of inefficiency and corruption. During their inspections of Hopkins's fledgling national relief operation in November 1934, they found much that made them cringe. Politics, for one, had naturally infiltrated the infant, ungainly, and highly vulnerable state relief administrations. Gellhorn complained that the Massachusetts relief show "was so definitely and blatantly bad that it was an object of disgust." Incompetence, she charged, "has become a menace. . . . Criminally incompetent men have been put into a job which demands intelligence, training, and disinterestedness. They are more than pitiful; they are criminally incompetent." Logically, in Gellhorn's eyes, an efficient and competent administration would be dominated by professionally trained social workers, not political appointees. It was a familiar theme in all the reports.[56]

Their common orientation predisposed the reporters to share several concerns. They anguished over the deteriorating moral fiber of the worthy poor, and harbored few illusions about the character of the unworthy poor, a class of people that, to borrow a phrase from Gellhorn, "frankly considers that society owes it a grocery order." What astounded and perplexed every member of Hopkins's coterie was the steady erosion of home values and psychological stamina among the white collar and professional classes. "They look for jobs," lamented Gellhorn, "but find none. How long will they go on looking; how long they'll be able to keep the pride which makes them hate to ask, I don't know."[57]

Confronting the jobless day after day not only shocked the sensibilities of the middle-class reporters but also afflicted them psychologically. The jobless seemed in such "bum shape." Many were ill, or else "their morale had so decayed that they were really not much use as human beings." But, if the reporters were depressed on the one hand, they were disconcerted, even terrified, on the other. This cauldron of social despair and suffering could seethe only so long before erupting into conflagration. Parrish found the conclusion inescapable that there was presently "growing unrest. . . . Clients are critical [of relief], more complaining, more ready to react." Steep was equally convinced that "any curtailment of relief or change in the face of continued unemployment would provoke demonstrations of a violent nature." However, despite her upper-middle-class, even aristocratic past, Gellhorn was essentially skeptical about the imminence of a radical revolution. She didn't believe it. Yet, if she was skeptical about a "red" revolution, nevertheless, she was a dour prognosticator of the American future. "It takes time," she explained, "for all things including successful rebellion; time and a tradition for revolution which does not exist in this country. But, it's far more terrible to think that the basis of our race is slowly rotting, almost before we have had time to become a race."[58]

Her message, like the messages of the other reporters, rang clearly in Hopkins's ears. The quality of American life teetered on the brink, and federal action was required to buttress the nation's cultural ramparts and protect the American Way. What the reporters regarded as the "American Way" was transparent. It consisted of a shared devotion to middle-class values, including hard work, intensive family life, education, the system of free enterprise, and clean, wholesome living. The subscription to this fundamental body of belief, the reporters assumed, bound Americans together, regardless of race, ethnicity, or social class.

The written accounts of Hopkins's reporters comprised an important body of information and opinion. From these descriptions of life in Great Depression America, as well as from the constant stream of more objective information received from FERA regional reporters and from Department of Agriculture rural surveys, Hopkins constructed a social profile of America that enabled him to campaign successfully for a Works Progress Administration, for Old Age Insurance, and for Aid to Dependent Children (now Aid to Families with Dependent Children, AFDC).

On the other hand, these reports constituted the grist for other less charitable positions occasionally taken by New Dealers. The reporters' concern about the relationship between poverty and venereal disease and poverty and emotional health reflected the same middle-class progressive mentality widespread in the 1930s that helped undergird the famous Tuskegee syphilis experiment launched by the United States Department of Health. National pessimism and the belief that social engineering could reinforce the frayed fabric of American culture encouraged state hospitals in the 1930s to perform hysterectomies on the mentally retarded, screen soldiers for "low IQs," and use public housing projects and the Federal Housing Administration to firm up the boundaries of racial segregation in northern cities while keeping the ranks of the United States military well-segregated during World War II. In other words, the reports enable us to glimpse the dark side of the New Deal as well as to refresh our understanding of its deep wellsprings of compassion.

3

City Streets and Slouching Men

■ One gets a clear impression of a community that has suffered so heavily and so long from the depression that it is almost losing heart.

Lincoln Colcord, from Detroit

■ The great crime is that the biggest bulk of these men are not the usual municipal flop house addicts. Once, and not so long ago, they were citizens.

Lorena Hickok, from Philadelphia

■ They are children really. If anything is being given away, they want some too. They are accustomed to having things handed out to them by white people.

a New Orleans relief administrator

■ America became an urban nation in the 1920s, and American cities became showplaces for the achievements of modern technology and the display of modern marketing principles. In fact, in the popular mind the word *civilization* created images of the modern city with its skyscrapers, paved streets, and palatial department stores which seemingly epitomized the consumption ethic of the New Era society. The Great Depression, however, shattered any illusion that this urban civilization implied unending prosperity, making a mockery of its glitter while underscoring the hazards and trauma popularly associated with city life. Plainly, an undercurrent of disillusionment verging occasionally on bitterness underlies the FERA reporters' exposition of life in urban America in 1934.

Unlike the earlier depressions which had struck in 1873, 1893, 1914, and again in 1921, the Great Depression of 1929 stalled America's industrial machine and paralyzed her cities. The resources of private voluntarism, which once enabled cities and their jobless to weather cyclic economic storms, failed. Soup kitchens, missions, ward relief organizations, family societies, and ancient poor boards collapsed under the weight of mass poverty. Faced with the spectacle of long bread lines, incidents of actual starvation, and the portents of popular insurrection, in 1931 President Herbert Hoover had attempted to coordinate the disparate ranks of voluntary relief, first through the President's Emergency Committee on Employment and then through the President's Organization on Unemployment Relief. Furthermore, seeking to bulwark voluntarism, cities such as Philadelphia appropriated emergency funds, and states like New York established the first state welfare agency, the New York Temporary Emergency Relief Administration (TERA). However, by 1933, with the urban poor scavenging city docks for bits of rotting vegetables, it became clear to social workers, civic leaders, mayors, and economists that without bold federal intervention cities were defenseless against the enormity of the Great Depression.[1]

In 1933 the administration of Franklin Delano Roosevelt became the first in American history to acknowledge the special predicament of the city in a period of economic crisis. Indeed, many of the early New Deal agencies—the National Recovery Administration (NRA), the Federal Housing Administration (FHA), the Home Owners' Loan Corporation (HOLC), and the Federal Emergency Relief Administration (FERA)—were created with the intention of bolstering the faltering urban economy.

As one aspect of this concern for urban America, New Dealers hoped to modernize the creaky, antiquated machinery of city unemployment relief. To that end, Harry Hopkins instructed his roving investigators to seek information on the size of the urban relief population, the pace of urban industrial recovery, the struggle of the urban jobless to exist, and the effectiveness of federal relief in suppressing what the observers perceived as a rising tide of social disorder and radicalism.[2]

Hopkins dispatched his reporters to all the nation's major cities and to many smaller urban centers as well. Lorena Hickok visited New York, Philadelphia, and Baltimore; Thomas Steep surveyed Chicago, Milwaukee, and Gary, Indiana; Louisa Wilson and Lincoln Colcord spent time in Detroit, Akron, and other Ohio cities; and Edward Webster studied conditions in St. Louis. At the same time, David Maynard concentrated on Cleveland, Cincinnati, and Indianapolis, and Ernestine Ball on such upstate New York cities as Troy, Jamestown, and Buffalo. In every city the reporters interviewed industrialists, small local businessmen, federal relief officials, local political and civic leaders, social workers, and, of course, the jobless themselves.

Doubtless, their reports reflect their individual social and political preoccupations; nevertheless, the descriptions furnish a valuable portrait of urban American culture during the Great Depression. Enfolding eloquent and perceptive assessments of the urban prospect, the reports registered a grim verdict on the possibility of the modern city as an engine for industrialism and working-class opportunity. At the same time the reporters described the social impact of industrialism in an era when—unlike the nineteenth century—cities could no longer easily employ the large labor pools of unskilled workers. This concern for the urban jobless led the New Deal to institute innovative social welfare programs such as FERA which would sustain the unemployed physically, while preserving their moral and psychological fiber and, thus, preventing anarchy and urban revolution.[3]

Whether the city visited in 1933 and 1934 was a large metropolis such as Philadelphia or New York, an industrial center like Milwaukee or Gary, or a smaller city such as Troy, New York, or Waltham, Masschusetts, Hopkins's reporters were decidedly pessimistic about the future of urban industrialism. Although New Deal emergency measures appeared to be relieving some of the panic which had gripped cities in 1931 and 1932, when hunger marchers invaded the downtowns of urban America, reporters like Hickok demured: "The emergency [may be] over," a Bronx social worker had told her, "but," as Hickok too believed, "the Depression lingers on." Wayne Parrish reinforced this growing impression on one of his several visits to Harlem, East Harlem, and the Queens section of New York. "With no private jobs in sight," Parrish witnessed relief rolls rising steadily in 1934. Among the workers he talked to, Parrish discerned "a complete lack of faith . . . that private jobs [were ever] coming back. Scores of employers had given up their businesses," and of those still operating, "most are willing to take back their people if business picks up; but they are not hopeful."[4]

Perhaps an even darker pall hung over Chicago. Having just interviewed managers of city department stores and mail-order houses in November 1934, Thomas Steep mailed to Hopkins a very discouraging report on the prospects for reemployment in those businesses. The president of Marshall Field and Company, John McKinley, had confided to Steep that while the company was actually selling more goods, it was doing so at lower prices. This had resulted, he said, in a third-quarter (1934) loss of over $175,000 for Marshall Field. Consequently, explained McKinley, "the company's tendency is to cut down employment." He also confessed that Marshall Field had been employing girls "at $8 a week to assort cards and so forth. We raised their pay to $14 [as required by new labor statutes] but immediately found a way of doing without them altogether."

Like Marshall Field, Chicago's Sears and Roebuck Company had increased working hours and reduced its working force by 1,700 employees in 1934. Sears's vice-president of operations told Steep that he saw "no prospect for a pickup. Our calculation is for a decline." When Sears, despite the depression, opened a new retail store in Chicago, a desperate crowd of 6,000 people applied for the 500 jobs. "There had been no advertising for help wanted," a Sears official told Steep.

Chicago's large industrial plants presented equally dismal prospects for reemployment. In November 1934, fewer than 10 percent of the Pullman Car and Manufacturing Company's normal work force of 8,000 were on the job. The company in 1934 operated 4,300 sleeping cars, but in 1929 it had had 8,800 in service. Railroad porters employed by Pullman dropped from 12,000 in 1929 to 8,000 five years later. During the same time, Pullman reduced its complement of conductors from 2,400 to 1,600. Thomas Steep sensed a "graveyard quiet" pervading the Hog Capital of the World. Driving through the streets of Pullman, Steep "did not see half a dozen people and no automobiles. . . . Most of the tenants [are] on relief." He observed that many of the large brick buildings of the Pullman operation were silent, without a single workman visible, and the spaces between the buildings were now filled with an autumn crop of weeds. Steep talked with a plant manager who lamented that he once saw "as many as 13,000 men employed" there, but now, instead of the din of machinery, all was silent, and a somber hopelessness prevailed.

It was perhaps even worse in Chicago's building trades. Of the 30,000 carpenters, 22,000 painters, and 73,000 other members holding cards in the Chicago Building Trades Council, only 10,000 worked regularly. All the others, Steep reported, "live on odd jobs and relief, occupying homes in which two or three families combine and pool their food."[5]

Here, then, in the heart of urban America, Hopkins's reporters discovered a stranded population, superfluous people, apparently adrift in the swirling tides of an urban industrial culture. Assessing the consequences in the 1920s of the efficiency to be gained by industrial modernization, many later New Dealers such as Rexford Tugwell had early reached the solemn conclusion that textile workers and other mechanics engaged in outmoded trades were permanently unemployable. He felt that, like sharecroppers and tenant farmers in rural America, these superfluous laborers contributed to excess production and thus fueled cyclic economic dislocations. In Tugwell's mind the Great Depression vindicated his

theory and confirmed the need to resettle these stranded urban populations in rural areas where they could subsist by raising their own food and
engaging in small craft enterprises. This belief that urban economies had
exhausted their potential for fostering employment opportunity helped
stir other early New Deal experiments such as urban garden plots and cooperative enterprises for canning vegetables and manufacturing mat-
tresses. Of course, the most singular outcome of these doubts about the
viability of the urban economy was the Resettlement Administration,
which proposed to build a series of planned garden towns along the urban
periphery.

Undoubtedly, the evidence from social workers and other observers of
urban America in the early 1930s reinforced this grim verdict on the economic future of the city. Among the jobless textile and metal workers of
Philadelphia, hope barely flickered. Although the businessmen and civic
leaders reporter Julian Claff interviewed believed that the worst was over,
none envisioned a bright future for the city. Instead, they predicted that
the city's economy would merely "limp along" indefinitely. Businessmen
grumbled to him that "labor troubles, heavy taxes, and a rotten city government" had already driven many factories out of Philadelphia, while "others
are only too eager for a chance to get out." In his observations, Claff
sounded the theme uttered again and again in the reports that "this decen-
tralizing trend stranded many thousands here who will never get work."

Likewise, across the Delaware River in Camden, New Jersey, Martha
Gellhorn found bleak economic conditions exacerbated by an expanding
corps of stranded people. Camden had three major employers: Campbell
Soup, New York Ship, and RCA Victor. All three firms had been laying off
people steadily since the depression began. Of the three, only Campbell
Soup continued to thrive. Yet Gellhorn discounted even Campbell as a
source of much future employment. All over the city, scores of young men
confessed to her that they "will never find work." Older workers lamented
that "even if there was any work, we wouldn't get it—we're too old."
Gellhorn, who would later embark for Europe to cover the civil war in
Spain, likened Camden's situation to "the third year of a war when everything peters out into a gray resignation." [6]

In cities with less diversified economies such as Detroit, joblessness
and poverty seemed so ubiquitous that a mood of unmitigated helplessness enveloped the town. Despite some slight improvement in the automobile industry, in the spring of 1934 Lincoln Colcord described Detroit's
economy as still languishing in "a condition of deep depression. . . . Traffic on the downtown streets on weekdays [was] noticeably light. Merchants," Colcord wrote, "report that sales of low priced goods are fairly
steady, but these sales are attributed . . . to the underlying support of relief funds. . . . [Detroit] does not seem so much disturbed as it seems

prostrated. One gets a clear impression of a community that has suffered so heavily and so long from the Depression that it is almost losing heart."

Colcord labeled America's automobile capital "the spear point of the Depression." But the lance was pierced as deeply into the heart of smaller industrial cities like Gary, Indiana, where in 1934 mills such as Illinois Steel operated at 22 percent of capacity and hosts of smaller plants were shut down entirely. Thomas Steep found the Gary region "dotted with silent factory buildings." One industrial survey he consulted questioned seriously whether most of the thousands of Gary's jobless would ever be reemployed. Steep quoted an employment survey that listed Standard Steel Car Company—"Closed Down for Good"; Hammond Pattern and Foundry—"Closed due to Bank Foreclosure"; and Gary Screw and Bolt— "Closed, No Business." Even those plants that were still operating suffered hard times. For instance, Universal Atlas Cement only employed 350 men out of its normal work force of 1,600 and for the future "did not anticipate . . . ever hiring as many men as it [the company] did in 1929."

Compared to Gary, with its many acres of idle plant facilities, the southern industrial city of Birmingham, Alabama, seemed well off. Still, Lorena Hickok could not find anyone there who believed that employment prospects were looking up. Nobody, she wrote Hopkins, "seems to have a banjo on his knee." Although few of Birmingham's mines, coke plants, pipe companies, and steel mills were actually idle, they were, Hickok observed, "mostly running on a greatly reduced schedule . . . and there's no prospect of [business improving soon enough] to make a dent in that 90,000 relief roll unless PWA [Public Works Administration] gets going."

In New York State, reporters in large cities such as Buffalo and Rochester, as well as in smaller ones like Troy and Jamestown, encountered the same gloom. "It's going to be a hard winter," was a familiar refrain. While some city industries reported slight upswings, businessmen continued to substitute machines for men "so that each city has a body of unemployed now on relief who very likely will never get back their old jobs because these jobs have vanished." In Jamestown, Martha Bruere found a dreadful situation "which will not be cured by a general renewal of business throughout the country. . . . [Jamestown's] problem is to find a new basis of livelihood for over 7,000 people formerly employed in establishments which have either moved away, gone into bankruptcy, or been torn down; it is a problem of reconstruction."[7]

In all the cities they visited, large and small, the reporters found the horrendous economic conditions exacerbated by a disturbing business-as-usual attitude among the employer class. Many businessmen publicly distrusted the programs and goals of the early New Deal: the federal monetary policy, the work relief projects, national wage scales, and the labor provisions of the National Industrial Recovery Act. Despite the severity of the Great Depression, business interests remained motivated by the lure of profits and in many cases seemed bereft of even the slightest sense of altruism. In Rochester, New York, reporters wrote of a "contented conservatism," the determination of businessmen that "the only danger is that business will lose confidence if the [Roosevelt] Administration makes more concessions to labor or moves further to the left." After a few days in Columbus and Cleveland, Ohio, David Maynard found "plenty of money on hand for business expansion, but industrialists and bankers [are] uninterested in investing because of a lack of confidence about what the government will do next and a general feeling that there is very little chance of profits."

Often, this lack of confidence and conscience manifested itself perniciously in company policy. When Campbell Soup's economic position improved, the company reduced its labor force and sped up the work pace rather than reemploying workers and expanding production. Several examples from Baltimore illustrate the invidiousness of business's "lack of confidence." Cynical Baltimore employers converted the National Recovery Administration's minimum wage provision into the standard hourly rate; in other words, the minimum rate became the maximum hourly wage. Department stores in Baltimore paid their clerks "only for the time they actually work[ed] and sen[t] them home during quieter hours." Montgomery Ward there hired waitresses for three hours a day at twenty-five cents an hour, a practice legal under the NRA's Restaurant Code but ruthless on the waitresses, who had to pay twenty cents for streetcar fare to get to work. Then, too, department stores frequently hired the hapless unemployed to peddle electrical applicances door-to-door on a commission-only basis. As Lorena Hickok bitterly observed, "If he sells anything, that's just gravy to the department store." At the same time, Baltimore auto mechanics were paid only while actually working on a car; when not working, they were required to "hang around without pay." As one employer put it: "If they don't like it, [they can] go somewhere else. Plenty of labor available these times!"

Baltimore business practices were not unique. Lincoln Colcord charged Akron, Ohio, businessmen with "living in the past." He insisted that industrialists there "were preoccupied with their . . . efforts to maintain the arbitrary economic position to which they have become accustomed. They [want] the government to furnish a huge public works program and to keep hands off in every other direction."[8]

Saddened by what they saw in these cities, the reporters poignantly reflected upon the social cost of the Great Depression. The American worker had historically been heralded as the bone and sinew of the nation. According to the popularizers of the American Way, it had been the nation's workers, the men who made steel, mined coal, built automobiles, and ran the railroads, who had exchanged their wrenches and drill presses for rifles and defeated the Kaiser in World War I. How completely had the depression obliterated that Bunyanesque image of the American worker? In 1934, a local social worker told Steep that "the men who have found their efficiency impaired no longer take chances of getting off relief." Elsewhere the jobless wandered as human flotsam drifting from city to city and flopping for months at a time in shelters for homeless men. Julian Claff branded Philadelphia's shelter "a genuine plague spot." All seven hundred residents of the shelter—located in a brick building which had once housed the Baldwin Locomotive Works—"appeared to be fixtures" in Lorena Hickok's eyes. "Nothing more can be done about them" she reported to Hopkins, "they can't handle themselves any more. They have slipped so far down the scale that they are content to rest and throw the responsibility on the flop management, while they spend a little spare time in digging up an occasional pint of gin." The real crime, Hickok wrote, was that most of these men were not the usual municipal flop house denizens. "Once, and not so long ago, they were citizens."

For the majority of the jobless, still rooted in family units, months, even years of joblessness had exhausted their savings and driven them to seek the cheapest and most dilapidated housing. Moldering tenement units, once considered unfit for human habitation, became homes for not one but often several families who sought any, even the barest excuse for, shelter. Hickok toured Philadelphia's notorious "bandbox" slums where the poor were crammed into tiny, boxlike, three-story structures—one 10 by 10 cubicle teetering above another. These antiquated rookeries lacked not only gas and electricity but also the plumbing necessary for basic sanitary facilities. Likewise, Thomas Steep found housing in Gary, Indiana, "pretty terrible. Some buildings are stuffed to suffocation with clients (the jobless) while hundreds of houses are empty because they have been taken over by banks and insurance companies and no one can pay the rent asked. . . . As elsewhere, scores of jobless men who formerly thought they owned their own homes have been evicted and have judgments hanging over their heads for balances due. . . ."[9]

Despite both federal and state efforts to undergird the emergency relief efforts of financially beleaguered cities and towns, by 1932 the whole voluntary relief structure had crumbled under the weight of mass joblessness. Consequently, the Federal Emergency Relief Agency undertook to build a new welfare edifice in America. Under Harry Hopkins, FERA employed a staff of efficiency-minded professional social workers determined to establish rigorous national standards of professional casework, including uniform rules for client eligibility and relief adequacy. By the time Hickok was in Philadelphia and Steep in Gary, FERA was operating as the central relief agency dispensing federal welfare funds and coordinating relief activities at both the state and municipal levels. In cities such as Philadelphia, Chicago, and Baltimore, FERA had supplanted a motley array of charitable agencies which ranged in efficiency from Philadelphia's highly professionalized Family Welfare Society to the makeshift soup kitchen and the ancient township and neighborhood-based poor board.

However, in November 1934, FERA's welfare edifice remained incomplete, while the size of the urban caseload rose. Over 131,500 families crammed Chicago's relief rolls—11,000 more than in 1933. Lorena Hickok found 1,250,000 New Yorkers—men, women, and children—totally dependent upon public funds for their subsistence. Many more of her citizens, Hickok confessed, should be getting relief and undoubtedly would be were the money available. These, she added, "are skating along on thin ice, barely existing, undernourished, in rags, . . . utterly wretched and hopeless, their nerves taut, their morale breaking down." Moreover, "the great majority of these people—those who are on the relief rolls and those who should be there—are in this plight through no fault of their own. They are entering this third winter of their distress." [10]

Significantly, the reporters in late 1934 predicted little abatement of the crisis. After touring St. Louis, Kansas City, Tulsa, Dallas, and Fort Worth, Edward Webster was more appalled than ever at "the scale of relief," "the magnitude and the complexity of the task," and the "disposition of America to interpret it all with placid fatalism." Webster believed that the relief population in St. Louis and other cities would increase "because of continued unemployment, increased unemployability, exhaustion of resources, loss of aid from relations and friends, and the trek from the land to the towns and cities [due in part to the drought, federal farm legislation, and the attraction of work relief wages]." In fact, "unless a definite upturn in employment occurs," Webster warned, "the relief population will tend to include practically all the unemployed." Not only were persons "from the high socioeconomic strata [now] forced to ask for help, as are more elderly and disabled persons," but, reported Webster, "all forms of chronic dependence . . . which were ordinarily cared for by relatives, friends, private welfare agencies, and public welfare agencies . . . have been dumped into the lap of the Federal Government." Besides these, he wrote, "have come the vast numbers of socially inadequate . . . , who have never known anything but poverty." [11]

During the first years of the Great Depression, American cities were totally unprepared to deal with mass unemployment in an urban-industrial society. In 1933, for example, New York City's entire caseload consisted of under half a million persons whom the city aided at a cost of slightly over $30,000,000. Then, in the first six months of 1934, the city's combined public and private caseload skyrocketed to over 1,500,000 people, whom it now cared for at a staggering cost of $50,524,309. Lorena Hickok termed New York's relief crisis as "breathtaking." One city block she visited housed over 200 relief families.

Like the professional altruists who administered private and public welfare in the city, the reporters regularly bemoaned the inadequacy of urban relief funds and criticized the inefficiency of politically motivated local relief agencies. Not surprisingly, in New York Hickok found lack of money to be the problem which "has been and still is and will continue to tower above all others." Even with the new "triangular system" whereby federal, state, and city governments each contributed a third of the welfare costs, Hickok figured that New York would still require $10,000,000 a month for relief; yet, she reported, the city "ought to be [spending] $15,000,000 a month, and even that would be barely adequate."

While admitting the frustration and enormous complexity of relief, the reporters reflected a liberal faith that bureaucratic efficiency offered the best solution to the urban welfare crisis. Robert Washburn, for one, regretted that local public welfare programs in states such as Connecticut and Massachusetts were quite separate from FERA and "coordinated only to the extent that it has been possible [for FERA] to wrangle cooperation." Yet, even slight success in "wrangling" cooperation enhanced local welfare standards, both by improving the administration of programs and, more important, by assuring the adequacy of relief services. Based on her observations of Akron, Ohio, reporter Louisa Wilson proposed that the efficient, professional administration of relief would streamline welfare services, ferret out the notorious welfare "chiseler," and hopefully reduce costs. Skyrocketing relief costs usually resulted in a reduction in the size of casework staffs and increased individual caseloads, thus compounding the crisis. Wilson noted that in Akron caseloads were so high that "with the time caseworkers spend writing orders for shoes, jackets, stoves, etc., they do not scratch the surface in checking on the resources of the unemployed." Nevertheless, many "workers believed that check or no check, chiseling goes on in less than five percent of the families."

Nothwithstanding the shortage of funds, urban relief administration under FERA became increasingly bureaucratized, efficient but less tempered by the philanthropic impulse to be emphatic which still colored the professional altruism of the 1920s. Wilson made this point in describing her visit to relief headquarters in Detroit. After informing Hopkins that the top women in the city's social service division resented the professional inadequacy of the staff and the low salaries (beginning caseworkers earned as little as twelve dollars a week), Wilson applauded the division's "healthy lack of over-paternalism." The director of training, whom she described as "a product of private agencies and the conventional training," told Wilson that the "new lot of social workers had a more healthy attitude toward the unemployed than the old group of caseworkers . . . , since they had not the same desire to do a thorough job of [client] reform. Lack of paternalism is a policy here." [12]

Heirs of the progressive ethos, social workers in the 1930s were dedicated to utilizing scientific welfare to buttress the institutional fabric of the nation. Despite the extreme clinical objectivity that Wilson found among the Detroit's staff, most modern social caseworkers distinguished scientific welfare from older, discredited charity while emphasizing the social-psychological needs of client families. Rather than serving the material needs of the jobless for food and clothing, caseworkers stressed the adjustment needs of poor families and used material relief as an instrument to assist families to adapt more successfully to urban industrial society. In accordance with this emphasis of social work on psychiatric principles, the best form of material relief was seen as aid that helped families adjust and conform to the American Way. In response to social worker Hopkins's great concern for the psychological health of the unemployed, the FERA reporters sought information in particular on the mental outlook of the jobless. At Chicago Commons in November 1934, Thomas Steep heard the director, Lea D. Taylor, express her fear that prolonged idleness had become destructive of the capacity to work. The jobless, she lamented, had become "muscularly soft and unconfident of their ability to work." Whenever they obtained temporary jobs, she said, "they are so fearful of making mistakes that they make mistakes and are promptly fired. The men who have found that their efficiency is impaired no longer take chances of getting off relief."

However, in his conversations with relief workers in Chicago, Steep found conflicting points of view about the degree to which relief had dulled the edge of the work ethic. For example, despite her pessimism Lea Taylor still felt that "a large percent—perhaps 90 percent—of those on relief would rather work." On the other hand, some Chicagoans, especially businessmen, told Steep that "too many people are beginning to think they can live without working." The director of the Illinois State Unemployment Service advocated taking all the employable jobless off relief and forcing them to work. He believed that relief discouraged people from seeking work. In Detroit, almost everyone Lincoln Colcord talked to warned that "public welfare was creating a permanent relief class . . . , that the psychological basis for it has already made its appearance, and that relief must continue to be undesirable."

Louisa Wilson's conversation with "two high-type service men who were applying for relief in Detroit for the first time" seemed to strengthen the familiar "permanent relief class" hypothesis. One of the two applicants, "still looking the gay blade even in the relief office, was obviously suffering at the idea of applying for welfare but said for himself and others: 'People don't think the same about welfare as they used to. I would have starved before applying three years ago. I wouldn't apply if so many others didn't.' His companion brashly interjected that 'They say welfare's pretty good this year.'" In Columbus, Ohio, David M. Maynard found cases where clients viewed relief triumphantly. Rather than feeling abashed, they flaunted their relief status. "Look what we've been able to get out of the government this year," gloated one client, "and we're going to get more." Many recipients were demanding, reported Maynard; one burst into the Columbus relief office shouting, "I've come for my mattress!" [13]

Deeply concerned about the moral deterioration of the unemployed and wary of the modest success of the communist-sponsored Unemployed Councils, FERA struggled to fashion a welfare program that conformed to the American Way. Not surprisingly, Hopkins promoted work relief as the centerpiece of his program. In late 1933, FERA unveiled its emergency Civil Works Administration (CWA), a jobs program aimed at carrying the unemployed through the coming winter months. By the time Hopkins terminated CWA in the spring of 1934, the $900 million operation had employed over four million persons and produced, among other things, over 255,000 miles of roads and city streets, 12,000 miles of sewers, and the construction of 469 airports. But not all CWA workers labored on visibly beneficial projects such as schools and airports; many men spent tedious hours raking leaves in city parks, while hundreds of jobless women toiled on large mattress-making or other sewing projects. Sewing, leaf-raking, and such make-work projects as one involving research on the history of the safety pin—while therapeutic for the unemployed—invited charges of wastefulness and were perhaps politically untenable.

To replace CWA, Hopkins established within FERA a smaller Local Works Division. However, politics notwithstanding, Hopkins and others increasingly determined that for the employable jobless a large-scale works program must replace federal participation in direct relief. Therefore, he sought evidence to undergird his resolve. Consistent with bureaucratic practice, Hopkins's reporters turned up information and opinions that basically reinforced his arguments. In Akron, Louisa Wilson discovered almost unanimous opinion among labor people, lay people, and relief workers in favor of work relief. She did uncover slight disagreement in Detroit and Flint, Michigan, where social workers felt that work relief "tended to make the relief person self-satisfied with his status and not look for [real] work." Elsewhere in Ohio, David Maynard talked with casework visitors, clients, and relief administrators who believed that a work relief program should be launched. But "in contrast to the earlier CWA program—workers in any new program must feel that they are doing something, if anything really worthwhile is to be expected." Maynard disclosed that "CWA left a terrific reaction against work relief," which he found revealed in the outburst of one typical businessman: "Oh, they just sit around and loaf on the job." In Detroit, Lincoln Colcord recorded the same mixed reaction to work relief. People surveyed by Colcord complained that "ill advised and poorly conducted work relief had a demoralizing effect on a man's standard of citizenship. In work relief projects on an emergency basis [like CWA] there is always a tendency to do things of questionable practical value and this creates a backfire of public criticism." [14]

Julian Claff detected a similar backlash among Philadelphia businessmen. A Chamber of Commerce spokesman dismissed CWA projects as "not worth a damn." The CWA "develops leaners," he insisted. "There is something pathetic about a gang of ragged laborers puttering around a bridle path, which they will never use, in a section of town in which they have no interest [perhaps his section of town?], for a few cents a day more than they would get out of jumping on direct relief." A Birmingham, Alabama, businessman uttered the most widely held viewpoint that the 60 percent of the cost of work relief that went into materials should be spent "reviving private industry, providing *jobs*, eventually reducing our relief load."

Yet, throughout the reports the positive overshadowed the negative side of the work relief argument. If many businessmen in Philadelphia and Birmingham derided work programs, others in Worcester, Massachusetts, confided to Martha Bruere that work relief was "worth the extra cost in keeping up people's work habits and physical capacity to work." In Jamestown, New York, Bruere visited a park project, "a lovely thing of which any city can be proud." The foreman eagerly pointed out the park's outstanding points—the wading pool and the bridge—and asserted that he had not had trouble with his men. "They didn't loaf on the job any more than anyone would. . . . He said the men were proud of the way the park looked." [15]

Who were the thousands of people whose impoverishment and misery overburdened the finite resources of city welfare funds and taxed the ingenuity of Harry Hopkins and the Federal Emergency Relief Administration? According to Hickok, New York City's relief rolls encompassed over thirty nationalities: "Thousands of them," wrote Hickok, "cannot speak a word of English," but, she added, "among them are business and professional men whose incomes five years ago ran into many thousands of dollars." [16]

As can be seen in Hickok's observations, just below the surface of these reports on America's cities there seemed to be an undue preoccupation with the ethnic, racial, and class identity of the unemployed. Unquestionably, the reports embodied an expression of ethnocentrism, symptomatic of what historian John Higham identifies as the American propensity for ethnic and racial "boundary-building" that flourished during the

Harry Hopkins in his Washington office, 1933. (*The Franklin D. Roosevelt Library*)

Lorena Hickok traveling with Eleanor Roosevelt, Miami, Florida, March 1934. (*The Franklin D. Roosevelt Library*)

Martha Gellhorn, circa 1933–1934. (*The Franklin D. Roosevelt Library*)

A Pittsburgh soup line, early 1930s. (*Archives of Industrial Society, University of Pittsburgh*)

Dispensing bread to the poor, Pittsburgh, early 1930s. (*Archives of Industrial Society, University of Pittsburgh*)

A Pittsburgh Hooverville. (*Archives of Industrial Society, University of Pittsburgh*)

A Bronx, New York, slum, mid–1930s. (*Photo by Russell Lee; Library of Congress*)

Black housing in Chicago during the New Deal. (*Photo by Russell Lee; Library of Congress*)

Poverty in New Orleans, mid-1930s. (*Photo by Walker Evans; Library of Congress*)

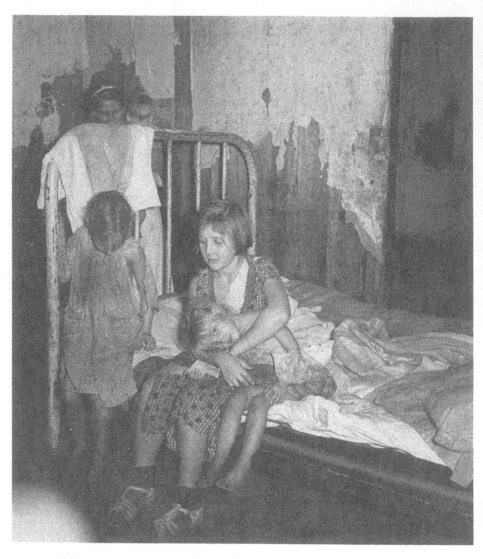

Children of a coal miner, Scott's Run, West Virginia, 1938. (*Photo by Marion Post Wolcott; Library of Congress*)

Main Street in a coal patch, Chaplin, on Scott's Run, West Virginia, 1938. (*Photo by Marion Post Wolcott; Library of Congress*)

Children at play in Manchester, New Hampshire, 1937. (*Photo by Edwin Locke; Library of Congress*)

twenties and thirties. Significantly, the reporters' interest in and intolerance for patterns of ethnic and racial behavior strongly suggest that the social and economic stresses of the Great Depression exacerbated already existing urban racial and ethnic tensions. This presaged on the one hand the racial violence of World War II and, on the other, the trend toward black ghettoization and white suburbanization that characterized the postwar era.

The reporters' ethnocentrism revealed itself in the way they categorized the victims of the depression. Generally they divided the urban relief rolls into two distinct client groups: the worthy, who deserved assistance, and the unworthy, who did not. In 1934 the unemployed white-collar worker, the hapless civil engineer, the jobless salesman and his advertising executive neighbor, the out of work store clerk, and waitress, all easily qualified as worthy—that is, they were "jobless through no fault of their own." Vagrants, derelicts, criminals, and the sporadically jobless laborer—the traditionally wretched poor—were labeled "undeserving." But also stigmatized among the latter were the recent black migrants to the city and other "new migrants"—the southern Italians, Greeks, Ukranians, Russian Jews, and Polish-Americans who began crowding America's urban slums in the first decades of the twentieth century. At the very least, Hopkins's correspondents accused these new immigrants of ignorance—an incapacity to cope effectively or efficiently with modern urban civilization. At their worst the reporters branded those whom Jacob Riis had called the "Motley Crowd" as being blatantly inferior, and the corpus of America's incipient "permanent poor."

Some of the reporters displayed an intolerance for the plight of the immigrant poor. Touring Buffalo, Martha Bruere found Italians and Poles "most content with home relief, and making the greatest demands on the [relief] staff—a condition," she added, "which seems to be the same everywhere that I have seen." Robert Washburn had his prejudices sharpened by a Boston "cop, who knows the affairs of everyone in the Italian North End of the city." According to the policeman, half the Italians in that neighborhood were on relief and, moreover, "they were contented with it and would never stir a stump again unless forced to. . . . When all due allowance is made for the vivid disrespect of foreigners [in Boston] there is a large section of the population," Washburn noted, "where the old abhorrence of going on welfare has died out." Among the Sicilian population of Bridgeport and New Haven, Connecticut, Washburn found "a premium placed on lying and concealing; these people follow the line of least resistance—to relief that is."

Thomas Steep displayed some generosity in his treatment of the ethnic groups who lived in the shadow of the Chicago Commons. "The clients in the neighborhood are largely Italian, Polish and Greek," he wrote, and "are known as an excitable people. For the most part they don't know what the Depression is all about and think the capitalist class is merely taking a rest, indifferent to what happens to poor people." [17]

But while Steep forgave the poverty of Chicago's ethnics, he, like his colleagues, never extended the same sensitivity to urban blacks. In city after city he and the other reporters entertained complaints about the size of the black relief population. For example, Philadelphia's black population was 11 percent; yet, blacks comprised 40 percent of the relief rolls. "Only about one-fourth of the entire relief load is white or 'American born,'" wrote Julian Claff from the City of Brotherly Love. In Detroit, where 10 percent of the population was black and blacks made up 25 percent of those on relief, Louisa Wilson uncovered "a certain amount of 'man-on-the-street' resentment at the high proportion of Negroes on relief." She found the "stigma of relief practically non-existent among Negroes and Negro politicians alert to see that there is no discrimination." Not surprisingly, disdain for blacks on relief bristled most in southern cities such as New Orleans, where caseworkers and supervisors alike concurred that the Negro caseload was much larger than it should be. There was little doubt in Lorena Hickok's mind "that thousands of these Negroes in New Orleans are living much better on relief than they ever did while they were working. You hear the same stories over and over again— Negroes quitting their jobs or refusing to work because they can get on relief." Perhaps only half of these stories were true, she offered, "but that's bad enough." A local relief supervisor believed that the high black caseloads were the result of "the Negro psychology. They are children really. If anything is being given away they want some too." Besides, she told Hickok, "they are accustomed to having things handed out to them by white people."

On the other hand, some reporters were tempted to explain—even to justify—the black relief problem. Lincoln Colcord blamed companies like Ford Motor, which during the boom years of the 1920s bused "colored labor" from the deep South into Detroit. "Many of those workers with their families are now on city relief," declared Colcord. "They were brought up on a low standard of living, and present relief standards are a luxury to them. They certainly have no incentive to get back to work." In a similar vein, Thomas Steep bemoaned the plight of black migrants drawn into the Chicago, Gary, and Milwaukee labor markets during the boom years. "Their chance for jobs is practically nil. . . . People in Milwaukee look upon them as a permanent object of relief."

Of course, the black neighborhoods in cities such as Detroit, Chicago, and Gary "were pretty awful," to use Steep's words. In 1934, both Wilson and Steep found tuberculosis cases so high among urban blacks, "particularly the importations from Georgia and elsewhere, that workers [were] instructed to map out adequate diets . . . weaning them away from steady beans." The prevalence of TB among Chicago blacks became part of the unemployment crisis. According to Steep, the jobless black in Chicago "has no money for medical service at the incipiency of his disease; moreover, he is compelled to double up in already overcrowded houses which have no running water, are insufficiently ventillated and devoid of sunshine, and have only one unspeakably filthy toilet for several families." Steep wondered why Chicago's public health department failed to care for such cases. The answer, he discovered, was that there were no facilities for hospitalizing them. The municipal tuberculosis sanitarium had a waiting list of 800 black patients, "but in the last year," Steep wrote Hopkins, "not one Negro patient has been accepted." [18]

However the reporters characterized poverty and relief, they appreciated the potential of joblessness for social and political disruption. Radical political activity in the cities had begun as early as 1930 when the Communist International, alert to the political importance of mass joblessness, abandoned its subtle strategy of working from within the American labor movement and formed the jobless into Unemployed Councils (UC), organizations which would move the unemployed into socialism. In 1931 and 1932 the Unemployed Councils conducted frequent demonstrations at city halls and state capitals, and at the scenes of tenant evictions, which were occurring with great frequency. Although the crowds at these demonstrations were small, their potential for social revolution worried many Americans, including Harry Hopkins. For Hopkins the future of the republic and the free enterprise system hinged on devising a successful response to the nation's relief crisis. Yet, by 1934, neither Hopkins nor the reporters expressed much confidence that the present relief system, which relied heavily on cash grants, food, and clothing orders, could allay the so-called "thunder on the left." Wayne Parrish's assessment of New York City seemed particularly ominous. Present conditions, Parrish wrote Hopkins, had brought relief clients "to the frame of mind where they will follow a leader. Clients are more critical, more complaining, more ready to react." The social workers Parrish contacted in the city "seem to sense the feeling that something is going to happen." One of them feared the making of a "new social order—unless the trend begins back toward private jobs."

Although a number of other groups in addition to the Unemployed Councils sought to organize the urban jobless, including the Unemployed League of A. J. Muste's Conference for Progressive Labor Action, most of the reporters focused on the Unemployed Councils which, according to Wayne Parrish, caused the bulk of the trouble in New York City. Councils were growing stronger, especially in Harlem where their effectiveness attracted large numbers of blacks. When the councils complained to relief administrators, they got results. Yet, one official in Harlem "said she felt like she was sitting on a volcano and expected things to begin happening."

Among the "vast majority [of jobless] who have grown up under the American tradition of opportunity," Parrish distinguished a growing discontent with relief as now administered, and, he added, the demand for jobs was bound to grow. "A great majority of people on relief for two years are reaching the cracking point," he wrote, "and have got to have jobs or go to pieces. The security of a minimum subsistence on relief is not enough."

The Unemployed Councils demanded jobs or more adequate relief, and to underscore their seriousness they staged demonstrations, often marching on the offices of relief administrations and threatening relief officers with a choice of either improving welfare services or facing violence. "We cannot hold our thousands of marchers back much longer," thundered the council leader of a midwestern city. "We expect an answer in the mail before Tuesday night. . . ; we have exhausted our patience trying to keep relief clients from storming the warehouse." [19]

In Chicago, the UCs beseiged a relief station, and "despite the presence of police reserves, subjected the supervisor to physical violence." Occasionally, these violent tactics met with success. In Detroit, UC violence forced the relief administration to supply groceries to single men who formerly had been required to live in the city shelter.

However, it was not among single men or among the jobless mill operatives that the Communist party recognized the grist for its revolution; instead, the party singled out black America and there focused the brunt of its organizing activity. The UCs militantly upheld the right of urban blacks to have equal access to relief. In Harlem the councils vigorously championed the cause of blacks not only against discriminatory relief policies but also against arbitrary and brutal evictions from their apartment dwellings. The UCs didn't just work in the metropolises such as New York, Chicago, and Philadelphia; they also championed black rights in smaller cities. In Sioux City, Iowa, Hickok was told that the councils frequently picked up blacks and took them to public swimming pools where they would be denied admission. There would be a disturbance, the police would arrive, "a few heads would be cracked," and the "Communists" and "Negroes, too," would be jailed. "Whereupon," she wrote, "they all became martyrs and the lot of Negroes became good Communists." [20]

Actually, the story Hickok was told was probably exaggerated. Despite the publicity given to the Unemployed Councils, despite the ominous threat they posed for the welfare administrators, and despite the fear they aroused in established society, FERA and the reporters discounted their threat. For example, after receiving repeated inflammatory reports concerning the spread of communism among the jobless in Oregon, Howard Meyers of FERA's Washington office wrote to the Portland field office:

"We have received with much interest the account of 'communistic demonstrations' in Portland." While Meyers might have been interested, he was mostly skeptical of the real meaning of such activity in the Northwest. "We are led to wonder," Myers confessed, "whether these demonstrations have a very definite philosophy of changing the form of government and therefore merit the name communist," or "whether they are naive and misguided individuals who feel that this type of demonstration will get them what they want in terms of food, shelter, and the like." For Meyers, it was difficult to distinguish between and among all the different organizations demonstrating through one form or another.[21]

Other Hopkins reporters were equally dubious about the radicalization of the jobless. Edward Webster portrayed the mass of jobless he encountered in Kansas City, St. Louis, and Dallas as "stunned, confused, and complacent. One hears far more expression of radical thought from those administering relief than from those receiving it." After eavesdropping at a UC-sponsored rally of the jobless in Camden, New Jersey, Martha Gellhorn, somewhat dissapointed, described it to Hopkins as "an eye opener." She caricatured the people at the meeting as "sad and dispirited." The main speaker, Gellhorn recalled, "tried very hard to get up a little enthusiasm from the audience," but failed to do so.

Thomas Steep found a similar malaise even in Hamtramck, the working-class suburb of Detroit. Although "reputed to be a hotbed of Communism," Steep reported to Hopkins that recent relief cuts had "brought out a demonstration of only two hundred or so." When he sought an explanation for the modest turnout, Steep was told that "the whole political philosophy of the (large Polish population) of Hamtramck is against Communism."

Julian Claff arrived at similar conclusions. After investigating jobless organizations in Philadelphia's working-class Kensington-Richmond neighborhood, Claff wrote Hopkins that the jobless groups "had passed the nuisance stage and were developing into a real impediment," and he denounced "the communist group as the noisiest and least considerate." But, adjudged Claff, "their active membership does not exceed 200." Nor did reporter David Maynard discover Communists mounting a significant front in industrialized Cleveland, where the Unemployed Councils represented fewer than 150 of the city's 3,800 relief cases, and where the biggest jobless demonstrations attracted fewer than 700 of the unemployed. Maynard offered that "there was little likelihood of serious trouble [in Cleveland] this winter [1934] unless a serious cut in relief was necessary."[22]

Yet, clearly the FERA reporters believed that the United States was deep in the throes of monumental social change. In the light of modern technology and the trend toward industrial and bureaucratic efficiency, the reporters doubted that industry would ever reemploy the mass of jobless presently on the relief rolls. Accordingly, the reporters agonized over the prospect of a corps of "permanent unemployed." They worried, too, about the erosion of skill among the long-term unemployed, and they frequently digressed about how joblessness affected the urban moral order.

What impact did unemployment and relief have on the fabric of American urban life? In pondering the "cross currents of public opinion" encountered in his visits to many western cities, Robert Washburn set forth eloquently and insightfully the crux of the problem facing America in 1934. "Too much of the analysis of opinion abroad and in urban America," he observed, "springs from the forlorn hope of recovery in terms of the prosperity of bygone days. Many [people] continue to look backward to the old order rather than forward to a new order representing adjustment to changed conditions." Consequently, surmised Washburn, "the relief situation is not being intelligently faced. All too many persons focus attention upon the possible abuses of relief and forget the major problem at hand."

Steep, Colcord, Wilson, Gellhorn, and Hickok joined Washburn in advising Hopkins about the gravity of the urban social crisis—a crisis, said the reporters, whereby the growing ranks of the "unworthy," usually unemployable poor contentedly accepted relief while the salvageable poor, those with enough wits and skill left to work—if work could be found— "bitterly chafe under it, ready to revolt if they [see] anything to be gained that way. [Others are] just sinking into apathy, which is perhaps worse." "As for the future, any effective relief policy," Colcord reflected, "must be self-liquidating lest a too liberal relief program would be likely to build up this minority into a permanent relief class." Choosing to slice through the gloom of the depression and end her report on a more optimistic note, Louisa Wilson tossed Hopkins first a bouquet, than a last note of warning: "Your best publicity," she wrote, "has been yourself; most people, unemployed and employed, agree with you that work is the only answer. Anything else is just peanuts, and their ropes are getting thinner and thinner." [23]

4

Beleagured Households

The Agony of the American Family
and the Unattached Person

■ I didn't feel he was a sane man
as he talked to me. He was a husky man, with lots of initiative, crazy
to work."
Louisa Wilson, from Akron

■ The men have nowhere to go.
They walk around the block, go to the relief station to gossip or to file
fancied grievances, and return to resume quarrels with their wives.
Thomas Steep, from Chicago

■ The mere fact of his having re-
sponsibility and a pattern of routine for existence completely changed the
man. He went around whistling. His wife was happier.
A psychiatric caseworker

■ In the center of the raging eco-
nomic storm swayed the American family, tattered, bent, but more or less
intact. America had long enshrined the family as its quintessential institution; in it reposed the heart of the nation's system of values and norms.
Through it America socialized its young and perpetuated the democratic
way of life. Naturally, every wound the depression inflicted upon the family aroused a heightening of social concern.[1]

In her studies of working-class families in Boston and Manchester, New Hampshire, Tamara Haraven has made clear that time spent in the family as well as at work had traditionally defined member roles. Males were breadwinners while women, even when they labored outside the home as mill operators, as in the Manchester textile mills, retained their primary work role as housekeepers. However, during the late nineteenth century these roles became increasingly ambiguous for both working- and middle-class families. Modern factory and office work offered less distinctive, sexually differentiated occupational tasks, while in middle-class households, technology freed women from much of the drudgery and tedium of traditional chores. Therefore, during the 1920s, not strangely, efficiency-minded social scientists castigated the traditional family—and in particular its role-fixing function—for retarding progress.[2]

However, the Great Depression, which triggered a revolt against the false promises of civilization, restored the family to its central place as the anchor of culture. During the 1930s, social scientists, the media, and opinion makers in general rallied to defend the modern family as an adaptive mechanism providing nutrient socialization for the young and emotional support for members enduring the trauma of economic change.

Typically, American families by 1930 were nuclear—mother, father, and the 2.3 children of the union. Middle-class families tended to be both more nuclear and somewhat more intensive than families comprising working-class and immigrant enclaves. Being more intensive, middle-class families sought emotional support and recreation within the womb of the family unit. Few middle-class families ventured much beyond home to enjoy the sociability of friends, work groups, fraternal organizations, or the neighborhood.

From as early as the 1840s middle-class Americans extolled the values of hearth, health, home, and family. Ideally, within the middle-class home, the Victorian family nurtured its children and cultivated the American Way. As a "cradle of domesticity," the middle-class family played a crucial part in determining its members' role and place in society, bestowing upon members not only their status but also their personal identity. The linkage between family and personal identity tightened around the family's role as a vehicle for consumption. Mass production, mass advertising, and mass media all forced the family to become a center for the consumption of an endless array of merchandise. Spacious suburban homes, appliance-centered kitchens, stylish mahogany radios, luxurious automobiles, and modern home laundries became status symbols identifying a family's success or failure in achieving an "American standard of living," and in a land where morality and material progress were historically connected, society ritually penalized families unable to compete effectively in the race.[3]

The economic upheaval of the Great Depression severely taxed the family's identity-fixing role. Nevertheless, despite the technological revolution of the 1920s, work, as occupation/vocation, survived unblemished into the depression as the principal definer of family member roles and as the adhesive for family solidarity. Thus, while the Great Depression tended to strengthen the image of the family as a cultural symbol by spawning mass joblessness, at the same time it removed the major prop assuring the cohesiveness of the family unit.

Hopkins's reporters joined a host of American writers and social scientists who expressed concern about the social and psychological resiliency of the nation's basic institution. Since few questioned the basic values of the culture, social observers increasingly measured the caliber of individuals and families by their ability to adapt or adjust to economic or social stress. For example, prominent social psychologists of the 1930s such as Karen Horney, Elton May, and Alfred Adler argued that success or good mental health hinged on adjustment or adaptation to the prevailing pattern of culture.

In the reporters' view, the high rates of unemployment and the enormity of the impoverishment caused by the Great Depression clearly challenged the adaptive powers of the American families. Indeed, the depression turned the quest for family status and member identity into a treacherous obstacle course where millions—among them even the presumably most fit—failed to negotiate the barriers. While on the one hand society still encouraged habits of consumption, on the other hand it challenged families to endure poverty and adapt to reduced living standards. Many young people delayed marriage as a coping strategy. Others who opted to form households delayed childbearing or responded to the trauma of lost or slashed wages by doubling up with relatives or taking in boarders to expand the circle of breadwinners. One recent study of the working patterns of middle-class women during the depression found that despite traditional middle-class disapproval of working wives and the weak market for female employment, the percentage of job-holding wives increased significantly during the thirties, even among families where husbands earned over a thousand dollars a year. In her article on working women during the Great Depression, Winifred Bolin, for one, rejected "pin money" as an explanation and made a strong case that the middle-class wives worked during the depression mainly to uphold the family's standard of living.[4]

However, what of the many families or family types that seemingly lacked the resources for any kind of adjustment—mining families, families living in dying New England textile villages? It is apparent from the testimony of the reporters that the New Deal came to regard these people as marginal, superfluous, stranded beyond the normative pale of American middle-class culture.

In some respects, the depression afforded a broad arena for testing the adaptive skills of American families. But the reporters' excursion into this labyrinth of American culture revealed an important feature of the social scientist's heightened fascination with the family in the 1930s. They harbored serious anxieties about the durability of the American social fabric and therefore probed deeply for evidence of pervasive archaic or dysfunctional family forms. What if, they feared, dull-witted or occupationally superfluous families should contaminate the emerging pattern of their culture? Such speculations reveal the propensity of progressive-minded Americans of the 1930s to dabble in social engineering, to proffer, that is, the devices of governmental power on behalf of strengthening the nation's social and moral fiber and promoting the American Way.

Therefore, in their quest for data on the impact of the Great Depression and of New Deal relief programs, Hopkins's reporters carefully scrutinized the American family, examining it for evidence of undue stress, moral deterioration, ruptures, and other signs of weakness. Everywhere they traveled the reporters discovered evidence corroborating their fears. The economic pummeling of the Great Depression—the loss of income, the depletion of savings, the surrendering of insurance policies, and the ignomy of it all—was immobilizing the family, suffocating it in despair. Martha Gellhorn told her boss that the condition of families in Boston, Lowell, and Lynn, Massachusetts, was so grim "that whatever words I use will seem hysterical and exaggerated." After spending one week "case visiting" with a Massachusetts social worker "seeing about five families a day," Gellhorn groaned at the enormity of the tragedy. Fear was driving these people "into a state of semi-collapse; cracking nerves; and an overpowering terror of the future." These people seemed more intelligent than the unemployed she had encountered in the South, and Gellhorn concluded that "the price of this intelligence is consciousness. They know what they're going through. I haven't been in one home that hasn't offered me the spectacle of a human being driven beyond his or her powers of endurance and sanity. They can't pay rent and are evicted. They are shunted from place to place and are watching their children grow thinner and thinner. . . ."[5]

In the face of this evidence the reporters raised serious doubts about the family's capacity to function effectively as a socioeconomic unit; but in doing so, they identified particular family forms that seemed more vulnerable than others. Noteworthy among these were families headed by older, even middle-aged men and "white-collar families" whose more "refined temperments" ill prepared them for the stigma attending acceptance of relief. Likewise, the reporters agonized over the plight of individual family members, particularly adolescents and young, unmarried offspring who were caught adrift in the swirling currents of a turbulent world.

This differentiation of families by social class and occupational status characterized the bureaucratic approach of the period and seemed typical of many local welfare administrations. Lorena Hickok marveled at the sophistication of Tuscon, Arizona's hierarchical class-ranking system, which was executed "so quietly that people didn't even know they were being classified—they divided their case load into four groups, Classes A, B, C, and D. They have about 2,800 families on relief there: 1,200 Mexicans, American citizens, but with a low standard of living; 800 Yaqui Indian families, political refugees from old Mexico; 800 white families." There were sixty families in Class A, mostly professional and business victims of the depression. Each group had its own intake. "No mixing," Hickok pointed out.

Families in Class A received a maximum $50-a-month relief grant, half of it in cash. "It took care of them fairly adequately," Hickok believed, "rents, clothing, and everything." Work projects were established for them, and although they were required to work only a few hours a week "for what they were getting,' Hickok was pleased to inform Hopkins that "these people have been giving full time, voluntarily."

Class B had 250 families, on a maximum of $36 a month, from 33⅓ to 40 percent cash. It consisted of some white-collar people—clerks, stenographers, bookkeepers, and so on—and skilled labor. Many of these people were able to augment their incomes by a few days' work now and then.

Class C included 1,000 families, on a $25 maximum, 30 percent cash. It consisted of white unskilled labor and Mexican and Spanish-American unskilled labor with standards of living higher than those of most Mexicans. "And into Class D went 1,490 families, on a $10 maximum all in kind [groceries, clothing, etc.]. These were the low class Mexicans, Spanish-Americans, and Indian families. . . . 'Now this all may seem pretty bad to you,' the relief administrator told me, 'but you're going to quit some day and leave us, here in these communities, to carry on. We'll never be able to carry on under the conditions Washington is imposing on us now.'" [6]

New Deal relief administrators were hardly alone in their class-based assessment of the impact of joblessness and poverty. Indeed, most contemporary studies of the family and unemployment, including Mina Komarovsky's *The Unemployed Man and His Family*, Robert C. Angell's *The Family Encounters the Depression*, and Ruth Cavan and Karen Ranck's *The Family and the Depression*, recognized that working- and middle-class families reacted differently to the trauma of lengthy unemployment. Findings based upon analysis of quantitative data from the Berkeley Guidance panel study of 112 families who experienced income loss between 1929 and 1933 support this contention. Sociologist Glen Elder's research, using the Berkeley data, disclosed that middle-class families during the Great Depression were more vulnerable to the threat and stigma of income loss even though working-class families experienced much greater and more prolonged income loss. Elder found that hard times exacted social stress on males and marital bonds at all levels of the social structure; however, heavy income loss, argued Elder, represented more of a "disturbance of habit" among middle-class families and therefore precipitated more incidents of neurotic behavior among middle-class males and more marital disruption.[7]

Long before Angell or Komarovsky published their findings concerning the effect of the depression on family functioning, the reporters were divulging similar information to Hopkins based upon their subjective observations. Concerned not only about joblessness but also about the effect of relief, they carefully inspected the middle- and working-class families they encountered for signs of psychological stress and tensions producing family instability. For instance, in his tours of St. Louis and other cities of the South Central states, Edward Webster observed the plight of many working-class families and lamented what he called the "double tragedy attending prolonged unemployment; first the family morale suffers from the loss of a job; to this is added the loss of morale attending the relief which must be given." From the trauma of joblessness, Webster saw "inevitably emerging a large number of maladjusted, more or less disorganized persons." He argued that "both common sense and common decency . . . dictate that a responsible society shall be vitally concerned to reduce to a minimum the untoward consequences of relief and shall take no attitude toward the victims of such circumstances that will break down the bulwarks of personality and destroy those incentives without which no man or woman can carry on."[8]

Similarly, Martha Gellhorn blamed the invidiousness of the relief system for demolishing the fabric of working-class family life. In Massachusetts, Gellhorn found once stalwart, hard-working families forced by circumstances "to be beggars asking for charity; subject to questions from strangers and to all the miseries and indignities attached to destitution. Their pride," pleaded Gellhorn,

> is dying but not without due agony. I get these comments constantly: 'We can't live on that $12 (family of ten)—we're going to starve and my husband can't find work—he's out every day looking—and I get afraid about him: he gets so black. . . . If anyone had told us a year ago we'd come to this I'd have said he was a liar; and what can we do. . . . It's a terrible thing when decent people have to beg. . . . We always tried to be honest and decent as we could and we've worked all our lives; and what has it come to. . . . What's the use of looking for work any more; there isn't any. And look at the children. How would you feel if you saw your own kids like that: half naked and sick. . . . It seems like we're just going backwards since the last two years. . . . We can't go crazy; we've got the kids

to think about. . . . I don't want to ask for nothing. I hate this charity. But
we haven't got any shoes; do you think you could get us something to put
on our feet. . . .'[9]

Frequent references in the reports to personal disorganization indicate
that joblessness undermined a principal element of the psychosocial support system of the modern American family—the nexus, that is, between
the breadwinner role and male identity. A psychiatric caseworker found
that an atmosphere of irritability had developed in a man's house because
his wife had become tired of seeing him. "The man begged us to give him
something to do; he didn't care what it was so long as it took him from
home." The caseworker decided to experiment. She "got him a job as a
utility man in a hospital. The beneficial effect was immediate. The mere
fact of his having responsibility and a pattern of routine for existence completely changed the man. He went around whistling. His wife was happier. You can find infinite variations on this instance."[10]

In Detroit, Michigan, and Akron, Ohio, Louisa Wilson also witnessed
the agony of working-class families forced to swallow their pride and beg
for help. For Hopkins's benefit, she noted the disappearance of many of
the traditional resorts of the jobless family: "Grocers and landlords, no
longer feeling optimistic about the economic possibilities of their debtors,
will not extend credit as they used to. . . ." Wilson observed that "workers in Detroit used to [be able to] run up debts between employment—
run up rent for several months, owe the grocery bills for several months,
and borrow on the furniture. . . ." A former Ford worker reminisced to
Wilson that he "used to be able to pick up odd jobs such as washing cars.
My wife did, too, then. We used to worry along." Wilson bemoaned that
the workers in Detroit "don't do that any more. When their money is exhausted, they come to relief."

After a few days in Akron, Wilson observed that she had glimpsed the
"climax of despair" in the faces of many families. Relief workers in the
Ohio industrial city found unemployed families "less and less embar-
rassed to ask for relief and becoming more and more dependent on it as
security against times of unemployment as well as in some cases a bulwark
forever." Public employment interviews attested to "the almost un-
bearable despair of many who see themselves drawing nearer to the relief lines."

What most grieved Wilson about the sights of poverty and joblessness
in Akron and Cleveland was the coalescing of relief and despair into a tor-
pid human condition. Families "cry" the first time they seek relief, explained Wilson, "but by the third order they become demanding. They
don't feel it's worth the effort to work out their own salvation. If they don't
have to keep on begging, I don't know what will become of them. . . ."

Wilson found that the only hopeful ones were those who had just been laid off. Those out of work for four or five years were deeply bitter. "Many of them are rebellious," she wrote, "without being actively so." In one family she visited, "a wild-eyed young man was holding his child as his wife tried to get someone to pay the rent so they would have their water turned on again and not be evicted." Because this particular family had been evicted before, the father had lied about his name and had assumed his wife's maiden name for reference. He told Wilson: "You can't expect a man to keep sane under these conditions." As for Wilson: "I didn't feel he was a sane man as he talked to me. He was a husky man, with lots of initiative, crazy to work." [11]

In the opinion of the reporters, the age of the breadwinner made little difference. In Chicago, Steep spent an hour with the Reverend James Franklin Clancey, who for nineteen years had served the Methodist Episcopal parish in the notorious stockyards district. Steep noted that the church maintained welfare activities and for that reason had close contact with the neighborhood's unemployed. "Dr. Clancey was concerned over reports he had received from various quarters that the stockyards would not hire men over 40. This is a complaint that crops up everywhere," related Steep. "There is a growing belief that we are reaching a stage in industry when a man is out of a job at 40 he might go out and shoot himself, because whether he is physically able or not, industry does not want him."

To reinforce the point, Steep offered the case of a forty-two-year-old man with a wife and two children. Out of regular employment for three or four years, the man had worked at odd jobs and had come to "accepting anything in a low grade of work." Wherever he had sought work, he told Steep, he found that "the younger man beats him to it." Although no one actually tells him that he is too old to work, the effect is that even though he is physically able to hold a job, "he goes home day after day convinced that he is an old man." Already superannuated at an early age, he is convinced that industry has no place for him and that he and his family have become permanent dependents. Sadly, Steep concluded: "No use, he thinks, for him to plod the streets only to come home wearier and hungrier than ever and be assailed by his wife with a lot of questions to what are the chances. Better stick to relief and possibly supplement it (without telling the relief worker) by making 10 cents, 50 cents, or a dollar at odd jobs now and then."

Nor did the younger jobless whom Steep encountered on Chicago streets perceive themselves as any less superfluous. Steep sketched for Hopkins the picture of a "man in his thirties with a family who is on relief. He is growing timid about accepting a job for fear it may prove to be temporary. His experiences [have] taught him that if he loses a job it takes him a week or more to get [another one] and even though the job paid a little more than the relief . . . he loses out in the long run and has more to worry. . . ." [12]

Eventually as in middle-class families the stress of long-term jobless-ness affected domestic tranquility. Regardless of a family's income level prior to 1930, during the Great Depression the heavy loss of income in-creased conflict between husbands and wives. Yet, financial tensions not-withstanding, the Great Depression witnessed relatively few divorces. Some scholars argue that in the 1930s most aggrieved husbands and wives could not afford the costly litigation associated with divorce. Rifts, how-ever, occurred.

Thomas Steep saw these financial tensions at work straining marriages in Chicago working-class neighborhoods. Steep found "people [in Chi-cago] because of their idleness, . . . tend[ing] to manufacture complaints and to engage in domestic upheavals." Two or three women told Steep "that the worst of their troubles was to have their husbands sitting around the kitchen stove. The men have nowhere to go. They walk around the block, go to the relief station to gossip or to file fancied grievances, and return to resume quarrels with their wives." Steep concluded that not-withstanding the men's settled conviction that government owed them a living, "they would greatly prefer the independence that goes with receiv-ing pay for work done." [13]

However, there were thousands of unattached men and women who had neither spouse nor stove to hang around. Rather than face the respon-sibility of marriage and fail as a breadwinner, over 800,000 couples can-celed or postponed marriage during the 1930s. The impact of those thou-sands of decisions not to marry not only lowered the nation's birthrate but also swelled the population of single men and women. Unfortunately, single persons, male and female, fared poorly in depression society. Many became the tramps, the hoboes, the vagrants whose presence indelibly marked the 1930s. Historically, America neither trusted unattached per-sons nor felt any special obligation to extend to them the hand of assis-tance. Nevertheless, by 1934 "the problem of the single man" attracted attention. Rochester, New York, counted 1,300 single men between the ages of sixteen and eighty, 620 of whom were sheltered at either the Lodg-ing House or the Men's Welfare Bureau. Martha Bruere informed Hopkins that 130 of Rochester's single men scrounged for their own housing; 200 others, mostly those between sixteen and eighteen and those who were old and feeble, lived in dingy hotel and boarding-house rooms paid for by the welfare department. These people, explained Bruere, were

> given no cash relief, but are provided credit for two meals a day at not more than 15 cents each. Almost 30 percent of them are good-type men who have learned trades and had good positions. . . . They adjust to this

low standard of living and sometimes are able to help themselves out with odd jobs that put a little money in their pockets. The professional bums are content with what they get and help themselves by begging. It is the younger group which present [sic] the most serious problem. Some of them are just out of school. There is no place for them. The YMCA has fallen down on the job of helping them. The old Railroad "Y" building, which was once used as a lodging house for railroad men, can accommodate a few, but it is so dirty and so vermine infested that they will not go there if they can find any place to sleep, a barn or an entryway.[14]

In 1935, FERA was told about a "dark and dreary" hotel for single unemployed men operating in Great Falls, Montana. The old commercial hotel had sixty-three rooms but only five bathrooms. "The unkempt condition of the kitchen," noted Lea Howard, author of the field report, "would destroy a normal healthy appetite. . . . In the dark halls piles of soiled linen were waiting to be sent to the laundry. The food closet or storage space was a small inner room. Opened boxes of prunes and quantities of food were sitting around." As for single women, the Rochester city welfare commissioner told Bruere that he did not know of any provision that was being made for single women aside from home relief. "I found, however, that the YMCA was providing shelter for a few, where they could work for their room and board."[15]

FERA's Women's Bureau in Houston counted some five-hundred jobless unattached women. A caseworker informed Hickok that "most of the younger ones have lovers or are prostitutes. She is inclined to think—and from what I know of the younger generation I am inclined to agree with her—that most of those who have lovers would anyway, that the Depression or the inadequacy of relief would have nothing to do with it. But about those who have become prostitutes—we both wonder."

"Not long ago," continued Hickok from Houston, "one of the men in the transient division put on old clothes and went down and mixed with the transients to see how they were getting along. As he walked along the streets in the tougher part of town, he was frequently accosted by young women. To one of them he said: 'I can't. I haven't any money.' 'Oh, that's alright,' the woman replied wearily, 'It only costs a dime.'"

Hickok also heard a story about a young single woman who was not a prostitute. She was twenty-eight years old and had taught school but lost her job when cuts in local appropriations eliminated her position. Then she had been on and off relief. For a while she worked as a servant but, as Hickok relayed the story, the woman was terribly depressed when the caseworker tried to raise her spirits: "Oh, don't bother," the girl said impatiently at last. "If, with all the advantages I've had, I can't make a living, I'm just no good, I guess. I've given up ever amounting to anything. It's no use."

Curious about the plight of the single person elsewhere in America, Hickok decided to discover what was happening to unattached women in the nation's largest city, New York. She spoke with Mary Simkhovitch, the director of the Greenwich House settlement, who "seemed to know more about them—than anyone else." Simkhovitch's reply to one of Hickok's queries underlined the callousness with which Depression America treated the problem. "Single women? Why they're just discard," exhorted Simkhovitch, a pioneer advocate of progressive labor legislation and urban reform including public housing. "I'll tell you how they live," she confided. "Huddled together in small apartments, three or four of them living on the earnings of one, who may have a job. Half a dozen of them, sometimes, in one room. Sharing with each other, just managing to keep alive. They've left the YWCAs and the settlement houses. They can't afford to live in those places any more." [16]

Writing to Hopkins in February 1934, a deeply concerned Pierce Williams emphasized that the majority of these single homeless people were "not in the transient class. . . . If we do not care for them, we shall find ourselves later on responsible for the demoralization of a large group of potentially fine citizens." [17]

Although they were greatly concerned about the dilemma of the growing population of unattached men and women and about the plight of working-class families, the reporters' attention fixed disproportionately upon two other concerns: the social maladjustment and mental anguish of jobless white-collar families and the crisis confronting America's youth. Sociologists during the 1930s identified middle-class families by their greater capacity for parental "sacrifice." Other studies contrasted middle-class with working-class norms and emphasized that working-class families more carefully delineated family authority roles while less carefully differentiating economic roles. For instance, except for the Italian-Americans, whose family norms confined women within the household, working-class wives in the 1930s frequently toiled outside the home. Moreover, recent studies of nineteenth-century working-class behavior by Stephan Thernstrom, Tamara Hareven, and Caroline Golab disclosed that such families customarily forfeited their children's education for the immediate goal of modest property mobility. However, in that same nineteenth century, intensive middle-class families established woman's place in the home, emphasized her role in mothering, and urged family sacrifice for the welfare of the offspring. If, during the 1920s and 1930s, time-saving appliances and the competition to achieve a higher standard of living had driven middle-class wives into the job market, the values placed by the middle class on domesticity stayed unchanged. Accordingly, Hopkins's reporters deplored the fact that the depression weakened the economic base of the intensive nuclear middle-class family, challenged its role in providing

member support, and undermined its function in providing generational
mobility for the offspring.[18]

While middle-class reporters such as Steep smugly assumed that the
ranks of labor were somewhat hardened to the sting of unemployment,
they cringed at the prospect of white-collar families bearing the cross of
poverty. Well-educated professionals and managers peopled the ranks of
the esteemed bureaucratic middle class. Presumably, it was these people
who would spawn the embryo from which would emerge America's future; these were the technocrats who in more halcyon days scouted the
frontiers of science, explored new electronic communications technolo-
gies, and evolved modern systems of scientific management. However, although American society may have entrusted its future to these technocrats, during the 1930s, it failed to shelter them from the plague of
joblessness.

The dilemma did not escape notice. Indeed, Hopkins's reporters were
deeply exercised about the nationwide plight of the middle class. As evidenced earlier, Lorena Hickok constantly espoused the "special case" of
the white-collar jobless. In Alabama's largest cities she discovered over
10,000 unemployed white-collar families scraping to preserve their dignity. As elsewhere, white-collar families in these cities joined the relief
roles very reluctantly. One reason for their unwillingness, Hickok explained, involved complicated eligibility rules; another "is an almost fa-
natical objection to the 'idea of relief'—investigations, for instance, the
idea that they become objects of charity, the idea that they must 'stand in
line with Niggers' at the relief stations." According to Hickok, "the eligibility rules versus the standards of living" of the white-collar families
caused the most trouble in Montgomery. No family could receive any cash
assistance where family income was above the minimum relief allowance
of $7.20 a week for a family of six. "For a white-collar family that is pretty
low," she wrote Hopkins. "It will buy food and that's about all." These
families, Hickok explained, "want supplementary cash from us, so that
they may keep their standards of living somewhat near normal. And obviously if we start in on that sort of thing relief costs will mount rapidly."

Eligibility regulations sometimes seemed unfair. Because of economic
conditions, many families moved in together and doubled up. Often these
families were related. The problem here, Hickok told Hopkins, was that
if someone in one of the families was working and earning more than the
minimum subsistence requirement for all members of the household,
"none of the household is eligible for relief, although the income of the
person working may be very little above the minimum."

Generally, however, Hickok reported, the difficulty "is over the idea of
taking relief. They want to work, or they want to borrow money to live
until they can get work." She was told that "many [white-collar] cases

have gone to agencies like the Morris Plan—where you borrow money, usually at an exorbitant rate of interest, on your personal credit, getting two people to endorse your note." Some people took these notes again and again, often "in order to save the face of some friend who was out of work and couldn't stand the gaff of going on relief."

"So the situation in Alabama now is this," concluded Hickok.

> You have 10,000 white-collar people [on relief]. About half of them have no training that will fit them into our work relief program. . . . Half of them cannot be reached through any professional societies because they don't belong to any. Most of them need help and need it badly. Probably 2,500 will be forced to go on relief under conditions that they bitterly resent. The other 7,500 will stay off relief and try somehow to struggle through, growing more resentful all the time. And, if this is the situation in Alabama, imagine what it must be like in places like New York, and Chicago!

To gain deeper insight into the relief psychology of the white-collar jobless, Hickok interviewed fifteen white-collar unemployed in their homes. Her list of interviewees included a certified public accountant, an insurance man, a pharmacist, two engineers, an architect, a pawn shop clerk, and a masseur, "who extends his income a little by peddling in a basket around Montgomery the whole wheat bread his wife bakes at home." Generally, observed Hickok, "I'd say they are numb with misery. . . . I asked them for suggestions on how we could best take care of white-collar people." One man volunteered that "I'd rather stay out there [in a ditch-digging project] the rest of my life than take one cent of direct relief." The most nagging problem in connection with white-collar relief, as Hickok saw it, was its inadequacy. "The white-collar middle class wants to cling to some semblance at least of their normal standard of living." [19]

Accepting Hickok's challenge to investigate the situation in New York, Wayne Parrish called on the jobless white-collar residents of Manhattan's Upper West Side, a district which included Columbia University. Parrish found the unemployed professors, clerks, and architects who lived in the shadow of the university violently opposed to dependency. These people, according to Parrish, believed that private business would revive the economy and provide new jobs. But most of all, they accepted relief only "as a last resort." Parrish discovered many cases where men in the area would pass the local relief office "six or seven times before getting the courage to walk in and ask for relief. There is still much stigma attached to it." One relief investigator in the Columbia section told Parrish that almost every one of her clients had spoken of suicide at one time or another. Like Hickok, Parrish was especially sensitive to white-collar victims of the depression. "Work," he wrote Hopkins, "an extremely simple thing in words, would have done wonders and still can do a lot." One man who had formerly held "pretty big jobs," Parrish wrote, "is slowly going to pieces in his furnished room."

> . . . In this white-collar neighborhood, those on relief are too depressed
> and 'bowled over' by the shock of going on relief to take any action. Only
> the younger ones would follow a leader. Most still feel their problems are
> individual ones and don't blame anybody in particular. Relief checks are
> extremely inadequate for this white-collar group, but the feeling is that if
> checks continue to come there will be no outward trouble, only serious
> psychiatric problems.[20]

Hickok talked with a New Orleans newspaper editor who offered a final word on the subject of the sad fate of the white-collar class. The New Orleans editor told her about a man, now jobless, who formerly was president of the National Association of Electrical Contractors. He lost his home, and he and his wife were living in a small room in the French Quarter. "It's not only men like him who are out of work and broke, that worry me. It's the whole white-collar class," bemoaned the editor. He had had to cut his staff on the *Item-Tribune* and those still working were on salaries "way below normal. And there isn't much chance of their getting back to where they were. They know it." Before the depression, the editor told Hickok, his people were independent and whenever they were refused a raise many would say " 'to hell with you, mister,' and take the train for the next town." But now: "They're whipped, that's all. And it's bad."[21]

Closely linked to their compassion for the white-collar class was the reporters' anxiety about the dilemma of America's youth. After all, if Hickok, Steep, and Gellhorn lamented the waste of human resources represented by unemployed engineers, how much more emphatically would they decry the spectacle of an entire generation of youth cut adrift in a stagnant economy. A nation that believed its youth embodied the future now anxiously watched its next generation slouching idly on street corners, or perhaps listlessly tinkering at menial tasks, or, worse, doing nothing.

Hazel Reavis testified that everywhere she traveled she witnessed the sad plight of the young. She found a "general acceptance of the fact that leadership must develop from the educated young people who are [now] mingling on the only jobs they can get with embittered unskilled laborers and absorbing their point of view." Reavis visited the house of a skilled Pittsburgh engineer who had "been out of work two years and where the son, a scholarship graduate engineer from Carnegie Tech [Carnegie-Mellon University], was supporting the family shovelling sand for the Penn Railroad." At the rooming house where Reavis stayed in Pittsburgh, the landlord's son, "two years out of college and an electrical engineer, is also doing day labor checking freight cars." Teachers, exhorted Reavis, "are alarmed at increasing delinquency. Settlement house workers report trouble with neighborhood groups." In the black sections of Pittsburgh, she wrote, "the young people leave home without regret. In the foreign slum sections, young men move out of the family house and sometimes out of town so that their earnings will not cut down relief for their parents." [22]

In New York City, Wayne Parrish detected a deep streak of restlessness among the youth idling on the streets. They feel "cut off from the future." A New York social worker, described by Parrish as "an ardent communist," called them "the lost generation." But, confessed Parrish, "the truth is . . . nobody really knows what is happening to the young, and it is no small job to find out. They are rarely at home, and not many of them are working." Parrish might have freely speculated that these youth were drifting, hitchhiking on the road, riding the freights; they were a generation of youthful hoboes, searching for what they used to be. [23]

Much less reticent than Parrish and freely brandishing a bow armed with deadly sociopsychological arrows, Martha Gellhorn propounded a grim explanation for the debacle of the young, generously punctuating her exposition with references to human pathology. The reporter most concerned about the behavioral consequences of the depression, Gellhorn unfolded the major elements of her psychological theory on a tour of Providence, Rhode Island, where she spent much of her time interviewing staff members of the Providence Neurological Clinic. The hospital staff's observations concerning the increase in nervous disorders among children reinforced Gellhorn's own more inchoate notions regarding orthopsychiatry and the Great Depression. For example, one mental hygiene specialist at the clinic explained to her that the hospital was seeing "a better class of people" now. Most of them were not on relief, but were "starving." These were white-collar people who avoided relief, "whose pride remains stronger than hunger." The more serious effects were on their children, with malnutrition widespread, as to be expected. But worse, the children were developing a neurotic condition "produced by hearing and being constantly part of the parental fear. The child grows obsessed with the material problems of the home and mentally shoulders them; and the nervous system cracks." He told Gellhorn of "little boys earning pocket money by perversion" and "little girls stealing in the five and ten cent store."

The doctor's revelations profoundly affected Gellhorn and prompted her to pen a startling and eerily prescient finale to her report on Rhode Island: "I don't want to howl doom," she wrote, "but it is really a horrible mess. And what can these men and women do; what will these children grow up to? *I should think it would be a cinch to run a war these days, with a good many of the world's young men having nothing better to do anyhow than get shot; and at least fed a bit beforehand, and busy*" (emphasis added). [24]

The symptoms of emotional stress and mental disorders among youth were hardly confined within the walls of neurological clinics. A relief mother in Akron, Ohio, told Louisa Wilson that one reason for her compulsion to abjure the relief roles was that "children of relief families were humiliated." Wilson talked with a young boy at the Akron relief office who blurted out that "he like others his age were growing determined to live their own lives without assuming the overwhelming responsibility that support of their families now on relief lists would bring. If my father ever could get work again I'd turn over everything I earned to the family, but he won't find anything. I can't give up life." Another caseworker told Wilson that "the pride of the children has been bitterly hurt, but that they did have some luck at odd jobs, the young girls going in for maid work. Parents are particularly worried about the effects of idleness on the boys. Many of them who left home during the summer [of 1934] to try and pick up some work are back."

The obsessive fear depression youth harbored about the pitfalls and uncertainties of their future ultimately engendered a gnawing, perhaps neurotic self-doubt. According to the reporters, the neurosis was widespread and produced erratic behavior patterns. Wilson was told about a federal relief program class in Detroit that taught young girls how to approach employers. "Are there any questions?" asked the instructor. One girl's response was taken very seriously by her classmates, for they felt the same way. "How," she inquired sheepishly, "can you go up and apply for a job without crying?"

Psychiatric caseworkers spoke about "employment fear," about young girls ailing constantly until they are assured that they won't have to go through the experience of looking for jobs. But not all the behaviors were diagnosed as mild paranoia. A caseworker recalled a fourteen-year-old girl "who stole a bathing suit and sold it for twenty cents, using the proceeds to treat another girl at school who had given her things." "'Out-of-school' children are special problems [in Detroit] as elsewhere," remarked Wilson. "They no longer have the recreational facilities that they did and can't afford the 'Y.' Publicity was given recently to a gang in which boys of relief families . . . who were 18 and 19 . . . stole 26 different objects, opera glasses and other things almost as useless." [25]

Gellhorn's graphic vignette of youth in Providence related a similar story but much more poignantly. In her words,

> the greatest single tragedy in this whole mess . . . are the young men and girls who sit around the home waiting for nothing at all. I find them really hopeless; much more hopeless than the older people, who can remember an easier life, a less stringent world; and refuse to believe that the end has inevitably come. But these young people have grown up against a shut door. A boy of nineteen said to me, 'Why the hell should I get up in the

morning, lady; what am I going to do with all these days. . . . I've been looking for a job for four years. I've had two; five months I've worked in all. After a while you just know it ain't getting you anywhere. There's nothing for us.' I would find it hard (not being a good enough writer) to describe the understandable and terrifying cynicism of these children. One said to me, 'I'd steal if I had the guts.' A very pretty Italian girl of twenty-one, saying, I'm young; it seems to me I got a right to something, if it's only one dress a year. . . .' I don't know whether this hopelessness will turn into suicidal depression or into recklessness. It depends on the individual probably. But at the moment, I think the best ones would do anything (what moral standards can be expected of people who have been cheated of the right to live and go on); the girls definitely would take to the streets if they could make anything out of it; and the boys would go in for the petty gangsterism which might at least provide food.[26]

A poem written by an eighteen-year-old boy and handed to reporter David Maynard by a social caseworker most eloquently captured the despair of America's vagabond youth. It was titled the "Prayer of Bitter Men":

We are the men who ride the swaying freights
We are the men whom life has beaten down,
Leaving for Death nought but the final pain
Of degradation. Men who stand in line
An hour, for a bowl of watered soup,
Grudgingly given, savagely received.
We are the Ishmaels, outcasts of the earth
Who shrink before the sordidness of Life
And cringe before the filthiness of Death.[27]

In addition to describing the tribulations of the working class, the agony of the jobless white-collar family, the unattached persons, and the odyssey of American youth during the Great Depression, the reporters dealt at some length with those Americans living on the margins of society. In this venture the reporters revealed a tendency to distinguish between acceptable cultural forms to be included within the pluralism of America and those deemed unacceptable. Notwithstanding a generation of progressivism and the commitment of the New Deal to environmentalism, these excursions by the reporters into the social underworld underlined just how tenaciously Americans in the 1930s still clung to the Victorian dichotomy between the deserving and the undeserving poor. Not surprisingly, therefore, that dichotomy encysted itself in the so-called modern welfare legislation enacted in 1935. Enlightened compared to the ancient edifice of poor laws they replaced, nevertheless, the Social Security law of 1935 accepted national responsibility only for particular categories of relief: the blind, disabled, and dependent children. The needy and the just plain poor tumbled back into the lap of the states, which continued to regard them as defective, slothful, and dangerous.

Gellhorn, Webster, and the other reporters had discovered America's unwanted poor not only in city slums but also in small mining villages entombed in the misty hollows of southwestern Pennsylvania, West Virginia, and Kentucky and in the forlorn textile towns of Rhode Island and North Carolina. In these towns and villages, as in the urban tenderloins, resided the "wretched refuse" of American industrialism, the stranded mining families, the "undernourished chaff" of textile peonage, black sharecroppers, superfluous agricultural workers, and the vagrant poor.

These stranded families whose plight is further discussed in chapters 5, 6 and 7, seemed to their progressive-minded beholders to be both culturally flawed and the victims of degenerative physical ailments. At best, they were families who lived beyond the normative boundaries inscribed by middle-class convention. Rarely did Hopkins's reporters display appreciable compassion for the plight of these hapless families. More characteristically, the reporters seemed to regard them as anachronisms, "human flotsam" to be ignored or jettisoned.

Some of the reporters found a rewarding explanation for the plight of the downtrodden in the marriage practices and sexual customs of certain families. Here the reporters' reactions loom as interesting and as important as the actual phenomena they observed. Most of the standard historical and sociological scholarship on families and sexuality during the Great Depression emphasize a decline in procreative activity. Couples deferred marriage, postponed childbearing, and experimented with contraception. Women lengthened their hemlines and adopted sexless, somewhat masculine clothing fashions. Social data notwithstanding, the reporters noted an alarming increase in procreation among the poor. Martha Gellhorn, who investigated relief conditions among stranded families in North Carolina and New England mill towns, communicated highly subjectivized observations about working-class sexuality. In fact, Gellhorn and to a lesser degree Edward Webster correlated the incidence of poverty with the rate of fertility and from there proceeded to link excessive fertility with mental retardation.

Noting that American youth had been "crushed" and had "nothing to look forward to," Webster observed that "it would be interesting to know just what the tendency of some young relief clients to marry really represented. That such marriages produce genuine adjustment or solve any basic problems is," reasoned Webster, "highly improbable. It is believed that the marriage of a considerable number of transient relief clients on extremely short acquaintance may involve an economic motive." By "economic motive," Webster alluded to the greater access to relief gained by married couples over single persons.

Gellhorn, on the other hand, objected less to the marriage practices of the jobless than to the subsequent consummation of their unions. Contrary to the demographic evidence on the 1930s, Gellhorn fancied the poor in droves heeding the Biblical injunction to multiply; moreover, she insisted that her view of the copulating poor was popularly held. It was, she asserted, the conviction of all the informed people she spoke with that if this class of people continued to reproduce at their present pace the government could not hope to cope with the situation. The poor, Gellhorn insisted, were the most prolific, and "as long as these people are undernourished and undereducated, I don't see what can be done about them. Benevolent despotism is fine; but they have to be able to do something for themselves and at present they are pretty incapable." Even more frightening to her, Gellhorn wrote, was that the eighteen-to-twenty-five-year-olds were "apathetic and despairing, feeling there is nothing to look forward to, sinking into indifference." [28]

After studying relief problems in the New Hampshire industrial towns of Manchester, Nashua, and Concord, Gellhorn—prone to dabble in eugenics—proffered her own answer to the question about children of poverty. In her view the poor were reproducing future generations with low intelligence, and the consequence of their uncontrolled childbearing could be eugenically explosive. Her speculations rang of a familiarity with Robert Dugdale's nineteenth-century sociological classic *The Jukes*, about a prolific, dull-witted family that produced one generation of criminals after another.

Wherever she traveled, Gellhorn uncovered more evidence seemingly substantiating a link between poverty, fertility, and mental impairment. At New Hampshire's home for the feebleminded, the director told her about the mounting incidence of serious retardation. Gellhorn noted that on every visit to the home she encountered "more actual cases of cretins [cretinism] than in previous visiting." After visiting the state home, she stumbled on another "nifty local problem." A social worker led her to the nearby town of Seabrook,

> which had a special area given over to halfwits. The entire population had intermarried in this district, and they can trace their cretins back for several generations. In my own limited experience I came across three families, in which three generations of imbeciles lived together. Each generation had been wonderously prolific. It appears there is a certain amount of intermarriage in these groups of 'old American stock.' (Very good news, isn't it.) The head of the State Home said that he believed much more of the feeblemindedness was due to syphilis than could be shown or proved. None of this has any special bearing on ERA [Emergency Relief Administration], but it certainly brings up again the necessity for birth control.

Gellhorn, for one, promoted birth control; she also quietly advocated sterilization laws, at least in places where such draconian measures might be necessary. In her opinion, Gastonia, North Carolina, qualified. Syphilis, or "bad blood," as the people in North Carolina called it, ravaged the local mill population. Doctors in Gastonia told her that "they have one child a year born to syphilitics, just as nicely as to the others. Which," reiterated Gellhorn, "brings us to birth control. Every social worker I saw and every doctor and the majority of mill owners talked about birth control as the basic need of this class." Gellhorn herself witnessed "three generations of unemployed (14 in all) living in one room; and both mother and daughter were pregnant. Our relief people have a child a year; large families are the despair of the social worker and the doctor." Doctors told her that the more children in a family, the lower the health rating. Likewise, the larger the family, the lower the intelligence rating. "These people regard children as something the Lord has seen fit to send them, and you can't question the Lord even if you don't agree with him. There is absolutely no hope for these children; I feel that our relief rolls will double themselves given time. I know we could do birth control in this area." It would be slow, and trying, Gellhorn wrote, but with education one could fight "superstition, stupidity, and lack of hygiene." Without some success with birth control among "these people," Gellhorn insisted, "we may as well fold up because they cannot be bettered under present circumstances." Their housing she found "frightful," their health "going to pieces"; they were "ignorant and often below par intelligence" and "will be useless human material in no time." It seemed that all the government could do was feed them beans and corn bread "and watch the pellagra spread." And: "in twenty years, what will there be; how can a decent civilization be based on a decayed substrata which is incapable physically and mentally to cope with life." [29]

Gellhorn's enthusiasm for a scientific or medical solution to deep-rooted poverty was fairly widespread among the social engineers of the 1930s. In his study of the now famous syphilis experiment conducted during the 1930s at Tuskegee University, the historian James Jones observed that the scientists of the Public Health Service who conducted the Tuskegee research—for many years with the support of the Institute's administration—believed that poverty and "bad blood" were linked. In fact, social planners in the 1930s viewed venereal disease, prostitution, juvenile delinquency, and other social problems as cancers destroying the cultural fabric but removeable through government research and federal programs. [30]

Stranded miners, textile villagers, and black sharecroppers were not the only cultural subgroups whose values and atypical family patterns were perceived by the reporters as a threat to American culture. In beating the bushes in remote parts of Utah, Lorena Hickok discovered a nest of actively polygamous Mormons. She was not particularly discouraged. "I'm told," explained Hickok, "that it is practiced to a greater extent than anyone would believe. And all sorts of difficulties arise, and the more ignorant of them still think that the air is just filled with little souls flying around waiting to be born, and that it doesn't matter how they're born, so long as they are born." The church, she explained, "had discarded polygamy and excommunicated those known to practice it. But little sects grow up, here and there, and return to the old ways." A social worker told her that they were usually started by men, "but the women take it Godawful seriously. The law can do very little about it, apparently, for they don't take out marriage licenses, so in the eyes of the law, no bigamy is committed. Really they are just common law marriages."

Hickok found a number of these polygamists on relief. One man had four wives and nine children, the eldest nine years old. He had two wives "living together in one house on one side of town and two living together on the other side of town. All four families are on relief. Case workers report that the wives get on perfectly amicably, believe they are obeying the will of God, and are dead in earnest about it." The latest bride, she reported, was a school teacher.

> And she presented the "community husband" with a house and lot and an automobile! And apparently there is nothing to stop him from going on and siring four children a year until he reaches senility! The man, a social worker told her, had two years of college.
> "What's his occupational background?" I asked.
> "He gave his occupation as promoter," she replied, her eyes dancing with glee.[31]

Likewise, Mexican-Americans joined the parade of subcultures branded by the reporters as normatively suspect. Investigating the relief population of New Mexico, Hickok discovered Spanish-Americans comprising the heaviest part of the caseload. "Unfortunately, . . . from an economic standpoint . . . [they are] helpless . . . pleasure-loving people, with a standard of living a good deal below our own. . . . Their relief needs, because of this standard of living, are low, if you want to consider it from that standpoint. . . . They all raise a little food. Their adobe houses are cheap and comfortable. A Spanish/American can build a house simply by digging up dirt out of the front yard and moulding it into bricks which he dries in the sun. Good houses, too." Hickok portrayed these Mexicans as "interesting people. Most of the adults seem to be illiterate peons, very low grade mentally. Sort of childlike. They grow old very rapidly apparently, especially the women." But, she added, "the children are usually bright and attractive—more so than American children on the whole. Somewhere, in the process of growing up, they seem to lose it all!"

Although Hickok minimized the Spanish-American relief problem, she was convinced that "we'll probably have them on our hands forever unless we try to rehabilitate them in some way. It's largely a matter of education. They need to be taught what [crops] to raise, how to raise it, how to take care of their stock. It's going to be a hard job, I gather. They're so perfectly docile but not particularly energetic."[32]

This concern for the social transgressions of the lumpen classes degenerated into an unveiled contempt that occasionally bordered on revulsion. Like other middle-class Americans in the mid-1930s, the reporters feared that the army of the poor had entrenched itself on the American scene, and, therefore, contrary to Calvinism—albeit Biblically sound—the poor rather than the hard-working seemed to be inheriting the earth. Such a prospect appeared too nightmarish for these guardians of culture and civilization to accept with equanimity. Many promptly manned the bulwarks in defense of manners, good morals, and good breeding. Ironically, in the 1930s the armies of the poor posed little, if any, threat to either society or middle-class standards. Contemporary studies of the unemployed emphasized that the rich and the poor, the employed and the jobless alike, had internalized the same work ethic, and both classes shared the same abhorrence of government welfare. If joblessness was socially disruptive, the pathology gnawed most at the psychological fabric of particular families, especially families socially and emotionally unprepared to cope with the stress attending joblessness.

Time and again the reporters confronted people victimized by their own guilt and sense of personal inadequacy. A Civil Works Administration project supervisor told Ernestine Ball about a relief worker employed on an airport project who "seemed to lay around on the job." The project head explained to Ball that the man didn't look healthy, "and after the first hour the boss of the gang thought he was faking, but he [the relief worker] looked kinda peaked to me and I told him if he was sick to lay off. He said he'd rather die than quit. It felt so good to be working again." Two weeks later the man died. According to the supervisor's story, all the time the man was home sick he kept talking about "how he had a job at the airport. He sort of died with his boots on—if you know what I mean."[33]

Clearly, the reporters' principal finding—the one duly conveyed to Hopkins—supported the need for expansion of work relief programs and the provision of adequate direct assistance to families where, through death, incapacity or inability to find employment, a primary breadwinner did not exist. Above all, it was work relief which in the reporters' mind represented the American Way, and assured the strengthening of the moral and emotional fiber of the family.

"The jobless want work," stressed Ball. While many Americans refused to believe that all the relief clients were sincere in their desire for jobs, "they grant that most of the men (they know) would grab at a chance to work. And there is no substitute for a job." Relief condemned a man and his family to widespread opprobrium.

The variations on this theme seemed endless, and the reporters entertained them all. In Jamestown, New York, Martha Bruere talked with a woman who was trying to get work, any sort of work, even work relief, anything to get off home assistance. Her husband, she moaned, was "on the verge of suicide from the shame of it. [He went] out of the house many times saying he's not coming back—and what I feel till I hear him coming in again."[34]

Of course, families succumbed to relief. They had to. They swallowed their pride and resigned themselves to defeat. Some, very few, "bit by bit," reported Robert Washburn, "came to realize that their situation was the result of social conditions and not personal failure." Yet, the relief that the reporters described operated dysfunctionally for too many families. In many cases it arrived too little and too late. Frequently, relief worked in such a way that a family head was forced to sacrifice family well-being in order to return to work. Washburn noted this wrinkle while analyzing the relief set-up in New Haven, Connecticut. Throughout the nation, explained Washburn, "relief cases are multiplied by more than four [the average family size] in order to get the [actual] number of people involved, while there are only approximately two-and-one-half people in the country for every one gainfully employed in normal times. Industry never did support these large families, even at subdecency levels, on the wages of only one family member, and it is hopeless to expect it to do so now."

Take the case of a man making $12 a week on FERA, Washburn went on, and receiving supplementary aid of $18 a week to meet his budget. Naturally the man would be reluctant to take a job for $20 a week; this would deprive his family of $10. The relief program also discouraged his children from seeking work. In Connecticut, Washburn wrote Hopkins, two-thirds of whatever they earned was subtracted from the family budget. Thus, in the above case, if a daughter obtained an office job for $12 a week, $8 would be taken from the family budget. "But the four that is left her," he pointed out, "may be insufficient for carfare, lunches, and extra clothes she needs to hold the job, so she is not only working for nothing but may actually find that the whole family is worse off than before."[35]

While most social critics objected to the inadequacy of relief, Lorena Hickok demurred. She openly worried that if relief became adequate, private industry could not compete with it. "It sounds funny," mused Hickok, "but it is beginning to be a real question." She referred to the case of Syracuse, New York, where "relief was more adequate than anywhere else in the states. Under the individual family budget system there, a man with a large family . . . may get as much as $16 a week on relief. The average minimum wage in private industry is $14." Under those conditions, she asked "what incentive is there for a man who is getting $10 or $12 a week on a part-time relief job? Why should he be interested in going back to work on a full-time job for $14?" She knew that the "labor crowd" was demanding higher relief wages, but "Damnit, man," she wrote Hopkins, "our job is to feed people and clothe them and shelter them, with as little damage to their morale as possible." FERA, she asserted, was not instituted "to fight the battle of the American Federation of Labor. . . . [T]he less we interfere with the normal lives of these families, the less damage we're going to do to their morale." [36]

However, notwithstanding the highly touted attraction of relief under the circumstances, few jobless families willingly submitted to it. In Chicago's Halstead Street neighborhood, famous for Jane Addams's Hull House, black, Italian-, and Polish-Americans abominated the boxes of groceries distributed by the FERA. While these grocery orders were

> theoretically adapted to families of different nationalities, [they] contained much that the families did not know how to cook or did not like; for instance, the Negroes did not like what the Italians liked, and the Jews would not eat things given to them, yet the things were common to all boxes. Miss [Lea D.] Taylor and Mrs. [Ester] Kohn [Assistants to Jane Addams] contended that the giving of goods deprived the housewives of the privilege of shopping and in a sense destroyed their responsibilities as housewives.

Dorothea Kahn, head administrator of the Philadelphia County Relief Board, fully concurred with Taylor and Kohn. One of the nation's most prominent social workers, Kahn argued that relief in kind—food, clothing, and other items—robbed the family of its autonomy and forced it into dependency. Families, pleaded Kahn, "have always managed to raise their children and feed them without help from [the] outside; they naturally aren't going to take kindly to it now. . . ."

Hickok joined the chorus of protest. "I'm darned sure," she declared, "that if I were on relief myself, I'd be quite miserable enough without being told what to eat or what to feed my children." Hickok also wondered just "how much is this whole business an emergency?" Would people stay on relief so long that the very health of their children would be permanently impaired "by insufficient and unscientifically balanced diets?" And finally: "Is the health of the children of more importance than what happens to the morale of their parents?" [37]

Observed from the eye of the Great Depression, where Hopkins's reporters stood, the American family teetered precariously amidst the depression. Although many families effectively sheltered their members and remained intact, as Hopkins's reporters discovered, too many families emerged from the storm physically and emotionally debilitated and in disarray. The reporters found a disproportionate number of these families in mining communities, mill towns, impoverished rural areas, and in the tenements of blighted inner-cities. They viewed the weakened family as symptomatic of a larger problem, the problem of people living marginal existences stranded beyond the pale of traditional American middle-class norms and values.

The 1930s exposed the frailty of these stranded as well as economically better off families in a post-modern world and begged a larger government role in providing rewarding work programs, adequate family welfare service, counseling, and family research programs. After World War II, all of these programs became familiar items on the liberal agenda for preserving the American Way.

5

Of Mill Towns, Mine Patches, and Stranded People

■ Thirteen people sleeping in three rooms amid filth. Three adults in one bed is fairly common. Bedding is terrible.

Henry Francis from Isabella,
Pennsylvania

■ They're marked for death here, marked by the hundreds.
Francis from Dilworth, West Virginia

■ It is probable—and to be hoped— that one day the owners of this place will get shot or lynched. Their workers resemble peons I have seen in Mexico, who are eaten away by syphilis and pellegra.

Martha Gellhorn, from North Carolina

■ During the 1930s, mill and mine towns moldered in the backwash of American civilization, lost beyond the main highways, trapped in time and space somewhere between the city and the small picturesque towns and villages immortalized by Sinclair Lewis, Grandma Moses, and Norman Rockwell. Isolated spatially, populated largely in the 1930s by Southern and Eastern Europeans, rife with unemployment, these communities impressed Harry Hopkins as serious problem areas that demanded close surveillance.

During the early New Deal, Hopkins invited a stream of intelligence about mill and mine towns, especially details on the size of their populations and their potential for reemployment. In the quest for facts, reporters like Henry Francis, Martha Gellhorn, Ernestine Ball, and Lorena Hickok steered their automobiles off main highways such as U.S. Route 40, which meandered through mountainous southwestern Pennsylvania southward into West Virginia. After bouncing along isolated, dusty, and poorly paved roads, the exhausted reporters arrived in grimy places such as Scott's Run, West Virginia, and Isabella, Pennsylvania—company-owned mine villages called "patches."

These typical mining towns along with mill towns such as Gastonia, North Carolina, and Homestead, Pennsylvania, as well as fishing and lumbering villages in Maine (discussed more fully in Chapter 6), belonged to a genre of industrial community that shared characteristic features. In addition to being small and isolated, all were dominated by one or, at most, two major industrial employers, and during the Great Depression all experienced a significant transformation in their social, economic, and political structures.

Among the most seriously depressed small industrial towns were the company-owned mining patches that pockmarked the quasi-rural countryside of the nation's bituminous coal regions in West Virginia, southwestern Pennsylvania, and Kentucky. These mining communities housed populations in 1930 ranging from 345 in little Reidsville, West Virginia, to 3,000 in Daisytown, Pennsylvania, and 4,189 in Dunbar, West Virginia. Non-mining industrial towns were somewhat larger. Messina, New York, for instance, home of the large Alcoa aluminum plant, had a population of 12,029 in 1930. On the other hand, steel towns such as Homestead, Duquesne, and Butler, Pennsylvania, sheltered populations of 20,141, 21,396, and 23,568, respectively.[1]

Whether the overlord was Bethlehem Mines, United States Steel, Jones and Laughlin, Dan River Fabrics, Alcoa, or Hershey Chocolate, the company wielded baronial power over its domain. The company ordered the rhythm of community life, controlled local politics, sculpted the dominant civic institutions, and effectively laid out the boundaries of local culture. On the one hand, spatial isolation preserved a lively ethnic organizational structure and, therefore, perpetuated the continuity of ethnic traditions and values. On the other hand, the isolation and company domination stultified local political life and retarded the development of modern social and cultural institutions such as schools, libraries, and welfare agencies. For example, company power precluded the creation of independent social and political organizations that might have linked the town organizationally and culturally to the wider network of communities. Mill town isolation facilitated the feudal domination of the company by consolidating corporate power and authority. It made possible the employment of industrial police—the so-called "Yellow Dogs"—and assured the traditional hegemony of the company store. Finally, company suzerainty welded the brutal nexus between company management and public poor relief that forced cowed relief supplicants to prostrate themselves before the awful majesty of company control.

However, as the reporters described it, the depression had devastated the industrial economies of mill and mine town and, by interposing the power and protection of the federal government between employee and employer, freed the worker from the historic domination of the company. In some respects, this federal intervention involved bonding the distended elements of society to the fabric of the mass society. One by one the enactments of the New Deal breeched the walls separating mill and mine towns from modern urban society. Federal relief agencies, for example the Federal Emergency Relief Administration, bypassed company-controlled poor boards, and federal officials working with local politicians orchestrated the election of union representatives whose presence weakened company domination. Meanwhile, other federal agencies, the National Recovery Administration, the Civilian Conservation Corps, the National Youth Administration, and the Civil Works Administration, all impressed townsfolk with the looming importance of the federal presence. It was to measure the government's success in reviving local economies while easing the burden of local unemployment and relief that Hickok, Francis, and the other reporters negotiated the winding roads into the small mill and mine towns of America.[2]

In their reports to Harry Hopkins the correspondents described the severity of the depression in these towns, surveyed the wretched living conditions, examined the provisions for relief, and assessed the future of mill- and mine-town America.

Hopkins's reporters beheld mill and mine communities that had been brutally battered by years of social and economic change even before the onset of the Great Depression. During the "furnace stage" of nineteenth-century industrialism, towns like Alicia, Scottdale, Messina, and Gastonia had mushroomed on the frontier of the nation's mill and factory economy. Founded to exploit the nation's seemingly inexhaustible supply of human and natural resources, these towns ordinarily possessed only fledgling social and political infrastructures and proved highly vulnerable to the wild vaccilations of the late nineteenth- and early twentieth-century economy. In the decade before *le deluge* of October 29, 1929, mercurial changes in the textile industry, the shift from coal to oil as a principle source of en-

ergy, and the fluctuations in the demand for steel tested the frailty of mill
and mine town economies and produced a decade of poverty, joblessness,
and violent labor conflict.[3]

Probably the hardest hit by the tempests of the late 1920s and early
1930s were the notorious mining towns of West Virginia, southwestern
Pennsylvania, and Kentucky, where since the mid 1920s overproduction
and a declining demand for soft coal had prostrated the local economy and
bequeathed a grim heritage of violence and gnawing poverty. Henry
Francis pronounced these towns testimonials to man's selfishness and bru-
tality. Entrepreneurs had ventured into West Virginia from the East years
before and "hogged" all the hardwood that covered the hillsides, he
wrote, leaving an erosion problem that had to be faced later. This same
outsider then mined the coal "and for every hundred cars he took out he
left half an acre of dessicated spoiled land on the surface." He paid "starvation wages," Francis insisted, kept costs down, and realized considerable profit. "When the boom came and coal prices rose he multiplied his
depredations." At the same time, as Francis described it to Hopkins,
"flimsy company shack towns grew up around poorly equipped, poorly
protected shafts, slopes, and drifts. Men were brought in from Alabama,
from the eastern states, from Central Europe. City mechanics, country
laborers, and small farmers from the hills were lured into the mines by
'high' wages which had to be defended by fire and blood." In the end,
Francis wrote, "more than two-thirds of these mines and towns now are
down or abandoned."

In 1934, mine patches like Scott's Run and Scottdale counted nearly
97 percent of their people out of work. Streets and roads in these isolated
industrial towns disintegrated in the absence of repair funds. Utility companies shut off the water supply of defaulting towns, forcing the jobless to
bucket drinking water from polluted streams. In Fayette County, Pennsylvania, Lorena Hickok discovered a colony of "forgotten men" living in
abandoned coke ovens, a sight that provoked her to notify Hopkins that in
most mine towns the church poor box is "the last bulwark against riot and
disorder."[4]

It was impossible to exaggerate the enormity of the depression in
Fayette County mine patches. Although Hickok's reports embodied at
least flickering hope, Henry Francis's evoked little more than doom.
Again and again Francis sounded the tocsin, telling Hopkins in one report
that "50 of the county's 150 mine and coke plants will never open."
Throughout the mining counties of southwestern Pennsylvania, Francis
discovered rampant unemployment. In small patches like Vestaburg
(Washington County), 140 families survived on scant relief. Those fortunate enough to have jobs worked only three days a week.[5]

Conditions in the small towns dotting the valleys and hollows of West

Virginia rivaled those in southwestern Pennsylvania. Over 90 percent of Logan County's 58,534 people lived off mining and few people farmed. Yet, fewer than one hundred mines operated in Logan County in 1934; moreover, the handful in operation did so part-time. Over 1,300 of the jobless lived on work relief. Francis pleaded that "thousands of men in the [West Virginia region] UMWA [United Mine Workers of America] membership must face the fact that, even with the Depression over, they will never be able to work again in the mines." The union estimated the number of these unemployed miners at about 5,000. The previous year, he was told, the number was nearer 7,000, but 1,500 or more had left the region and were looking for work elsewhere. Some, according to Francis, found it in glass plants in Washington County, Pennsylvania, and in automobile factories in Michigan. "They were the better class," he wrote. However, explained Francis, "those remaining [behind] are older men with larger families, and living in abandoned patches, some of them pay no rent, and having little gardens and perhaps a child working manage to keep off relief." He nourished little hope for the future of these forlorn people. Again Francis propounded the grim theme that reverberated throughout depression social thought: that these miners, like so many other industrial workers, were doomed to permanent unemployment. They were in fact, stranded people.

"Many of these [miners]," insisted Francis, "are above the 45 year age limit set by the companies; many have lost fingers or toes or suffered other minor mutilations which prevent them from passing the rigid physical tests to which applicants are subjected; many are known as poor miners or are branded as trouble makers as a result of previous strike activity. In any case," stressed Francis, "they are not wanted; nor will they be wanted."

Even if good times came to the coal industry, Francis lamented, "these people would still be a problem. A pick-up in existing industry would only partially solve it. A new 'out' for these people just must be found." [6]

Conditions were equally brutal farther south in the mining camps that dotted the rugged hills of eastern Kentucky. For years the coal wars between operators and miners had inflamed the Harlan County fields. Violent strikes, epidemic evictions, and charges of "red agitation," culminated by the Great Depression, carved a broad swath of poverty and unmitigated misery across the region. Hickok surveyed the social wreckage on her trip through Harlan County in the fall of 1933. In Middlesborough, she "heard of a miner's widow with six children who had nothing at all to eat that day and no prospects of getting anything the next day either. At the Continental Hotel in Pineville I was told that five babies up one of those creeks had died of starvation in the last ten days." [7]

Workers in the copper mining towns of New Mexico and Arizona were also hard hit, and Hickok predicted a grim future for them. "Take out your government and railroad payrolls in New Mexico," figured Hickok, "and you have one mine and one smelter, working part time and employing part time, less than 2,000 men, instead of 7,000 or 8,000! Because of the merger [of railroad repair shop operations], the county relief director estimates that there are 1,200 heads of families who never will get their jobs back, no matter how much the copper industry picks up." The official told her that in Douglas alone there were between 600 and 700 men who would never get back into the smelter. "And seventy-five percent of these people are white American citizens," she complained.

At first they tried to find work in other places, she was told. "Many went up to Boulder Dam, and hundreds of them did get work there. Many started wandering. They're coming back to us now—some of them have been from coast to coast—penniless, tired out, old, discouraged."[8]

Nor did the more modern industrial towns in Texas oil-producing and refining areas escape the plague of unemployment. Even in such oil-rich fields as those surrounding Beaumont and Port Arthur, Texas, reporters found strong evidence of strandedness. People there told Hickok that the old refineries would not take back men who were over thirty-five years old. In Casper, Texas, near Beaumont, the head of the local social service division had been asked by the superintendent of one refinery to move twelve families out of the company town. According to the superintendent, "the heads of none of these families would ever be employed in the refinery again." One or two had been blacklisted for involvement in a labor dispute, but the rest, charged the superintendent, "were over the age limit—that is, they were over thirty-five."[9]

In Braddock, Duquesne, and Homestead, Pennsylvania, the reporters found a "deathly pall" enshrouding the darkened sheds and shabby workers' homes that clustered there in the shadow of the mills. One-third of the families in Carnegie Steel's Homestead Works survived on relief. Not far away, 40 percent of Braddock's families and close to 50 percent of Duquesne's families clogged the relief rolls. In 1934, Braddock's famous Edgar Thompson Steel Works operated at only 20 to 25 percent of capacity. Once in the mid 1920s the plant had employed 4,200 men; now it had fewer than 3,000, and of these, close to 2,500 worked part time. Likewise, the American Bridge Works, the foundation of Ambridge, Pennsylvania's economy, limped along at under 30 percent of capacity. American Bridge kept its skeletal workforce four days a week producing steel girders for the gigantic Oakland-San Francisco Bridge.[10]

Textile towns shared a common fate. As in the mining and steel baronies, these towns were mill-dominated and likewise had endured serious labor struggles in the 1920s. Historically centered in northern cities such as Fall River, Lawrence, Lowell, Philadelphia, and Reading, by the mid 1920s the textile industry had fled southward seeking lower taxes and a less costly, more tractable nonunion workforce. Under the economic mauling of the Great Depression the social fabric of the old New England and Pennsylvania mill towns crumbled. As the depression wore on, conditions worsened. By 1934, 40 percent of the textile workers of Pawtucket and Woonsocket, Rhode Island, worked only part time, earning between $5 and $7 a week. Work hardly existed for men over forty-five years of age or youths under twenty-five, a social phenomenon that left the ravages of malnutrition rivaling the frequency of veneral disease.[11]

Paradoxically, Henry Francis failed to discover greener pastures in the southern textile town of Gastonia, North Carolina. As in Rhode Island, closed textile mills scarred the townscape. Men and women laboring in the mills there earned less than their hapless neighbors employed on emergency work relief projects. Everyone with whom Francis spoke in Gastonia seemed fearful of hunger, cold, and loss of employment. Poverty and despair were also prevalent in less isolated mill communities. For example, in 1934 Messina, New York, boasted the presence of one of Alcoa Aluminum Corporation's largest and most modern plants. Yet, Messina with 12,500 workers—mostly French Canadians—endured severe unemployment; in 1934, over 490 families (or 20 percent of the town's population) were on relief.

Possibly the hard data on joblessness and poverty conveyed a too-dispassionate view of how the Great Depression afflicted mill and mine towns in America. Closed mills, abandoned mines, stranded workforces, and starvation wages eroded the social as well as the economic and physical basis for community life. Isolated, victimized by absent or inadequate water, sewer, transportation, and educational services, these towns groaned under the weight of social paralysis and malaise. Faithful to their instructions, Hopkins's reporters explored this social-psychological dimension of mill-town life, mindful that their boss was deeply concerned about the potential effectiveness of federal welfare strategies in reclaiming the usefulness of "stranded populations."

Appalachian mining towns such as those visited by Henry Francis in West Virginia and Pennsylvania contained not only the most isolated peoples but also, considering their exhausted economies and large first- and second-generation Slovak-, Hungarian-, Polish-, and Italian-American populations, those deemed by the reporters most hopelessly "stranded." In 1934, these Appalachian coal patches bore many scars inflicted by a decade or more of cut-throat industrial competition and labor warfare. Usually, simple, often prefabricated frame houses were slapped together upon crude slab foundations arranged in a monotonous gridiron plan. Streets were usually unpaved. Open trenches doubled as storm and sanitary sewers. Set in the shadow of gray mountains of slate, patch towns afforded minimal aesthetic pleasures. Years of neglect caused by declining coal prices, low wages, and long strikes deepened the harshness of the town-scape. Not even a coat of paint or a new pane of glass brightened the stark ugliness of the scene.

Lowell Thomas, America's quintessential tour guide, assailed patches like Scott's Run, West Virginia, as the "foulest cesspool of human misery this side of hell." Motoring through West Virginia and southwestern Pennsylvania, Henry Francis found other patches just as foul. Chieftain, one of Harrison County, West Virginia's thirty "stranded towns," sheltered over seventy families. Francis painted Chieftain as a "buckled railroad platform of rotted planks, a closed company store with a window display of cobwebs, and a forbidding cluster of eighty-three company houses, held down by clotheslines, ly[ing] between hills of garbage strewn slag in the shadows of a rusty runway and an old fashioned tipple." A few garden patches, he continued, "with prone anemic cornstalks, lean toward the jaundiced, acid-poisoned creek as though bent upon slipping in and ending the effort to produce life amidst economic death."

Nor did Francis see hope springing eternal in the next generation. To Francis the youth living in these coal-scarred hollows seemed as socially and physically unredeemable as the land. Indeed, a hardly disguised contemptuousness tinctured his account of the miners' children, whom he described as "engaged in, for the most part, eating dirt or playing seven-up with matches as stakes. I noticed," he wrote, "that they are adequately covered with dirty clothes and all have shoes." [12]

At Isabella, a mine town in Fayette County, Pennsylvania, Francis encountered three hundred wretched families who had struggled to live on relief for over a year. In a labor dispute that pitted a local union organizer against the head of a rival company union, the UMWA leader shot and wounded his antagonist, and "now wherever Isabella men looked for work," allowed Francis, "they were informed that 'no Isabella men need apply.'" All families in Isabella were on direct relief. Although the company freely hauled away the town garbage and even contracted for cleaning the outside toilets ("for health consideration"), Francis deplored the squalid conditions he observed there. The slate roofs leaked, porches were dangerously shaky and lacked guard rails. "One woman fell off a porch a month or so ago and broke her neck. The Brownsville undertaker buried her on credit. The porch still lacked a guard rail to prevent one slipping backward to a 12 foot drop." He saw other more woeful conditions in this place. Francis recounted "thirteen people sleeping in three rooms amid filth. Three adults in one bed is fairly common. Bedding is terrible. Binion [a relief worker], who accompanied me, said people might clean up a little better but they've lost heart! Shoes, underwear, and bedding are urgently needed."

Similar conditions prevailed in Alicia, a mine patch owned by the

Monessen Coal and Coke Company, which had been shut down since December 1933. "When the mine closed," explained Francis, "all the men owed back rent and with no food credit available they went immediately on relief. Other mines refused to employ the men, the same discrimination being shown as in the case of Isabella." Fifty families, the total population of the patch, were on relief, and fifty-five houses were empty.[13]

Ultimately this poverty, hunger, filth, and lack of sanitation exacted a high price in poor health. In his study of Appalachian poverty and health, Robert Coles discovered that the final payment was often collected twenty-five to thirty years in the future. That is, it was the sickly, emotionally scarred offspring of this misery who paid the final installment on the harvest of despair.

Hopkins's reporters were appalled by the enormity of the squalor they encountered in the hollows and mountain ridges of Appalachia and deemed the health conditions there worse than in the slums of urban America. On the outskirts of Dilworth, West Virginia, in Williamson Hollow, Francis observed children sleeping on the cold damp floor of makeshift cabins and old shacks that were "rot-ridden, filthy, and open to the four winds of heaven. They're marked for death [there]," lamented Francis, "marked by the hundreds."

Reflecting his dim view of this culture of poverty, Francis blamed intermarriage for depleting the genetic stock and malnutrition for severely weakening it. He viewed these hapless mountain folk as both socially and physically defective, and "an easy prey to disease." Venereal disease was rampant and tuberculosis, cancer, and other diseases commonplace. Right now, reported Francis, "pneumonia is raging throughout these hills. People, lacking clothes but having relief coal or digging it in the hills, heat their hovels to suffocating temperatures. When the fire goes out at night the temperature inside the shacks, open as they are, is the same as the outside. Bed clothing is scant and they sleep cold. Children sleeping on the floor, can't help get pneumonia." Nurses told Francis of "numerous cases of typhoid due to insanitary conditions. 'Water supply, usually wells, becomes polluted from toilet seepage. We fill up the wells with rocks and make them get water elsewhere. Sometimes they have to carry it from wells a quarter of a mile away.'"[14]

While Francis discovered pneumonia and typhoid, Lorena Hickok found diptheria to be rampant in West Virginia mine towns. In fact, she heard that there had been so many deaths in Logan the past winter that "they established as one of their work relief projects the making of coffins! All the relief people, particularly the American Friends [Service Committee] representative in the county, begged [Hickok] to see if something could be done about opening a free hospital there."[15]

Such deplorable health conditions were not limited to the mine towns.

Wherever single industries such as steel, textiles, even fisheries dominated local economies, joblessness and poverty proved devastating. In the steel town of Homestead, Pennsylvania, for example, conditions in 1934 matched circumstances commonplace in 1911 when Margaret Byington, writing in the *Pittsburgh Survey,* disclosed grinding poverty, poor health, and social insecurity. The depression of the 1930s mired unemployed steelworkers deeper and deeper in poverty. Over 2,500 jobless blacks and Eastern European immigrants lived in one of Homestead's worst slums where, according to Hazel Reavis, decrepit housing "menaced the health of the whole community. Water was turned off months ago in most houses. Water is now brought in cans from the nearest fire station." Unchanged from 1911, latrines in the area were still "unconnected with the mains and are in use by whole communities of families. In one thirty foot square court five families in the most complete misery are on relief."

Just south of Homestead, along the Monongahela River in the Carnegie Steel town of Duquesne, 70 percent of the company's workforce lived on supplementary relief. To Reavis, Duquesne looked hungry despite stomachs shrunken by years of enforced dieting. "There is considerable begging," she wrote. "Clothing is ragged and inadequate, more conspicuously so than in the other mill towns visited." Men as well as scrawny children "have the listlessness of old people." [16]

Touring Gastonia, North Carolina, Martha Gellhorn saw "latrines drain-[ing] down a gully to a mill from which [residents] get their drinking water." Yet, Gellhorn evoked little sympathy for North Carolina's textile workers. She estimated that half of the textile families "are both syphilitic and moronic, and why," she wondered, "they aren't all dead of typhoid, I don't know. (It probably would be a blessing if they were.)" At one North Carolina village Gellhorn visited "the houses were shot with holes, windows broken, no sewerage, rats. The rent for these houses [was] twice as high as that of fine mill houses. It is probable—and to be hoped—that one day the owners of this place will get shot or lynched. Their workers resemble peons I have seen in Mexico, who are eaten away by syphilis and pellegra."

Gellhorn appeared obsessed by the prevalence of venereal disease in these southern textile towns, as well as the dietary deficiency, colitus, typhus, anemia, and other maladies that scourged mill workers and their families. But like the other reporters she harbored a low opinion of these victims, faulting them for their ignorance about disease and their failure to take even the minimal precautions.

In addition to assessing the extent of the joblessness and tabulating the cost of idle labor in mill- and mine-town America, Hopkins's reporters searched out evidence of political discontent or even overt revolutionary fervor. Earlier, in 1929, upon directions from Moscow, Communist Party leaders in America had formed the Trade Union Unity League (TUUL) as a rival to the American Federation of Labor. In southwestern Pennsylvania the collapse of the bituminous coal industry along with the concomitant decline of the UMWA prompted the TUUL to organize the National Miners' Union (NMU) as a Marxist alternative to the more traditional coal union. The NMU was involved in many strike and protest activities until it collapsed before the superior power of the UMWA in the mid 1930s. While they uncovered enough revolutionary fervor to warrant Hopkins's concern, it was a mood of despair rather than mordant discontent that informed their reports. Some of the reporters reacted more than others to the volatile potential of the Great Depression. After surveying the bituminous coal regions, Hickok read more anger than defeat in the miners' eyes. She found "vast numbers of the unemployed in Pennsylvania right on the edge. . . ." What is more, she exclaimed, "the Communists want bloodshed. They say so themselves. However, the people who go into these organizations [Unemployed Councils] . . . are the people most worth saving. They've got some fight in them."

Francis also discovered evidence of the miners' wrath surfacing in Brownsville, Pennsylvania, where Victor Kemonovich, a Croatian-American miner, had organized an active unit of the National Unemployed Council (UC). Not far from Brownsville, in Carmichaels, a physician, Dr. George Teagarden, organized the General Relief Committee of the UMWA. Like Kemonovich, Teagarden battled the "crooks and mine owners who for forty years have been exploiting miners," and, in Teagarden's words, "are willfully denying relief to those miners joining the union and giving relief freely to those who stand [with the company]."

But Francis's mine-town informants entertained only the vaguest ideas concerning the size of a "radical" constituency in southwestern Pennsylvania. One informant guessed that only 25 percent of the jobless miners belonged to the councils. However, Francis believed that UCs were active all over the bituminous coal regions and that the organizations thrived on the miner's dissatisfaction with the handling of relief—the standing in line for hours and the walking miles for clothing and shoes only to find that no clothing or shoes were to be given out.[17]

While Francis and Hickok vigilantly monitored the activities of the Communist-linked Unemployment Councils and the Marxist NMU, they expressed greater concern about the prevailing defeatism and about the numbers of dispirited people slipping beyond the pale of social and psychological redemption. In Fayette County, the economic collapse threatened to undermine an entire society. An employer told Francis that these miners were

> just flotsam by nature. Of course, [they] should have work for which [they are] fitted—that means grubbing coal underground—but [they] should

not be counted on in any fanciful rehabilitation schemes predicted on self-help. [They] simply will not fit in—[they're] miners by nature and nothing but mining at good pay will satisfy [them]; I tell you, this thing of lifting up the lowly can't be done. Not so darned high. Talk about self help; well you just don't know the class of labor we have here. All you can do with 'em is give 'em work if you've got it or food if you haven't. And pretty soon they'll want food without work.

This, declared Francis, "is verbatim from a man who has hired and known labor hereabouts for thirty-five years." [18]

Down in West Virginia, Francis found equal despair. The state had thousands of permanently displaced coal miners. There are, Francis learned, "a great number of mines which simply cannot be operated at a profit. Much of the coal was inferior, freight rates were against them, and where the coal vein was only 30″ deep as in Mingo County, it's obviously unprofitable and senseless to operate these mines. . . . The soft coal industry is dying on its feet—on its knees [a snide reference to the 30″ seam], and thousands of men will never get their jobs back."

Relief agents told Francis that "the aged and disabled will have to be helped until they die; they are dying pretty fast and the particular work division project which has to do with coffin making is behind in its orders." Thousands of younger people, he wrote, would have to be brought back to health before they can help themselves. "Employment will have to be found for thousands now denied it by existing industry or else people will have to be moved from the country to industry elsewhere." Francis detected more pessimism than hope among these West Virginians. "According to the 'best people,' these mine families have always lived the way you see them now. When the men were making a few hundred dollars a week in the mines they lived just the same way. You can't interest them in bettering themselves."

Despite wrath and despair, Francis caught a glimmer of hope stealing through the thick atmosphere of gloom. At Charley Zosky's house in the Alicia patch of Fayette County, for instance, Francis beheld the "cleanest object in the house," a lithograph of President Franklin Delano Roosevelt "wreathed with festoons of hand-cut colored paper." Zosky assured Francis that "'we've got 'em licked now. . . . New Deal give man work, that's all, no want relief if get work. There'll be work, alright now. There'd have been work long ago if the bosses had wanted to give it to us instead of trying to starve us out.'" Francis thought that since the November 4th (1934) election, "morale has been vastly improved." He reported that among miners, the election had vindicated their "struggle against oppression and dethroned the oppressor for all time." At the same time, Francis sensed that the protest groups would continue their activities "on the principle that the time to strike is when the iron is hot." [19]

The reporters found a similar mixture of anger and despair in America's steel and textile towns. Years of austerity had taught steelworkers how to gird themselves against hard times, but the Great Depression proved unprecedented. An enfeebled Amalgamated Steelworkers Union had barely survived the union busting of an earlier time, but the mass joblessness of the early 1930s stunned an already cowed union and robbed it of any will to be militant. In fact, Hazel Reavis was struck by the "sense of hopelessness on the part of many of the able but middle-aged unemployed—a fatalistic day-by-day point of view." Yet, the New Deal had instilled new hope among workers in Aliquippa, Pennsylvania, a town dominated by the Jones and Laughlin Steel Company. In Aliquippa a newly organized Amalgamated Steelworkers Union used the authority granted under Section 7a of the National Industrial Recovery Act (1933) to secure pledge cards from more than 90 percent of the company's 5,200 workers. Nevertheless, this was the only group that Reavis saw in Beaver County "which felt that it had any chance of bettering its condition," and, observed Reavis, "the effect was tonic."

The large jobless populations in towns like Aliquippa, Homestead, and Braddock swelled the ranks of the Unemployed Councils. But in these towns of the Pittsburgh area, as in the textile towns of North Carolina, the revolutionary threat posed by the UCs was too easily exaggerated. In Gastonia, Martha Gellhorn discounted the importance of the UCs. "I got a note from your office asking about 'protest groups,'" she wrote Hopkins in November 1934. "All during this trip I have been thinking to myself about that curious phrase 'red menace,' and wondering where said menace hid itself," she joked. Rather than outrage, she found reverence. "Every house I visited," Gellhorn wrote, "had a picture of the President. These ranged from newspaper clippings to large color prints, framed in gilt cardboard." The portraits held a place of honor over the mantel, "comparable only to the Italian peasant's Madonna. And the feeling of these people for the President," she observed, "is one of the most remarkable phenomenon [*sic*] I have ever met. He is at once God and their intimate friend."

This survival of hope surprised Gellhorn, who had seen people who, according to almost any standard, had little in life and "practically nothing to look forward to or hope for." For example, Gellhorn met one woman with five children who was living on relief ($3.40 a week). "Her picture of the President was a small one, and she told me her oldest daughter had been married some months ago and had cried for the big, colored picture as a wedding present. The children have no shoes and that woman is terrified of the coming cold as if it were a definite physical entity. There is practically no furniture in the home, and you can imagine what and how they eat."

Elsewhere, Gellhorn described men who faced hunger, cold, and the awful prospect of "becoming dependent beggars—in their own eyes." The threat of homelessness and the dispersal of their families was omnipresent. "What more a man can face," Gellhorn wrote, "I don't know." She had expected in her travels among these people "lawless talk," threats, "or at least blank despair." She did not find it, she reported. Instead: "I found a kind of continued and quiet misery; fear for their families and fear that their children wouldn't be able to go to school." From most of them, she heard: "All we want is work and the chance to care for our families like a man should." The only thing keeping them sane, "keeping them going and hoping," she believed, "is their belief in the President." [20]

Underscoring the reporters' concern about the economic, social, and spiritual malaise of these mill and mine towns was the enormity of the relief problem. Notwithstanding the grim portrait of tuberculosis and typhoid fever, open sewers and rutted roads, painted by his informants, Harry Hopkins measured the real plight and pathos of these industrial towns in terms of wasted manpower and unfulfilled lives. He was most keenly interested in data on the size of the relief load, the state of relief, and the steps being taken to keep the employable jobless physically and psychologically fit for work.

Prior to the Great Depression and the entrance of the federal government into the business of relief, the operation of public welfare had been highly decentralized. The distribution of relief fell to county "Directors of the Poor," politicos who were basically unschooled in the principles of modern "scientific" social work and who were scorned by welfare professionals for being philanthropic Neanderthals. In most cases the company dominating the town controlled the dispensation of relief. Ordinarily, mill-town unemployment relief amounted to extending credit at the company store or allowing jobless tenants to delay rent payment on company houses. As for poor relief, since the company dictated town policy, it decided who was eligible for the dole and what and how much would be granted. It can be assumed that frequently those who had been fired by the company, who were on strike against it, or who were openly critical of its regime were ineligible.

Workers and their union leadership perceived relief policy as critical to breaking the iron grip of the company. In Pennsylvania, miners ignored local and state governments and, according to Hickok, "looked to the federal government for aid." However, they were "inclined to hold the federal government responsible when it is not forthcoming." Consistent with what Martha Gellhorn found in North Carolina, Hickok reported bituminous coal miners having "no faith at all in anyone save the President." They "carry his picture in their picket lines, and [in] their little parades—with American flags and quaint little bands made up of saxophones and

accordians—when they [go] back to work. Stuck up on a window of the
home of a miner who had been out of work and nearly starving on inadequate relief for more than a year, I saw a newspaper clipping, apparently
out of an advertisement, of the President's picture and a Blue Eagle. . . .
All this," it seemed to Hickok, "puts the President, the Federal Emergency Relief Administration, and the Federal Government as a whole in a
pretty difficult and serious dilemma." Hickok repeatedly reminded Hopkins that the New Deal was raising great expectations; and to shatter
those expectations would invite violence, and perhaps even revolution.

Although the Federal Emergency Relief Administration strove to establish scientific standards of relief, the task of efficiently delivering relief to
four million jobless proved awesome. Following an established tradition,
FERA initially dispensed relief in kind—that is, food, clothing, shoes,
blankets, and other items. Faced with the size and diversity of the relief
population, even urban-based, efficiently administered agencies bogged
down, and small-town organizations were overwhelmed. Hickok reported
that relief in many small towns was "awful." Relief officials in Maine's
wood pulp-, fish-, and shoe-producing towns, for instance, were not only
inexperienced but unsympathetic in their attitude toward the poor.
"Weekly food orders [were] written out by men who apparently [hadn't]
the slightest idea of the food needs of a family. Nor," added Hickok, "its
other needs. It has never occurred to some of them that people need soap,
for instance."

One food order, turned over to Hickok,

> contained the following items: 1 peck of potatoes, [$].20; corn meal, .15;
> rolled oats, .25; two quarts beans, .20; pork, .25; two quarts of dried peas,
> .30; two cans of milk (and there are several children in the family), .13; 2
> pounds of rice, .15; 1 quart of molasses, .20; Total, $1.83. No soap, prac-
> tically no meat, no fish, no fruit of any kind, no fresh milk, no sugar. In
> fact, practically nothing except starch and a little fat and a little molasses!
> Pellegra, incidentally, has appeared up there. This order was supposed to
> last the family a week—and did. Across the bottom was written: 'Mr.
> Higgins left this order for you to be filled just as he gave it.'

A Maine relief official told Hickok that "last winter we used to give 'em
dried fish that would knock the plaster off if you threw it at the wall."
Complained a relief recipient, "Don't you suppose something couldn't be
done so they'd stop sending me half a pound of cream of tartar every week
and let me have some oranges . . . instead." [21]

Similar problems plagued clothing relief in Pennsylvania. Much of the
anger and militancy of the unemployed organizations—including the welfare committee headed by Dr. George Teagarden—stemmed from dissatisfaction with clothing relief. Henry Francis traced 80 percent of the

complaints from protest groups to the failure of the jobless to receive emergency clothing. One cold November day in 1934, Francis visited a relief office in Fayette County that lacked "the following articles: Women's winter suits, vests, bloomers. Misses' winter suits, hose, slips. Children's suits, 3 to 6 years; hose. Men's hose, pants, dress shirts, work shirts. Boys' hose, long pants, dress shirts, work shirts. Youth's dress shirts. . . . Of the 660 pairs of youth's shoes, 596 were in three sizes. Only 23 pairs of youth's high shoes were in stock."

In Washington County, Francis reported, the first need was "for a better clothing supply; the second is for a better system of distribution. The present one is too slow. The shoe department now is more than 7,000 pairs behind its orders. Good weather helps. Severe weather would bring trouble." Ernest Cole, a relief supervisor, told him: "The situation in Fayette is ready to boil over; there's the basis for a conflagration." [22]

Significantly, it was the professional competence of the relief workers, not their incompetence, which often drew the bitterest criticism from recipients. Pennsylvania's jobless families reviled the dispassionate professionalism and bureaucratic efficiency practiced by many relief staffers. Hickok overheard numerous complaints against investigators, yet her contact with the staffs in Washington, Fayette, and Indiana counties convinced her to discount them. "I honestly believe these complaints cannot be said to be generally justifiable," explained Hickok. "The people who are handling the job really do appreciate the viewpoint of the unemployed and do their best to meet it." Aside from specific complaints against individual caseworkers, she wrote, "the unemployed organizations are inclined to be rather bitter about the county and state boards. 'No person on that board has ever known hunger,'" said one of the groups from Indiana County. "They report some rather silly rules—such as taking a man's automobile license plates away before granting him relief." She heard about one single man, "living with his sister and her family, who was told that his relief would be cut off if he ate with the family. So he set up a table in the garage and ate all his meals out there!"

Union leaders and spokesmen for the organizations of the unemployed charged two other parties with culpability in the relief mess: politicians and company bosses. Henry Francis attended a UMWA meeting in Uniontown, Pennsylvania, called to "proclaim the prevalent injustice in the matter of miners' relief." Union officials railed that the "relief organizations in Fayette, Greene, and Westmoreland Counties are headed by men who have been and still are owners of coal properties, who have the operator's point of view, and are out of sympathy with the miners." Affidavits were available to prove the injustices. Francis was told that food had been "burned out on the foot of the mountain rather than applied for the relief of workers on strike at a mine in which the relief director had an interest." He did not know whether these complaints were fully justified or not. "What I am reporting," he carefully pointed out, "is discontent with everything. Relief is just another thing to grouse about." Anyway, Francis wrote, discontent "runs in the miner's blood; it always has. He goes down into the mine and never knows whether he'll come up again. The bosses don't go down; nor do the stockholders and the relief workers." Why should he not demand his share from all of them "and more than his share if he can," Francis argued, especially since his union is telling him "that he is getting less." [23]

Hopkins, for one, recognized the deficiencies of direct relief. He especially condemned what he saw as the psychological damage inflicted upon the recipients of the dole. Not even the substitution of cash for food and clothing orders would overcome the damage caused by dependency. Work, according to Hopkins had always been part of the American Way. Therefore, work as opposed to direct relief, he argued, preserved the moral and physical fiber of the jobless. Naturally, Hopkins sought intelligence from his reporters concerning the success of FERA's work division and of the Civil Works Administration (CWA) in meeting the social-psychological needs of the unemployed. [24]

These reports strengthened Hopkins's resolve to make jobs the centerpiece of FERA's war on poverty. From New York, Ernestine Ball informed him that the unemployed there "clamor for work relief. . . ." The jobless in Messina, New York, she noted, "believe that Uncle Sam has specifically guaranteed them work and their morale would be shattered if work relief were withdrawn for any but seasonal reasons."

Similarly, in Pennsylvania Hickok discovered that "apparently everybody—the taxpayer, the relief distributor, and the unemployed—would welcome . . . more made work." The taxpayer would be better satisfied, too, if "he thought he might be getting something permanent in return for the money that is going into unemployment relief; the people would be better if they had something to do; and the better element of the unemployed feel that they would have more self-respect if they were, however indirectly and inadequately, self-supporting." [25]

In 1935, Hopkins unveiled a massive federal works program that relinquished direct relief responsibilities to the states and to the new Social Security Administration. Replacing FERA was the Works Progress Administration (WPA), headed by Hopkins and armed with $5.5 billion to employ the able-bodied jobless. Earlier, Hopkins had struggled to launch a work relief program. During the winter of 1933–1934, his Civil Works Administration employed thousands of workers. CWA demanded no means test for eligibility, which greatly simplified the processing of men into jobs; but the task of finding work for all the unemployed forced CWA to create many leaf-raking, road-work, and mattress-making jobs. Barraged by criticism that CWA amounted to a colossal boondoggle, Hopkins terminated the program in April 1934, leaving only FERA's bureaucratically strait-jacketed Local Works Division (LWD) to keep some of the unemployed "working for their relief." LWD projects, especially in small towns, were mainly of the road-gang variety. Finding more creative work for the jobless in financially depressed industrial towns overtaxed the resources of FERA, whose main goal was to meet the immediate survival needs of the unemployed. However, LWD enjoyed some success. For instance, aware of West Virginia's desperate need for improved health services, one FERA project there employed hundreds of jobless nurses to do public health work. Everywhere Lorena Hickok traveled in the state she came upon "little clinics set up in abandoned stores, in empty miners cabins and school houses. It may not seem like much," suggested Hickok, "but in West Virginia it means a lot." [26]

Yet, FERA's requirement that states and municipalities furnish the material costs of work projects proved an insurmountable obstacle. After looking over FERA's work relief operations in Fayette County, Pennsylvania, Henry Francis evoked only dismay. He explained to Hopkins that the only organization that had any borrowing capacity at all in the county was the poor board! "Towns like Uniontown can barely pay their police, firemen, and teachers. Mr. Buttermore (the work relief director) figured out that after he had paid his labor and his administration costs, he'd have left just about enough for truck hire." According to Francis, work for ten thousand men in the Uniontown area was held up for want of trucks and materials. "'We have some 800 men at work on roads,'" Buttermore explained, "'only because the farmers give stone, etc. . . . With an eight or ten percent allowance for trucks and materials we could put ten thousand men on the road. A greater percent would permit work on sewer projects which are of vital necessity from a health standpoint. The creek running through Uniontown is an open sewer. . . . But we can do nothing. Finances are lacking.'" [27]

Nevertheless, Hopkins and his reporters doubted that work relief would be able to satisfy the material, moral, and psychological needs of jobless workers. All doubted the ability of even a resurgent American economy to fully employ the workforce presently "stranded" by reason of age, technology, or outmoded lifestyle. Rexford Tugwell, a Columbia University economist and Roosevelt "braintruster," urged the resettlement of these "stranded" people in planned, freestanding communities. Reflecting the Tugwellian concept, new towns such as Arthurdale, West Virginia, Greenbelt, Maryland, and Norvelt, Pennsylvania, sprang up just beyond the suburban fringes of cities. Some were "greenbelt" towns, planned communities based on the idea of a late nineteenth-century visionary, Ebeneezer Howard. These were human scale, school-centered towns that emphasized limited size and garden-like landscaping free of automobile traffic.

Others were not. For example, Arthurdale and Norvelt, smaller rural communities built by the Subsistence Homestead Division of the Resettlement Administration, featured Cape Cod cottages attractively arranged on lots spacious enough for extensive gardening. In addition to community buildings, health clinics, and modern schools, Arthurdale, for one, had a furniture factory giving it a modern albeit precarious economy.

Another manifestation of Tugwell's belief that dislocated and disinherited populations could be plucked from the cruel grasp of dependency and transformed into self-sustaining, productive citizens was the idea of subsistence gardening. Many industrial towns, like Messina, New York, for example, while dominated by a mill plant, were surrounded by rich farmlands. The inescapable contrast of industrial unemployment and the richness and workability of the nearby soil captivated the imaginations of conservatives and New Dealers alike. In fact during the New Deal the subsistence vegetable garden became a new frontier. The idea was so simple and so attractive and seemingly so American—let the jobless garden for their food. In Messina, Ernestine Ball found that the proximity of farmland challenged policymakers "to help clients back to the land where they could become wholly self-sustaining or at least raise enough subsistence to supplement occasional work in industry." [28]

Almost from the beginning of the Great Depression, relief officials were entranced by the idea of turning the jobless into subsistence farmers, not merely in small towns but also in large cities. For example, in Philadelphia, as early as 1931 gardens blossomed on vacant lots. By 1934 a FERA garden project supplied seeds and farming instructions to help the city's jobless produce their own food. Naturally, land-rich areas such as West Virginia afforded a perfect laboratory for testing the subsistence-garden strategy. In fact, one reason Francis journeyed to the coal-scarred town of Scott's Run was to inspect the progress of a FERA-sponsored subsistence garden project; another reason was to look at a related "cooperative" venture. Both projects were successful. Although work in the Scott's Run mines was extremely sparse, Francis rejoiced that "the men were kept off relief because thanks to the garden project last summer, most of them were well stocked up with canned vegetables." And because of the garden project, the miners of Scott's Run got involved in a rehabilitation scheme to resettle mine families on plots of land as part of a cooperative community. "Yes, sir," related an obviously enthusiastic Francis, "the men were all heated up over this housing scheme." Francis continued:

> I went on to see the [community] nurseries and playgrounds. In a tastefully decorated hut children were 'quiet-timing' on mattresses made by miners' wives on work relief. In an adjoining room older children were getting lunch. Still others were taking shower baths using clever home-

made plumbing. . . . The children were clean, healthy, and happy. In another building of rough, unplaned boards which had been made cheerful with gay curtains and a spotless lineoleum floor covering were women and older children sewing by hand and the 'community' machine. Outside in a green-flecked playground, sand boxes, games and a variety of 'exercisers' occupied other children. The whole place was an oasis, not so much of peace as of promise, amidst the gray dreariness of the unpainted company town—a spot redeemed and radiant, standing out against the forbidding blackness of the tipple.[29]

While reporters such as Francis and Hickok were enthusiastic about the prospect of gardening and other back-to-the-land projects, some like Ernestine Ball noted that there were serious, practical limitations and obstacles to their success, even in farm-crowned Messina, New York. Although Messina's garden project "under careful supervision produced good crops," alas, bemoaned Ball, "no clients came to the welfare office asking to be helped back to the land. In fact, one honest citizen with a vital vocabulary and a great interest in the clients called the whole scheme "cockeyed!" He cited the expense involved in months of effort which so far produced one family ready to go back to the land. In three shakes of a cow's tail that family will be back on relief. . . . A client who knew how to milk a cow when he was a boy won't [necessarily] make the grade as a dairy farmer."[30]

Apparently, other cow-oriented New Deal rehabilitation schemes met a similar fate. One plan called for jobless West Virginia miners to raise three hundred cows for market. Under the plan, FERA would supply the cows to the miners, who, after purchasing from two to five dollars' worth of soybean seed, contracted to plant the seed and harvest and store the feed crop. A group of West Virginia miners set out to do just that. They purchased the seed, planted the crop, built storage sheds, and in Francis's words, "waited expectantly for the cows to arrive. Time passed and finally the cow applicants received—not cows—but a few cans of roast beef. And now they are paying off their soybean debt at the rate of $.25 a month, taken out of their relief checks."[31]

Other subsistence ventures involved forming self-help cooperatives. In the euphoria of the early New Deal a sizeable group of avant-garde liberals believed that recalibrating American capitalism might require an occasional experiment with industrial or agricultural collectivism. FERA aided and encouraged the farming cooperative in Scott's Run. In Philadelphia the County Relief Board supported a cooperative canning factory; and in Dayton, Ohio, a self-help cooperative raised and canned its own food supply. Hopkins's reporters were attuned to cooperative ventures and did what they could to promote and encourage self-help operations.

The reporters found an interesting self-help venture among the unemployed steel and glass workers in Belle Vernon, Pennsylvania, a small industrial town in the Monongahela Valley. In Belle Vernon—"a hot bed of radicalism," according to Francis—FERA helped organize a self-help toymaking factory. It all started, explained Francis, "when over a beer Mr. Mingo, the relief worker," suggested that the idle working men of Belle Vernon have a Christmas party for the kids "and make toys out of ends of wood and cardboard. Shaping the toys with jack-knives was slow and hard and someone suggested 'Joe Thingamubob's' jig-saw, which they succeeded in borrowing, but only for a day. Instead of using the jig-saw the men made a copy of the borrowed tool. A penny collection was taken up and a dozen saw blades were purchased for $.25."

Work on a "mass production scale" was begun. A local hardware dealer sent a pound of nails; another store supplied a can of paint; and the five-and-ten-cent store sent broken "junked" toys to be repaired. "Things positively were humming," marveled Francis. "There wasn't a minute to listen to oratory imported by the N.U.C. [National Unemployed Council] and eventually the group seceded from the national body and formed the Unemployed Council of Belle Vernon which in its bylaws 'bans political and church arguments of all kinds.' The group made friends fast . . . [and] the electric light and water company [now] contributed light and water free."

Francis praised their product as "well made and so ingeniously contrived. Prancing horses have checkers for wheels; the hubs of wheelbarrows are made from cotton spools carved with jack-knives and sanded to a glass finish. Today all the talk in Belle Vernon is about the coming Christmas party. . . . It's not just a game," reassured Francis. "It's real self-help. One man is making bed quilts. . . , others turn out good tables, stools, benches. But the prize something-from-nothing-industry is Anthony Cuppola, who is making carved paperknives and really inspired Blue Eagle ornaments out of rib and shin beef bones which he gets free from the local butcher." [32]

In Belle Vernon the jobless expected the glass factory to reopen. But as described earlier such optimism was rare in mill- and mine-town America. Despite hopes raised by President Roosevelt's election, the reporters detected a deep underlying strain of defeat in these towns. Perhaps they were witnessing the death throes of a whole genre of American community—the industrial village. Hickok, Francis, Gellhorn, like others familiar with mining regions, doubted that the future scale of production and the pace of technological change would tolerate predepression levels of employment. The reporters conversed with older workers who never expected to be rehired, and youths whose joblessness robbed them of the

chance to acquire the necessary experience. Superannuation and skilless-
ness alone did not condemn small mill and mine towns to molder into
oblivion. Poor housing, absent or antiquated sanitary services, a long history of political oppression, and geographic isolation teamed with the economic catastrophe of the Great Depression to undermine the creaking social fabric of these towns and mark them for destruction.

However, in those industrial communities destined to survive, what the
reporters witnessed were towns in the throes of societal transformation.
Although company bosses struggled to retain their overlordship, inevitably the bosses' authority was attenuated by the operation of federal relief,
by new strong union organizations, and by the political gestation accompanying the rise to ascendancy of the Democratic party in places historically dominated by Republican politics. In fact, the reporters surveyed a
phenomenon of which they themselves were a vital part; that is, the arrival of modernization and the end of cultural and political isolation. After
World War II the surviving mill and mine towns would no longer be feudal
baronies but merely small towns in a modern mass consumption society.

Stricken Hamlets

Economic Hardship and Poverty in America's Agricultural Communities

■ Wouldn't it be a little better to make relief a little less adequate and therefore less attractive?

a small-town businessman in upstate New York

■ We don't want any dole. All we want is a chance to carry ourselves through the winter so we'll be able to become self-supporting next year if we have half a chance.

a South Dakota farmer

■ Three loud cheers for CWA! I may be wrong but I think probably it's the smartest thing that has been tried since we went into the relief business.

Lorena Hickok, from South Dakota

■ They all had a little money in their pockets. They were all going to have something in the house to eat for Christmas. You wouldn't have known them!

a Fairmont, Minnesota, coal dealer

■ Rural hamlets and farmsteads faced especially grinding poverty and social disintegration during the Great Depression. Washington had first evinced concern for the social and economic malaise eroding the quality of rural life in the early 1920s and this solicitude persisted throughout the so-called Flapper Era. After all, the yeoman farmer, the American Cincinnatus, who, according to Ralph Waldo Emerson, in 1775 guarded the "rude bridge which arched the flood," posed a powerful symbol in American life. Alas, in the twentieth century this rural American seemed more embattled by the forces of industrialization and urbanization than ever by British troops approaching Lexington Green. Modernization had permanently changed American agriculture. The old order was gone, a way of life was over. The reporters writing to Hopkins from Western New York, Maine and from the Big Sky Country of the Midwest and the Great Plains found farmers there confused, downtrodden, hurt, entrapped in the swirls of these changes. In describing the forces militating against the farmers' interests the reporters noted impatiently that the farmers' plight was further exacerbated by local political factionalism and greed. Finally, delays and bureaucratic inconsistencies in some New Deal programs drove farmers to near desperation.[1]

In 1930, when President Herbert Hoover's Commission on Recent Social Trends launched its survey of rural life, social scientists had prognosticated a dreary future for agricultural America. Essentially, social scientists and economists such as Rexford Tugwell, Carle C. Zimmerman, Edmund de S. Brunner, and Dwight Sanderson espoused a theory that pitted the tradition-minded farmer/ruralite against modernization. Sanderson argued that "unprecedented development in transportation and communications and in the mechanization of agriculture increased education, increased contact with cities, and the spread of urban ideologies and other factors were responsible for an unusual degree of social change in rural life." Economists such as Sanderson also hypothesized a decreasing national population, which would reduce demand for agricultural products. Consequently, "the Great Depression not only tolled the end of agricultural expansion," but it also, surmized Sanderson, made it evident that "much poor land unadapted to agriculture must be relinquished from the plow. . . . Agriculture and economic opportunity now lie in the intensive development of specialities and in moving from poor to better land."[2]

In the tradition of efficiency-minded bureaucratic reformers, these agricultural theorists promulgated a modern business model for agriculture. To make farming more efficient and profitable, they urged not only the retirement of submarginal land but also the institution of business management methods, the creation of farm cooperatives, and the formation of committee systems designed to encourage economical purchasing and the participation of farmers in the planning and administration of farm policies. Moreover, the social scientists contended that the effect of World War I and the Great Depression had accelerated the regressive tendencies in rural life, "rendering the once idyllic countryside poor, dispirited, and potentially volatile." The economic and social reclamation of rural society, they pleaded, demanded the massive intervention of the federal government. Both the American Country Life Association and the Commission on Rural Social Trends warned in 1930 that just as was happening in America's urban slums, living conditions where families farmed marginal or submarginal land produced delinquency, low levels of intelligence, lack of sanitation, miserable health, and an unprecedented burden of public relief.

Experts dated the beginning of the rural depression from 1921, when the index of farm purchasing power plummetted to 75, using the halcyon years 1907–1914 as the base of 100. As an indicator of farm health, 75 measured the ratio of prices farmers received for farm products to the prices that they paid for goods and services. Although the index had climbed to 90 in 1929, by 1932 it had plunged to 56. Accordingly, gross farm income, which had reached nearly twelve billion dollars in 1929, tumbled to seven billion in 1931. However, it was the frightening volume of forced farm sales that most graphically reflected the cataclysm overhanging American farm civilization. Bureau of Agricultural Economics estimates of forced farm sales per thousand total farms revealed that nationally the mortgages of 26.1 farms per thousand were foreclosed in 1931. The figure skyrocketed to 41.7 in 1933, then jumped to 54.1 in 1934. The data is more illuminating when viewed for individual states. In Montana during 1934, 109 out of every thousand farms fell under the sheriff's hammer; 86 per thousand were lost in North Dakota, 66 in South Dakota, and 68 in Idaho.[3]

By 1933, conditions in midwestern rural America conjured up visions of an impending apocalypse. Seething discontent arose from the accumulating grievances of farmer-businessmen who in the early 1930s faced not only steadily declining farm commodity prices but also wholesale foreclosures on their farm mortgages. Consequently, some of America's most conservative, tradition-minded people began voicing the ideas of political radicalism. In fact, it was the frequent acts of violence in northern Wisconsin committed by the followers of Milo Reno's Farm Holiday Association (FHA) that instilled an element of urgency in those New Dealers and social scientists intent on engineering a new, more efficient rural society.[4]

Under these circumstances, in October 1933 the Federal Emergency Relief Administration through its Division of Research and Statistics launched a comprehensive field survey of the effect of the depression upon rural economic life. After conducting a census of "Rural Families Receiving Relief," in the late fall of 1933 the Division inventoried the resources for the rehabilitation of rural relief families, concluding the survey by undertaking an analysis of rural social organization. Finally, in April 1934, in order to provide "expert criticism and discussion" of the organization and results of the several rural surveys, Hopkins's assistant at FERA, Corrington Gill, assembled an advisory committee composed of the "ablest and most distinguished" rural social scientists, Edmund de S. Brunner of Columbia University, John H. Kolb of the University of Wisconsin, Charles E. Lively of Ohio State University, Carle C. Zimmerman of Harvard, and Dwight Sanderson of Cornell.[5]

In contrast to this collection of hard data, the reports of Hopkins's 16 correspondents provided the soft side of FERA's rural survey. At the same time, the reports were linked to the broader social scientific inquiry and comprised a brief but important part of the New Deal's efforts to rehabilitate rural America. This chapter, like chapters 7 and 8, follows Hopkins's reporters through parts of rural America. Here, guided by the reporters, conditions in the Big Sky Country and in Maine and western New York are explored. Conditions in the South and West are covered in the following chapters.

As reported by Lorena Hickok, T. J. Edmonds, Clarence King, Winthrop Lane, Benjamin Glassberg, J.C. Lindsey, Pierce Atwater, and Pierce Williams, among others, hired to investigate economic conditions in the Big Sky area, the rural crisis of the early 1930s bespoke not only the waste and inefficiency of the small subsistence farmer who farmed submarginal land, but more importantly, the failure of American middle-class farmers to fully comprehend their role as businessmen in a modern capitalistic society. Despite access to agricultural education, utilization of improved farm technology, and the work of lobbying organizations such as the American Farm Bureau, the farmer/businessmen that the reporters met in their travels appeared unsure of their identity and wavered ambivalently between their hallowed if mythical role as yeoman and their modern role as entrepreneur. Thus, in 1934, bourgeois farmers were faced with a two-pronged struggle, attempting to preserve some dignity and status against the forces of both economic collapse and social change. Hopkins's reporters bemoaned their sad dilemma.

The reporters' itinerary in rural America ultimately took them from upstate New York and New England to the Midwest and the Great Plains, where they encountered some of the most severely stricken parts of agricultural America. Lorena Hickok launched her trip through the nation's rural countryside in upstate New York, from where she next traveled to see poverty conditions among Maine's potato farmers and fishermen. Farmers in New York and Maine seemed engaged in a futile struggle against both nature and the unfathomable, impersonal mechanism of the modern marketplace. Hickok discovered that in Clinton County, New

York, dairy farmers were only getting $1.40 per hundred weight for milk which, by the time it reached consumers in Plattsburg, cost $6.42. This situation, added to an early summer drought, led farmers to wonder if they would be able to feed their stock in the coming winter.

"Well, I know what we'll do," one farmer confided to Hickok. "We'll have to shoot our cows." Some had already been shot, and considering that it had taken years to build these herds, some of the finest in the country, Hickok allowed "it does seem pretty tough." One after another the farmers were losing their farms. Hickok claimed that 85 percent of the farms in Clinton County were mortgaged: "There are public auctions all the time."

Like upstate New York's "Northern Tier" farms, its resorts, paper mills, and other businesses were distressed. Along the St. Lawrence River the tourist business had been so poor that many local people had no incomes whatever. A few paper mills were operating, apparently benefitting from the reduced value of the American dollar which undermined the formerly cheap Canadian paper. However, business spokesmen held out little hope for any imminent revival of either the resort or paper industries.

Nevertheless, unlike the situation in many of the states to the west which she would later visit, Hickok found the adequacy and administration of public relief in New York "so far ahead of what I had seen in other states that there just isn't any basis for comparison at all." The state's Temporary Emergency Relief Administration had modernized its operation to the point where it had just about achieved what FERA was aiming for in the rest of the country. Clothing and rations, food allowances, and work projects—although still inadequate in some parts of the state—were generous enough in New York that one small-town businessman asked (or rather complained): "Wouldn't it be a little better to make relief a little less adequate and therefore less attractive?" [6]

While upstate New Yorkers were not prospering by any means, they were better off than most of their neighbors to the north and west. For instance, not that far from upstate New York, although thousands of miles from the drought and locust infestation of the upper Midwest and the Plains, Lorena Hickok discovered Maine's potato farming and fishing villages enduring the grievous tribulations endemic to rural society at large. Yet, Hickok particularly commented on the tenaciousness with which Maineites clung to their traditions of individualism, defying agencies of modernism such as government and technology even when it seemed against their economic interests to do so. Their quixotic behavior actually confounded Hickok; on the one hand, she applauded their steadfast commitment to self-reliance, thrift, and traditional virtues; but at the same time she questioned their resistance to modern efficiency and to meeting human needs.

Individualism aside, Maine's lumber, potato, lime, and fishing economy had proved a weak bulwark against the persistence of the Great Depression. In 1932, Aroostook County potato farmers had expected four dollars a barrel for their product but instead got twenty to sixty-five cents. Yet, each barrel had cost eighty-five cents to raise. In retaliation, Maine farmers dumped so many thousands of potatoes into rivers and streams that Maine officials feared damming and resultant flooding. Unprecedented indebtedness plagued Aroostook County. Seventy-five percent of the potato crop was under liens; hundreds of thousands of dollars were owed on federal land loans, fertilizer loans, crop mortgages, and bank debts. At the same time, potato farmers needed ready capital to begin next year's crop. For most laborers in the potato industry, the introduction of new harvesting machinery and a reduced crop meant no work for the first time in memory.

Like farming, the timber and wood industry in Maine floundered—reflecting not only the pummeling of the Great Depression but also changes in the technology of ship- and home-building. Most timber cutting in recent years was done in pulpwood, but because of labor conditions American pulp could not compete with Canadian and Russian cuts. In the absence of a protective tariff, the American paper industry purchased a cheaper wood product from abroad. The so-called "long timber" industry, which cut the boards used in home-building and shipbuilding, was in a sorry state. By 1930, few wooden ships were being built and the home-building industry had collapsed—and even should it revive, the modern tendency was toward using less wood in home construction. Although a lumber mill in Van Buren was running to capacity filling a Civilian Conservation Corps contract, in northern Maine thousands of timberjacks seemed permanently unemployed.

A similar story characterized the Maine fishing and canning industries, which complained bitterly about foreign competition for their sardine and smoked herring trade. While demand for sardines was rising (someone told Hickok that this was due to the return of beer!), activity in Maine's sardine fisheries still sagged. By the time fishermen netted their sardines, they were so large they had to be halved for canning, which depressed their dollar value.

In Rockland, the center of Maine's commercial fishing industry, fishing had not flourished for years. Most of the canneries were locked. One afternoon Hickok spoke with two fishermen who had just spent thirteen hours at sea. "They had used eight gallons of gasoline," she said, "at 19 cents a gallon and 100 pounds of bait at 2 cents a pound, bringing back 80 pounds of Haddock for which they got 4 cents a pound, and 220 pounds of Hake, which brought them 1 cent a pound. After they got all through," she wrote, "they had 20 cents apiece for their day's work!"

Rockland's historic lime industry fared no better. The primary use for lime being the production of plaster, the lime trade was dependent on the home-building industry, and collapsed along with construction. Besides, the use of substitutes for plaster had grown increasingly, further devastating Rockland's major business. Consequently, the lime quarry that once supported several hundred families had fallen into the hands of receivers and offered no hope whatsoever for reemployment. Maine's granite industry was in equally dire straits.

Throughout Maine, economic conditions were dismal. "Our Main Street is a mile-and-a-half-long," a small-town businessman told Hickok, "and on it there are thirty vacant stores." Fewer than 15 percent of the local merchants were within six months of paying their rent, most were a year or a year and a half behind. Poor business conditions contributed to a rapidly declining tax base. Hickok found the fiscal plight of most small Maine communities "pretty awful."

Everywhere, tax delinquencies were rampant. For instance, one quarry in Rockland owed $76,000 in back taxes; in the potato farming community of Presque Isle, delinquent taxes amounted to $125,000; and at Houlton, still in potato country, officials reported $50,000 in back taxes in addition to the $200,000 then due. Thus, rural towns were broke. When local officials at Allagash, far north in the timber country, asked Augusta (the state capital) for help, they had to borrow a postage stamp from another community to send the application! Of the approximately ninety families living in Allagash, all but three were on relief—the fire warden, the game warden, and the ferryman, and the last was being paid in food orders.[7]

While in Maine the reporters seemed most impressed by the persistence of rock-ridden individualism, in the upper Midwest and the Plains, the heartland of American agriculture, they emphasized the schism between the farmer as yeoman and the farmer as businessman. It was here, too, in the rich hills and lowlands of Wisconsin, the Dakotas, Iowa, and Nebraska, where they found farmer-businessmen so crushed by the counterblows of economic and natural disaster that to many, America's whole agricultural civilization seemed to be toppling. Beginning in 1932 and continuing into 1936 a severe drought ravished the plains from the Dakotas down to Texas, producing in its wake a huge "Dust Bowl." As if the Great Depression were not bad enough, more than a hundred million acres of land blew away in one of history's worst ecological disasters. Pastures and cornfields were scorched and wasted, and plowed land became sand dunes drifting here and there with the wind's direction. It was darkness at noon, though farmers could see their crops dying of thirst and could visualize their cattle perishing from lack of feed in the coming winter. They were particularly stunned by the plight of farmers in North Dakota. In Dickinson, Hickok spoke with a group of local husbandmen who had gathered

outside the entrance to a church. Clad in shabby denim, they shivered in
the cold wind which swept relentlessly across the open plains. Devastated
not only by the Great Depression but also by alternating plagues of hail
and drought, nevertheless, these formerly successful middle-class farmers
stubbornly shunned the relief office. Land they had—lots of it. In fact,
they were, in their own words, "land poor." For instance, a 640 acre farm
at about ten dollars an acre (the current value) was worth only $6,400 in
1933. Most of the men also owned an abundance of livestock, thirty to
forty head of cattle, a dozen to fifteen horses, a number of hogs and sheep.
But, thin and rangy North Dakota stock foraged "on land so bare that the
winds pick up the soil and blow it about like sand." Most of their livestock, already mortgaged to the limit, would probably die that winter.
Their cows had gone dry for lack of food, and their hens refused to lay
eggs. The situation was so near desperate that T. J. Edmonds reported to
Hopkins: "It would be very difficult to make a mistake in giving any
farmer relief because the entire state is on the verge of bankruptcy." [8]

Hickok's notes from "her West" poignantly reveal the indomitable—
often intractable—yeoman character of farmers, whose livelihoods hinged
precariously on the uncertainties of "Mother Nature" and of the modern
urban marketplace. One day in Williston, North Dakota, a quiet, mild-
mannered Scandinavian wheat farmer came into the Farmer's Loan Association office seeking a loan. "Hailed out again," he had not had a really
good year since 1916. "Why do you stick at it?" Hickok asked. "No place
to go," he said. He did have some assets—thirty head of cattle, sixteen
horses, a few hogs, some farm machinery, a tractor which he could barely
afford to operate, and 320 acres of land he had purchased years before for
$2,600. But his liabilities, including a bank mortgage on a quarter of his
land, back taxes, and a feed and seed loan, totaled $3,600. "How are you
fixed for the winter in food and clothes for your family?" a secretary asked.
The man did not answer, Hickok wrote. "Instead, his eyes filled with
tears—which he wiped away with the back of his hand. The question was
not repeated. And for the second time since I've been on this job I found
myself blinking to keep tears out of my own eyes." [9]

But, far more significant than the reporters' empathy for rural America
was their baleful ambivalence about its prospects. While evincing pride
and respect for the moral fiber, self-reliance, and irrepressible character of
the traditional rural family, the reporters generally expressed little hope
for its survival. Asked to view the prospects of rural America, to assess the
true condition of its people and its chances of fitting into a more socially
and economically viable future, the reporters offered a Janus-headed response. As writer-humanists, they pined for the rural idyll of the past, but
as progressive-minded agents of a New Deal modernism to be engineered
through social science, they offered harsh testimony about rural economic

and cultural weakness. As strongly as in their other New Deal epistolary, an elegiac strain infuses their discourse. They firmly believed that modern farm technology and newer marketing systems rendered a rural lifestyle unsustainable for all but an exceptionally efficient few.

Here and there in cattle and wheat country, Hickok reported ravages that could only have confirmed the social scientists' beliefs concerning the folly of attempting to cultivate marginal land. She found a majority of small North Dakota wheat and cattle farmers bankrupt; indeed, failures reached 95 percent in and around Williston, where depression, drought, hail, and grasshoppers had claimed a savage toll. One farmer there sold four cows weighing over 4,000 pounds and netted just $3.16. Another shipped twenty-nine head of cattle to St. Paul and pocketed a mere $200. Cattlemen in the area earned as little as thirty-five cents an animal! A carload of cattle, which had brought $600 to $900 the year before, went for $300 now.

Some farmers had nothing. One application after another contained such statements as "hailed out," or "no crop at all." One man, according to Hickok, who had planted 140 acres of wheat, 25 acres of oats, 20 acres of rye, 20 acres of barley, and 30 acres of corn, was only able to harvest a little corn, and at that he was luckier than some. Hickok drove past dozens of cornfields barren except for the limp remains; only emaciated stalks survived and those battered and beaten down by the hail. Here and there, half-starved cattle rooted around them. One old German farmer had worked 800 acres, from which he harvested only 150 bushels of wheat and 7 bushels of rye, all sold below cost. Out of two large groups of farmers Hickok spoke with one afternoon, only a couple had any incomes at all, and this they earned from cream checks, which would soon stop because their cows were going dry from lack of food.

In the wind-swept Dakotas, reporters found the condition of the livestock "pitiable." Farmers had only roughage to feed their cattle, and little of that. In desperation, they harvested Russian thistle, a plant with shallow roots that dried up in the fall and blew across the prairie much like rolls of barbed wire. The effect of dried Russian thistle on an animal's digestive system would be the equivalent of eating barbed wire, so farmers cut it when it was green, enabling their livestock to survive, if not prosper. A full winter later, Hopkins reporter Pierce Atwater found little improvement. All across the Dakota prairie he found land "so dry that there is not enough moisture in the ground to freeze the earth." He wondered "why more people rather than [fewer] are not on relief." [10]

Buffetted by both nature and depressed food prices, farm debt mounted year by year. A newspaperman in Dickinson, North Dakota, told Lorena Hickok that by the time most farmers brought in their first load of wheat they had six or seven mortgages to pay off. While some were able to hold back their wheat in hopes of selling it at a better price, most were forced to sell immediately in order to repay the loans. Hickok heard of one disgruntled farmer who carried an endorsed check in his pocket, refusing to cash it because he was not going to get any of it anyway.

It was much the same in other Big Sky areas. In eastern and central Montana a succession of dry summers had created a pre-depression depression for farmers. Hopkins reporter Clarence King spoke with a number of them, "farmer homesteaders who, after establishing their claims by years of arduous labor and sacrifice, have been glad to give their farms away to others who would assume the taxes." In contrast to Montana farmers west of the continental divide, where there was sufficient rainfall and possibilities for more diversified agriculture, King surmised that in eastern Montana "there would seem to be no permanent solution for these impoverished families other than relocating them in some other part of the country." [11]

But certainly not in Bottineau County, North Dakota, where Lorena Hickok found a submarginal farming civilization at its lowest ebb. Local farmers there had not harvested a decent crop in four years, and during the previous year, grasshoppers had devoured the entire crop. People needed bedding, clothes, even furniture and house repairs. Along with a relief investigator, Hickok stopped to see one of the county's "better-off" relief families. "In what was once a house," she found two small boys "running about without a stitch on save some ragged overalls." With no socks or shoes, "their feet were purple with cold." Light from the house escaped under the front door, plaster was falling off the walls about her, and old newspapers stuffed in the cracks around the windows vainly buffered the family from the icy north winds.

Worse, the mother of the little boys, who greeted them bare-legged and wearing a pair of ragged sneakers on her feet, was only three months away from bearing another child—"*in that house.*" Hickok confessed that she "could hardly bear it." Only a filthy ragged mattress and some dirty pillows, along with a few old rags of blankets lay on a single iron bedstead. The family's bed linen had given out over the year before. "Do you and your husband and the children all sleep in this bed?" It was then five degrees above zero in Bottineau, and, while Hickok wrote, a blizzard piled snow against the buildings. The year before on that date the temperature had dropped to forty degrees below zero and remained there while a sixty-mile-an-hour gale wind whipped furiously across the prairie. There were eight hundred such families on relief in Bottineau County.

After her trip through the Dakotas, Hickok wrote about the "Siberia" of America, an image conceived after driving mile after mile across the state's flat brown country where only an occasional snowdrift or blowing Russian thistle broke the scene. Her vignettes of dessicated fields, emaciated haystacks, and drab, weatherbeaten buildings surely provided grist for Washington policymakers intent on restructuring the social and economic landscape of rural America.

Yet, according to Hickok, large areas of rural states such as Minnesota, particularly those linked economically to the network of midwestern industrial cities, managed to escape the deep human suffering encountered in the Dakotas. For example, the depression hardly touched the iron-range town of Hibbing, Minnesota—"the richest village in the world"—where United States Steel Corporation taxes went into the town coffers and where citizens enjoyed a five-million-dollar high school. The Hibbing fire chief drove a Cord automobile "half a block long," and the town recorder's salary topped the Minnesota governor's. The town's medical clinic, observed Hickok, "would do credit to an up-to-the-minute metropolitan hospital!" A local doctor on a full-time salary examined every child in the school district and found no signs of undernourishment among his warmly clothed children.[12]

Conflicting attitudes about modernization affected relief activities in rural America. It remained assertively individualistic. Heavily laced with a tough, unyielding brand of traditional, farm-grown Calvinism, rural ideology rejected the modern concept of public relief. Farm-state conservatives could easily endorse New Deal farm credit programs, commodity price supports, and land bank systems while at the same time, on their own particular moral grounds, denouncing such federal relief programs as the "dole."

New York's Temporary Emergency Relief Administration (TERA), although a model of bureaucratic efficiency, reflected an ethic of relief-giving clearly tinctured by Calvinistic individualism. For instance, in the western part of the state Hickok spoke with subsistence farmers who complained about a special "escrow system" that allowed a man to work a full week on a relief project, while officials withheld part of his pay until sufficient money was accumulated for the man to lay off a week. It was paternalism run wild; TERA presumed that if a man received all his pay at once, he would not save enough to sustain him through the week he was forced to lay off. For these once successful farmers, being on relief was bad enough; being treated as children only deepened the frustration.

New York farmers experienced considerable difficulty paying taxes. Under the escrow, they never seemed to have sufficient funds at any one time to pay them. "I'll manage it by selling some of my trees for guide posts along the highway," one farmer told Hickok, "but it's a question whether they'll buy them in time so I can pay my taxes next month." If he could not pay, he lamented, "my place will be offered for sale. I'll have six months in which to redeem it, but I'll have to pay six percent interest."[13]

However, of all the places Hickok visited, Maine epitomized the persistence of premodern ideas about philanthropy and most vividly revealed the impact of Calvinistic notions upon charity and the administration of public relief. She described Maineites as "down East Yankees," thrifty, proud, reserved, independent, "shrewd, but honest." She applauded their ability to resist the "bigger and better madness" which she decried in most modern Americans, and she praised them for clinging to the "good solid virtues on which this nation was founded." Yet at the same time, Hickok deplored their intolerance of others who failed to live up to those virtues. They resented neighbors who accepted relief, particularly the French-Canadians along the state's northern border. Easy-going people often living from hand-to-mouth even in better times, these French-Canadians who accepted relief were villified as "white trash" by the Maine natives.

A belief in "rugged individualism" and an abhorrence of relief flowed deeply in Maine blood. The typical Maineite, observed Hickok, "would almost starve rather than ask for help." In fact, she wrote, "his fellow citizens would expect it of him." Among these people it was considered a disgrace to be "on the town." Officials at the state relief headquarters in Augusta told Hickok that it was difficult to find white-collar people for relief work because there were so few of them on the relief rolls. Officials lamented that there were probably thousands of such people literally starving to death, but refusing to ask for help, and thus virtually impossible to find. Those "Yankees" still believed that "there must be something wrong with a fellow if he can't get a job." They really believe it, Hickok wrote, even as they tell you how desperate their plight is and how hopeless the employment situation looks for the future. "It just don't seem right," one old farmer said, "for anybody to get something for nothing. It's pauperizing, that's all." Unfortunately, the officials administering relief in Maine shared these views. In handling relief, Hickok wrote, "they are apt to be honest to the point of fanaticism." One old man on relief told an official that he and his family were getting tired of eating only vegetables, mostly beans. "I can stand it," he said, "but my wife's getting ugly." When he told this to the town official who prepared the food orders, the latter said, "Good! I'm glad to hear it!" This general attitude, Hickok believed, accounted for the inadequacy of relief and its maladministration.

Maineites on relief had "to stand for a good deal of discrimination based on purely conventional moral standards." As for all the talk about "deserving cases," Hickok concluded that to be "deserving" in Maine a family had "to measure up to the most rigid nineteenth-century standards of cleanliness, physical and moral." There was nothing hyperbolic about it; women who failed as housekeepers had a tough time, wrote Hickok, and "Heaven help the family in which there is any moral problem!"

Local governments discouraged even worthy people from going on relief. Hickok found only seven Maine counties receiving state and federal relief monies and most of it aided northern Aroostook County's French-Canadians. Since most community leaders fretted that "all that money from Augusta and Washington is going to have to be paid back sometime," they refused help, preferring to "get along somehow."

Typical of such a community was Calais, where conditions were described by Hickok as "simply frightful." Despite some cries for aid at a recent town meeting, local officials stubbornly rebuffed offers of assistance. Those unfortunates on relief in Calais were subjected "to treatment that is almost medieval in its stinginess and stupidity." Yet, the mayor boasted to a bewildered Hickok that he was proud of the town's refusal to ask for help. "It has been a tough job," he said, and everybody had sacrificed, particularly school teachers, whose pay had been cut until they barely had enough to eat.

During Hickok's stay in Maine, only a half-dozen trained social workers administered the state's welfare caseload. Moreover, local officials in Maine, in the manner of rural relief officials in Pennsylvania and elsewhere, distrusted trained and salaried caseworkers. Alas, rural Maine's grassroots lack of generosity and harsh attitudes toward those who could not obtain jobs hampered whatever trained relief help that might have been available. That rugged Yankee individualism which, despite the Great Depression, thrived along Maine's rock-ribbed coast, made life a nightmare for the truly needy.[14]

For the most part, however, exhausted public coffers and incompetent public officials, more than rustic ideology, determined the meanness of rural relief policy. In Idaho, Pierce Williams told Hopkins that political infighting was inhibiting relief programs. In North Dakota, T. J. Edmonds and Lorena Hickok discovered county welfare offices where finances were "shamefully inadequate." In one county a thousand families, or a third of the population, mostly farmers, lived on relief. County commissioners who handled relief were given a budget of $6,000 a month, approximately six dollars per family. And because most relief families were large—eight to ten children—the commissioners devised a plan whereby indigent farmers could work on county roads for more adequate relief at about fifteen dollars a month. Sadly, on the day Hickok visited, the highway department had just told the commissioners to cease all road work and pay off the men—most of whom had only ten or fifteen dollars due them.[15]

Hickok constantly bemoaned the desperate need for clothing, especially since 1933–1934 was an extremely cold winter in the Dakotas. Even in her woolen dress and winter coat Hickok felt the bitter chill whenever she ventured outside. "How about clothes?" she heard a relief official ask a farmer in Dickinson. "Everything I own I have on my back," he replied, going on to explain that, having no underwear, he was wearing two pair of overalls and two ragged denim jackets. "His shoes," Hickok observed, "were so far gone that I wondered how he kept them on his feet." She saw scores of men without overcoats; most wore faded shabby denim that hardly kept out the wind. Once when she and a few relief workers went to enter their car outside an old church in Morton County, she found it full of farmers, the windows drawn tightly against the wind. "They apologized," she later recalled, "and said they had crawled in there to keep warm."

But it was the phenomenon of ramshackle, too often politicized relief offices operating on antiquated and unscientific principles that most infuriated the cosmopolitan Hickok. All too frequently she encountered relief "shows" in rural America that were battling a twentieth-century calamity armed only with an eighteenth-century mentality and nineteenth-century machinery. Even when on occasion she stumbled across an enlightened administrator, it only reinforced her low opinion of the archaic nature of the system.

One such administrator was Thurston County, Nebraska's Lowell Evans—one of her favorite "unsung heroes of the New Deal." A "mild-mannered little chap, about 30," Evans wore horn-rimmed glasses, dressed in an old army uniform, and walked about in boots caked with Nebraska and Missouri river-bottom gumbo. Evans was "just one of those little guys who have to do the job that the rest of us plan and observe." As a relief director working in the scrubby little county seat of Walthill, Evans was paid $125 a month in script claims, the currency issued by the county after it had exhausted its tax warrants. He cashed his county script at the local bank, taking a discount of around five dollars a month to operate his car, described once by Hickok as a "tired, wheezy Ford that could barely make some of the hills in the gumbo this afternoon." The money barely covered Evans's gas, nor did it compensate him for the ten dollars in repair bills "on what used to be a Ford." The Walthill relief director did wheedle a free office, but the county only paid his light bill, disallowed long distance calls to Lincoln, and made him pay for his own postage. While the county commissioners were willing to provide him with investigators and administrative funds, they made him about as welcome, Hickok wrote, "as a plague of grasshoppers."

"Oh, it's plenty tough, this job," Evans told her; but he would manage. It had been even tougher at the start. "The boss of the county commissioners doesn't believe in relief," Evans said. "He has told me more than once, 'Aw, let the damned fools starve! They never did amount to anything anyway.'" Every time Evans enrolled a family on relief whom the political boss had not recommended, the boss howled; yet, most of those the commissioners recommended, relief investigators soon discovered to be ineligible.

The county commissioners and the bankers, to whom practically everybody in the county owed money, comprised the relief committee. The banker who dominated the group did so because all the rest owed him money! In September, when the county had received its first $5000 allotment from Lincoln, the boss of the county commissioners simply turned it over to his son-in-law for distribution. When Evans then seized the money, he interrupted the politicians' plans. They had been "just itching to get their fingers onto that money," Hickok wrote. "Why, the very idea of having some young whippersnapper come in there and take it away from them? They'd soon fix *this* little bug."

Through it all, Evans persevered. When Hickok suggested that he visit Lincoln to get support when things were bad, he declined. "I don't want to admit to them that I can't handle this situation. I *can*." By the time she left Nebraska, Hickok was also convinced.[16]

While Nebraska, despite the successes of Lowell Evans, was bad enough, it was worse in North Dakota, where fierce weather and antiquated relief laws exacerbated the dismal economic conditions. Yet, T. J. Edmonds chose the popularity of President Roosevelt, the peculiar foods, and local customs as appropriate items to send along to his boss Hopkins. He determined that the people in the state had "considerable confidence" in the President; that a certain "sort of fish" that North Dakotans ate did "not taste so bad, but it looks something like the victim of a bad automobile disaster"; and that in mixed company in North Dakota one did not say "By God," but if one left off the "B" and merely said "I God," it was proper.[17]

But Lorena Hickok was more angry than curious. And it was in Bottineau County where she discovered the most backward relief conditions. "Pretty low in mind," she wrote Hopkins from Bottineau in early November 1933: "I've seen nothing, heard nothing save the desperate need for things to keep people warm up here in this ghastly climate." Bedding, fuel, and clothing were all in short supply. "And today, as if it wasn't bad enough already, there's been a blizzard." Although as evidenced before, Hickok tended to betray contempt for those she considered undeserving, she expressed anger in this case at the apparent lack of concern evidenced by incompetent Bottineau relief officials, whom she found

> inclined still to think there is something wrong with a man who cannot make a living. They talk so much about "the undeserving" and the "bums." No doubt expert investigators could reduce the rolls here in North Dakota, but, damn it—people are suffering from cold in this state *right now*. Terribly. And I feel this is not the time to be fussing about who should get relief and who shouldn't. They should have settled that a long time ago.[18]

Throughout rural America, state and federal relief officials confronted the paradox of the historically sturdy but nevertheless presently needy farmer. Was he the Jeffersonian bone and sinew of American democracy, the quiet, self-reliant individual, or was he in fact really a modern businessman with lobbyists in Washington, whose capital investment in land and stock needed propping up with federally underwritten loans? This was the essence of the somewhat vitriolic conversation which swirled about the governor's reception room in Pierre, South Dakota, one afternoon in November 1933 while Hickok listened and took notes. A delegation of angry farmers had gathered there, deeply concerned over the government's 4-4-2 limit of relief eligibility. The 4-4-2 rule stated that before a farmer could qualify for assistance, he had to divest himself of all livestock save four cows, four horses, two brood sows, and twenty chickens. The men she overheard in the governor's office that day were fuming:

> We believe that limit cannot be applied in our country, because we are not grain growers, primarily, but stock breeders. Our families cannot get along with only four cows apiece. . . .

> If you make our farmers reduce to that limit, they'll be on relief for years to come. You'll be making paupers of them. You'll be forcing them into bankruptcy. . . .

> We don't want any dole. All we want is a chance to carry ourselves through the winter so we'll be able to become self-supporting next year if we have half a chance. . . .

Farmers in Pierre considered their plight worse than that of the city poor. "We worked all summer for nothing," while the city man, they claimed, did not. "If prosperity should return next summer," they argued, "the city man gets a job and becomes self-supporting. But the farmer on that 4-4-2 basis can't be self-supporting." When the government "confiscates the factory where the city man earns his living," one bitter farmer declared, then "we'll be satisfied to let the government sacrifice our stock."[19]

It was not only in Pierre, explained Hickok, but throughout the northwestern cattle country that farmers protested against the inflexibility of the 4-4-2 rule. Most of the large cattle farmers insisted that the rule was more applicable to states such as Wisconsin, where farms were smaller and the farmers grazed fewer head. In order for Dakota farmers to comply, they had to sell their cattle in a nonexistent market. Therefore, they either had to give their cattle away, pretend to sell it and lie to authorities, or kill most of their stock. South Dakota farmers, afraid to cut their herds from forty head down to four, especially at the low prices, turned their cattle out to shift for themselves. Hickok saw the result of that practice firsthand during her trip through (the Rosebud country) and around Huron. There she observed livestock roaming the hills so scrawny that the sight "would make you sick."

Officials blamed confusions and contradictions in state and federal programs for much of the trouble. For instance, there was a law in North Dakota that prevented an elevator operator from selling grain stored by farmers in his elevator. The title remained with the farmer. Consequently, in the distribution of wheat in government programs it was found that while the elevators in certain towns were full, the wheat could not be sold and thus there was little room for the wheat sent in to be stored. This created a ridiculous situation where a cattle farmer might drive ten or fifteen miles past full elevators and on to another town to get his wheat. It seemed, then, that the Surplus Products Corporation and FERA were shipping wheat to counties where there were full elevators already.

Others blamed the perceived inequities and the general confusion of the farm loan program on its newness. Newness was also used to excuse the interminable delays in the program, delays that usually seemed intolerable to the farmers. In North Dakota, the secretary of the Farmers Loan Association in Williston told Hickok in November that he had processed 450 applications since the program had been established in June 1933. "I leave it to you," Hickok wrote her boss, "to imagine how a farmer would feel when he applied for a loan back in June and by the first of November still didn't know whether he was going to get it or not! Especially when the money was available all the time."

Delays were blamed on bankers in Minneapolis and St. Paul who "didn't understand and didn't try to understand" the conditions in the farm areas. Moreover, these bankers, whose approval was necessary for the loans to be finalized, regarded wheat and livestock farmers as "peasants," at least according to Hickok, who had worked for a decade on the *Minneapolis Tribune*.[20]

Elected political leaders did not always help, either. Hopkins's correspondents were both frustrated and fascinated by the "politics of relief" and the political volatility of the Big Sky states, particularly Idaho and the Dakotas. Arriving in North Dakota in the summer of 1934, after the CWA had been disbanded, T. J. Edmonds wrote to Washington in prosaic but nevertheless revealing language. "The sun blazed in the West," began Edmonds,

heating the North Dakota steppes to a temperature of 105 degrees in the shade; a crescent moon hung in the southeastern sky; one maverick cloud fled before the hot winds and finally dissolved against the stark blue sky and huge whirls of alkali dust shot up from the beds of dried-up lakes, as clad in a fur-lined sheepskin jacket, helmet, goggles and parachute strappings, I flew in an open military plane yesterday into the state that has two governors, a special session of the legislature about to convene on an illegal call, martial law prevailing from Fargo to the Badlands, rumors of thousands of Farm Holiday farmers converging on the Capitol. . . . khaki-clad boys with fixed bayonets . . . guarding the entrance to the state house, and ⅔ of the voters still believing that a man convicted of a felony by a federal court and deprived of his citizenship by a confirmatory ruling of the State Supreme Court, guilty of a still further offense of starting a riot of alleged relief clients, and described privately by the press as a double crossing son-of-a-bitch is God's own gift to the farmer, the laborer, and all the under-privileged and unfortunate of North Dakota.[21]

Edmonds referred, of course, to Governor William Langer, an aggressively independent Republican who was convicted of using relief funds for political reasons. Removed from office in 1934, he was cleared the next year and again elected governor in 1936. When Edmonds was in North Dakota, Governor Langer declared martial law and deployed National Guard around his office, which enabled him to remain in office despite the Supreme Court ruling that he was no longer governor. Ole Olson, "the other Governor," opened his headquarters in a hotel (also surrounded by the Guard) and attempted to run the state from his hotel room. He eventually assumed the office. While these events might have provided some comic relief for Hopkins's reporters, they hardly provided for effective public relief programs.

Hopkins's reporters found that almost all Big Sky state governors wanted a piece of the relief action. In Montana, Benjamin Glassberg reported, the governor "feels that every time a check comes from D.C. he is to have personal responsibility for its expenditures and that it should be spent by people loyal to him." In Idaho, T. J. Edmonds told Hopkins that the political use of relief monies by Democratic Governor C. Ben Ross, who liked to be called "The Abraham Lincoln of the West," was so blatant that "if real facts about Idaho were ever brought to light they would wreck the Roosevelt Administration." Perhaps only the fact that "Idaho is a long way from Washington and is buried among mountain fastnesses," Edmonds wrote, had prevented "an earlier explosion."[22]

Political machinations doubtless delayed relief and added to gnawing rural poverty. Yet, this wretched peasantry spawned negligible social unrest. Instead, contrary to the worst premonitions of New Deal "service intellectuals," the most violent rural protest sprang from among the ranks of America's farmer-businessmen, conservative Iowa, Nebraska, and Wisconsin farmers whose capital investment in land, buildings, and machinery was threatened by the low market value of farm commodities, and for whom mortgage foreclosure loomed as an imminent possibility. As the farm losses dashed one middle-class expectation after another, the accumulating social tensions transformed conservative farmers into violent activists. As early as 1930, at its Seventh Party Convention, the Communist party, USA (CPUSA) had observed that the forthcoming agrarian discontent would involve farmer-owners, the "Agrarian petty bourgeoisie," and not the agricultural wage workers. The party called for the formation of Committees of Action which would organize tenant strikes, mass refusals for paying mortgage interest, taxpayers strikes, and a physical struggle against foreclosures.

However, as the late historian John Shover has pointed out, the CPUSA merely "rode the crest" of a wave of rural rebellion that swept the Midwest in 1931 and 1932. In fact, it became part of CPUSA strategy to align itself with already existing protest groups such as the Farmer's Holiday Association (FHA) and the National Farmer's Union, groups whose strength in numbers of followers cast them in the forefront of the farm protest consuming Iowa, Minnesota, Wisconsin, and Nebraska.[23]

Traveling around Minnesota, Nebraska, Iowa, Montana, and the Dakotas from the fall of 1933 through the spring of 1934, Hopkins's correspondents heard a great deal about such groups, particularly the militant Farmer's Holiday Association. Formed in the summer of 1932 by Milo Reno, head of the Iowa Farmers Union, the FHA called on farmers to strike, demonstrate, protest, and withhold their products until they received a "cost of production" price. Reno's movement was centered in northeastern Iowa, perhaps the world's richest farm area. Clearly, there as elsewhere, Farm Holiday leaders were the formerly prosperous and respected members of their communities. As the Communist party sorrily discovered, these former pillars of respectability were hardly interested in overthrowing the America government; indeed, they considered themselves *as* the government, seeing justice as the community saw it, not as judges and politicians might.

Despite their conservative credentials, these farm protestors did not abjure the use of violence. Farm Holiday protestors spiked telegraph poles, punctured tires, smashed windshields, blocked highways with logs, threatened and beat sheriffs and local turnkeys who arrested them, attacked company agents and deputy sheriffs attempting to foreclose on farm mortgages, and in LeMars, Iowa, nearly killed a judge who refused to promise not to foreclose any more mortgages on their farms. Meanwhile, in Wisconsin the FHA gained the most notoriety for dumping milk along frigid state highways. Moreover, in Madison, FHA marchers assaulted the statehouse and occupied the Assembly Chamber, and in Minnesota and Iowa they overturned trucks carrying farm goods to market.

But not all the farm protest involved such violence. The Farmer's Holiday and other groups held conventions and demonstrations in areas where the reporters visited. For instance, in North Dakota, Lorena Hickok reported that meetings were going on all over the state. The Farmers' Union had a four-day convention in Williston; about 700 delegates and crowds as large as 1,500 attended. A few days later, five or six hundred irate farmers convened in Bismarck. Two hundred or so farmers stopped a foreclosure sale at Oaks, and then marched into Ellendale where they ran a field representative of the State Emergency Relief committee out of town.

But as J. C. Lindsey and Pierce Williams later reported from Idaho, there was, all things considered, much ado about nothing. It was perhaps true that Pocatello was "a hot bed of agitation and controversy . . . where congregate men from Utah, Idaho, Montana, and Wyoming." There were large numbers of enthusiastic union members there, "some of whom are on the radical side." However, Lindsey contended, there was "just enough local agitation to give the newspaper reports a color of truth, but no more than that." It was the same in Boise, where on one occasion it was reported that 350 people crowded the streets of the capital in a public protest against FERA policies. "I am told by reliable citizens," Lindsey wrote, "that this number did not exceed 15 or 20." [24]

Most farmers were frustrated rather than furious. Hickok was in South Dakota when a long-awaited farm strike began. She reported that most of the creameries along the Yellowstone Trail between Aberdeen and the Minnesota border were closed. Farmers who had taken chickens from Aberdeen down to Watertown had brought them back. Farm Holiday leaders were meeting in Aberdeen, Webster, and other towns. One of them, whom Hickok deemed reasonable and reluctant to strike, spoke with her at length about the farmer's plight. "Our feeling is that down there in Washington they don't understand us right," he said. "We have asked for things, but they just ignore us." Sadly, he lamented, "a lot of us don't want to strike, but we feel we've got to defend ourselves and somehow keep this part of the country going. We've done our part. Farmers have built up this country. We've built these churches and these schools. Somehow we've got to keep them going, too." All farmers want, he said, "is that we get what it costs to produce our crops. We don't even ask for a profit." Farmers, he insisted, "believe in our government, but we think our government should be made to fit us, as well as the people in the East." The farmer denounced Communists, who "want to make everybody as miserable as possible to get a revolution." They did not offer anything constructive, he told Hickok. "We don't feel that way. We think the way out is through cooperation between the government and the farmers." Unfortunately, he claimed, the farmers were not getting any cooperation now.

Although this farmer reflected the convictions of many in the Farm Holiday and other groups, their strike and their movement were actually in decline. In all the farm states Hickok visited in the fall, things had improved somewhat for the farmers. Farm loans were moving much faster, and local people were now serving as appraisers. In the Dakotas, wheat prices had risen almost to the cost of production, and wheat allotment checks were about ready to come through. Thus, the editor of a Republican newspaper in Fargo did not "expect to see North Dakota farmers blowing up bridges this winter."

The farm loan program and the Agriculture Adjustment Act had been designed to address the long-term grievances of farmer-businessmen and thereby silence the "thunder rolling from the rural left." And clearly, as John Shover has pointed out, the farm credit, crop reduction, and price stabilization programs helped assuage the angriest and most volatile elements in the rural community. However, for that hapless dispossessed segment of the rural population beyond the pale of farm loans or price fixing assistance, the only option remained thin philanthropy or public relief, a vile prospect among individualistic farmers. Therefore, as elsewhere in her travels but especially in rural America, Lorena Hickok was almost obsessed by the federal experiment with works programs as an alternative to the degrading experience of direct relief. In fact, it was while she was recording the terrible plight of poor farmers and their families in the nature-cursed regions of the Dakotas that Hickok first learned about the Civil Works Administration (CWA). She seemed ecstatic. "Three loud cheers for CWA! I may be wrong," she wrote, "but I think probably it's the smartest thing that has been tried since we went into the relief business." She thought that the CWA would "take away a lot of the bad tastes" associated with previous relief programs and reported that it "has been greeted with enthusiasm out this way."

Two days later, in Nebraska, Hickok received a large folder outlining CWA policies, material she needed since she knew very little about the program. Republican newspapers in the Dakotas and Minnesota, she explained, "don't do any more explaining or clearing up than they just have to!" In Nebraska and Iowa, she learned about CWA firsthand. First, she visited a CWA gang working on a road project. "It was a nasty morning," she observed. "Cold and sleet greeted the men at work. But they looked cheerful. Thirty-hour week, forty cents an hour—CASH, instead of grocery orders." [25]

In South Sioux City, Hickok again wrote rapturously about the promise of CWA. "Whose idea CWA was I don't know," she exuded, "but it's a honey!" She envisioned more people getting back to work at a much faster rate than was possible under FERA and PWA. Later, Hickok's enthusiasm dampened considerably, but at that moment she saw only a bright future. "It was truly heartening," she wrote from Nebraska, to see "thousands of men going to work NOW."

One of the "bad tastes" Hickok felt CWA would take away was the threat to the free enterprise system; the optimism restored by CWA counteracted the appeal of communism. That optimism had reached Fairmont, Minnesota, in time for Hickok's arrival. "Every Saturday there's a big crowd around there," a coal dealer informed her. "They've been a pretty gloomy crowd these last two or three years," he said, "but—say, you should have seen 'em last Saturday! laughing and joking—why, I hadn't had so much fun in years! They all had a little money in their pockets. They were all going to have something in the house to eat for Christmas. You wouldn't have known them!" While in Fairmont, Hickok visited an old friend, a district judge with wide acquaintance in southern Minnesota and northern Iowa. Only a year earlier, an angry mob had threatened to hang the judge in LeMars, Iowa, and, in fact, Fairmont had had enough of its own civil strife in the past year that her friend feared to leave the area "because no one knew what might happen next. But now he marveled at the changes"—quicker action on loan applications, wheat allotment checks, corn loans, and now, CWA. "'If any one had told me a month ago that things were going to improve as much as they have in the last three or four weeks,'" the judge said, "'I'd have said they [sic] were crazy. It's almost unbelievable.'" [26]

Although Hickok somewhat muted the theme, she portrayed CWA as modernizing the infrastructure of rural America; after 1935 the Works Projects Administration (WPA), which superceded the CWA, would intensify the process of building and rebuilding a more modern countryside. Throughout rural America, federal relief workers built roads, storm and sanitary sewers, waterworks, township and borough buildings, schools, irrigation canals, and other projects all of which upgraded rural health, sanitary, and educational facilities by thirty years. Towns anxiously sought the fruits of federal work relief projects, although in the countryside as in the city, politics and the requirements that the projects be labor-intensive and that the community absorb the bulk of materials costs frequently proved to be major obstructions.

In rural upstate New York, for example, Hickok reported that delays due to cautious politicians and slow-to-complain local officials often hampered public works projects. There was hardly a town Hickok visited that did not have a project on hold, either in Albany or Washington. Even towns that succeeded in raising their own share of project funds waited all summer to receive public works money from Washington. In one instance, the town went ahead on its own, extending its water and sewer systems, hoping to be later reimbursed from Washington. Upstate New York received some federal highway money, but for Clinton County in the Northern Tier, it came too late; unfortunately, by the time the head of the Federal Re-employment Bureau had 834 men ready to work on a road project, the contractor reneged because of oncoming winter weather.

Yet, on a smaller scale, many work relief projects were in fact underway in rural parts of New York. For instance, at Fulton, a local clergyman directed a very successful reclamation project using a homemade dredge (floated on empty oil drums) to clear the outlet from a lake. The now purified lake featured "a grand little beach." Small-scale sewer and road projects also provided aid for rural dwellers in upstate New York.

In Iowa, both cold weather and the prohibitions against the use of labor-saving machinery inhibited the works program; yet, Hickok still applauded the small successes. In one Iowa town, "practically every able-bodied man from the relief rolls" found employment on a local sewer project. Back in Nebraska, she informed Hopkins, over one hundred CWA and PWA projects were in the works; twenty-one had been approved by Washington, the work already started and/or the contracts let; and fifty others were awaiting action. "And the beauty of it," she wrote, "it's a planned statewide affair, with an objective—irrigation, to keep this state from drying up and blowing away as South Dakota is doing." [27]

Hickok's observations about the importance of CWA, together with her observations about rural poverty in Bottineau, North Dakota, rural individualism in Maine, and rural violence in Iowa reinforced the social scientific critique of rural America that Rexford Tugwell, M. L. Wilson, and the other New Deal braintrusters were constructing in the federal Department of Agriculture. From rural Maine and upstate New York to the Midwest corn belt and the cattle ranges of the northern Dakotas, Hickok had discovered farmers whose futile attempts to eke out a livelihood on marginal land eventuated in gnawing poverty. These farm families constituted America's rural proletariat, people whose weatherbeaten visages were captured most eloquently in the photographs of Dorothea Lange and other photographers commissioned by the Farm Security Administration. However, these yeoman sodbusters, who laboriously tilled the soil undaunted by plagues of bad weather and insects, represented to the social scientists not heroes, but outmoded vestiges of America's agricultural past.

Like her reports from America's cities and mill towns, Hickok's letters from rural America memorialized a way of life undergoing the upheaval of social and economic change. So, in the Midwest she glimpsed a countryside trembling from agrarian protest. There, in Nebraska, Kansas, Wisconsin, and Iowa—America's agricultural heartland—Hickok encountered traditionally conservative farmer-businessmen blocking roads, dumping milk, and threatening death to district judges who ordered mortgage foreclosures. However, rather than the apocalypse or the first violent engagement in America's red revolution, the actions of the farmers heralded not the emergence of agricultural collectivization, but instead the dawn of federal farm cooperation and the ensconcing of American agribusiness. [28]

As she had in urban America, Hickok discovered that in the Dakotas, Iowa, Montana and Minnesota the thorn of politics had obstructed the efficient delivery of relief, the issuance of farm loans, and other forms of federal assistance. In contrast to this political turmoil and the inefficiently operated federal programs she found in the Big Sky country, Maine and New York exhibited a persistence of Yankee conservatism where Maine fishermen and potato farmers and New York pulp mill workers and dairymen evinced traditional values of individualism and self-reliance. And, although economic conditions were as grievous in New York as in the large western states where she traveled, Hickok found that the administration of public relief was considerably more successful in the former than in the latter. Nevertheless, by late 1933, inefficiency and politics notwithstanding, Hickok espied federal relief and loan programs already defusing much of the violence and radicalism attending rural protest. Hickok's enthusiasm for CWA and her confidence that the forces of radicalism had been vanquished, seemed to affirm the belief that, shored up by the federal agricultural programs, a modern agrarianism would triumph over the forces of rural decay. Yet, Hickok's bursts of optimism often yielded to fits of gloom and depression, especially after wading in the squalor of rural poverty such as she had faced in Bottineau County. Such scenes reminded her that the struggle against retrogressive farming methods and rural poverty would be long and the victims of rural ignorance and despair legion. This certainly appeared to be her mood as she launched her tour of the American South.

7

The South

A Saga of Despair and Hope

■ He can't git no place to crop.
a North Carolina sharecropper's wife

■ This CWA wage is buzzing in our
Niggers' heads.
a South Carolina cotton grower

■ A Promised Land, bathed in
golden sunlight, is rising out of the gray shadows of want and squalor and
wretchedness down here in the Tennessee Valley these days.
Lorena Hickok, from Tennessee

■ If farm families in Maine, New
York, Iowa, Minnesota, and the Dakotas were suffering grinding poverty,
their counterparts in the South were mired in even worse economic straits
because for many of them the Great Depression had only made an already
bad situation worse. Ever since the Civil War the rural South had been
plagued by soil exhaustion, low productivity, and little income. Along
with miserable housing and sorely deficient diets, the rural South had the
country's highest rate of illiteracy, and its highest birth rate as well. By
almost every conceivable economic indicator, rural southerners were the
poorest people in the nation.[1]

The urban South fared little better. Backward and desperate rural migrants swelled town populations, and their increasing numbers strained the limited capacities of outmoded and outmanned relief agencies. Moreover, textile and industrial workers in towns such as Gastonia and Birmingham were working longer hours for lower pay; perhaps worse, in those towns and others, formerly successful professional and white-collar people faced the unfamiliar shock of reduced social status and economic destitution. At the same time, debt-ridden local governments were hardly prepared to deal with the ever increasing human distress. In Durham, Atlanta, New Orleans, and other southern cities, family relief funds were exhausted by early 1932, and the meager state and federal help of the Hoover years did little to ease the suffering there.[2]

Moreover, at the very moment that Harry Hopkins's correspondents were touring the Old Confederacy in 1933 and 1934, southern intellectuals were engaged in a great cultural struggle seeking to recast the South's past and to plan for a more modern and hopeful future.

While it would be a few years before he would complete his epic study *The Mind of the South*, North Carolina newspaperman Wilbur J. Cash was already agonizing over the South's past, present, and future. In articles for H. L. Mencken's *American Mercury* and in numerous editorials and book reviews for the *Charlotte News*, Cash grappled with such issues as lynching, labor violence, conservative religion, sluggish rural economics, and the New Deal.[3]

In *The Mind of the South* (his only published book, called by the *Atlantic Monthly* "a literary and moral miracle"), Cash rejected out of hand the notion that the Old South was a pristine land of rose gardens and crinoline and lace; he likewise denied that the New South was now a place where industrialism was dominant, a region of progress and modernization. At the same time, while sympathetic to the "Nashville Agrarians," a group of influential poets led by Robert Penn Warren, Donald Davidson, John Crowe Ransom and Allen Tate who implored their fellow southerners to eschew industrialism and the new modernization, Cash rejected their views as mere sentimentalism for a past that never was.

The Great Depression had been devastating to the average southerner's faith that his was the best of all possible worlds; it had created social as well as economic chaos. Thus, despite an apparent aversion to change and concern about continued Yankee economic colonization of the region, the South had accepted much of the New Deal and the changes it wrought, perhaps mainly because it came from a Democratic administration and brought with it desperately needed financial assistance. Cash's account of the effects of the Great Depression upon the South was particularly useful to his contemporaries because Cash insisted that fundamentally little had really changed. Despite federal largesse and the inroads of industrialism, the South had retained its traditional patterns: the economic and social order of the Old South's plantation system had been transferred to the New South's tenant farms, cotton mill villages, and industrial centers.

Cash described the modern descendent of southern yeomanry as the "man at the center," mannerly and proud, honorable and loyal, brave and generous. Yet he was also prone to violence, intolerant, and suspicious of new ideas. Incapable of deep analysis, he often possessed "an exaggerated individualization and a too narrow concept of social responsibility." The southerner's "attachment to fictions and false values," particularly his "attachment to racial values," led him to "justify cruelty and injustice in the name of those values."

However, while Cash, writing from Charlotte, a bastion of North Carolina conservatism, gloomily concluded that the region's future seemed imprisoned within its past, other southern intellectuals actually perceived an enlightened future. Not far away, at Chapel Hill, the site of the state university, a group of scholars was busily engaged in planning the New South. In 1933, one of these scholars, University of North Carolina professor Rupert B. Vance published a pathbreaking book, *Human Geography of the South,* in which he proposed a program for modernizing the South by blending orderly industrial growth with advanced agricultural techniques. This program, which Vance called a "New Regionalism," would be directed by civic-conscious citizens, urbane and public-spirited industrialists, and involved intellectual leaders trained in southern universities. Vance envisioned a program of research, planning, and implementation aimed at producing a material and cultural renaissance in the South.[4]

Although Vance carefully articulated the idea of New Regionalism, its most influential proponent at Chapel Hill was Professor Howard W. Odum, Vance's tutor and colleague, founder of the Institute for Research in Social Science and head of a virtual academic empire at Chapel Hill. In 1936, Odum published what many considered to be the Bible of the movement, *Southern Regions of the United States.* Odum's panorama of the contemporary South was a weighty volume, bulging with facts and figures. His statistics clearly portrayed the South as a distinct section. Yet, Odum's portrait of the South as a region differed from the older sectionalism which, argued Odum, while adequate as a historical foundation, did not provide adequate guideposts for future regional development. The old sectionalism was devoted to the past, to the sacred Lost Cause. It abounded in conflict and confrontation, demanded social and intellectual independence from the other regions, included notions of Anglo-Saxon racial purity along with anti-union and anti-radical rhetoric. It emphasized southern orthodoxy and suggested that such virtues as honor and gentility were properties of the South alone. The New Regionalism was much more hopeful. While recognizing the distinctive features of the South, even emphasizing them, the New Regionalism called for a more social and intellectual integration (not,

Rural Slums, Aroostook County, Maine, during the New Deal. (*Photo by Jack Delano; Library of Congress*)

The Dust Bowl, 1936. (*Photo by Arthur Rothstein; Library of Congress*)

Farm children, Williston, North Dakota, 1937. (*Photo by Russell Lee; Library of Congress*)

Black slums, Atlanta, 1936. (*Photo by Walker Evans; Library of Congress*)

Rural poor in Coffee County, Alabama, 1939. The children have hookworm, the mother pellagra and phlibitis. The father works on a WPA project. (*Photo by Marion Post Wolcott; Library of Congress*)

Rural poverty among blacks, Heard County, Georgia. (*Photo by Jack Delano; Library of Congress*)

The Mexican quarter, Los Angeles, early 1936. (*Photo by Dorothea Lange; Library of Congress*)

Hispanic children in the kitchen of their home, San Antonio, 1939. (*Photo by Russell Lee; Library of Congress*)

San Joaquin Valley, California, 1938. A World War I veteran turned migrant worker on Highway 33. (*Photo by Dorothea Lange; Library of Congress*)

A transient community located at the edge of a dump in Bakersville, California, 1936. (*Photo by Dorothea Lange; Library of Congress*)

Elko, Nevada, during the Great Depression. (*Photo by Arthur Rothstein; Library of Congress*)

of course, the end of racial segregation) of the South into the rest of the nation. New Regionalism called for considered social and economic planning and ultimately the modernization of the Old Confederacy.[5]

While Cash's work was reflective, guilt-ridden, and impressionistic, Odum's was statistical, optimistic, and programmatical. In that sense and others, both Odum and Vance could be counted among that group of activist and public-minded academicians including Rexford Tugwell and Dwight Sanderson whom Richard S. Kirkendall has termed the "service intellectuals," social scientists who, determined to follow their ideas with concrete programs, played a large part in shaping farm policies and politics during the New Deal. Rejecting a more cloistered life devoted to teaching, research, and writing on the university campus, the service intellectuals determined to utilize their academic standing in more open service to the state. The service intellectuals advocated government involvement in economic affairs devoted to the promotion of human progress. In the area of the agricultural sciences such men as M. L. Wilson, Mordecai Ezekial, and Howard Tolley promoted the application of modern social scientific methods in advocating farm reforms. Wilson, Ezekial, and Tolley even accepted positions in the Roosevelt administration. Although they did not do so, Odum and Vance had anticipated the New Deal through their humanistic studies of agriculture in the South and their support of regional planning. Indeed, features of New Deal agricultural policy such as farm diversification were popular in the South before the New Deal emerged.[6]

Significantly, while Vance, Odum, and others inquired into the mind and state of the South, the region's severe economic and social plight mollified its deep-rooted suspicion of federal authority. In fact, as the New Deal dawned, southern political leaders looked eagerly to Washington for help. Not only would New Deal programs be considered by a Congress now controlled by southern Democrats, but also President Roosevelt was openly sympathetic to the South's plight. For a decade Roosevelt had vacationed in Warm Springs, Georgia, seeking relief for his polio-stricken legs. He often expressed great affection for the place, its people and surroundings, and he regarded himself as "an adopted Southerner." Sometimes acting the gentleman farmer (he owned more than a thousand acres of timber and farm land in Georgia), Roosevelt was convinced that he not only appreciated the South's economic distress, but also knew as well some solutions to the region's problems.[7]

Yet, despite Roosevelt's sympathies and concern and despite southern control of Congress (nine of the Senate's fourteen major committees were chaired by southern Democrats), early New Deal legislation proved a mixed bag for the South. In some cases, recovery measures not only fell short of expectations but also further disadvantaged many of the South's most vulnerable people. For instance, the cotton textile code of the National Recovery Administration (NRA) included lower minimum wage provisions in the South than elsewhere; and on top of that, southern textile operators adopted methods that aborted any gains for workers. New labor-saving machinery reduced the work force, and speed-ups exhausted laborers and led to the dismissals of countless marginal workers. Moreover, the labor disputes these conditions sparked caused scores of ambitious workers to be fired for their persistent union activities. Soon, business and industrial leaders and their newspaper publishing allies, while appreciative of the New Deal for its economic stimulation, criticized NRA "coercion" and "oppression" and called for an end to New Deal "paternalism."

It was one of the predilections of the service intellectuals that the federal government had a responsibility to aid the American farmer by promoting research in land-use practices and in studies of present and prospective supply-and-demand levels. Another was for the government to adopt specific programs designed to produce regional farm efficiency in order to provide sufficient profits. In line with these predilections, the Agricultural Adjustment Act of 1933 was designed to limit production and boost the price of such farm products as cotton, wheat, livestock, and corn. But the farm program did not nearly answer the South's basic economic problems. While it helped the largest cotton growers, it hurt the region's already depressed poor white and black tenant farmers and sharecroppers. The NRA cotton contracts between the federal government and the landowners so favored the latter that endless numbers of farm workers were evicted from the land and left to fend for themselves.

A major part of the Federal Emergency Relief Administration's mission was relieving the distress of poor, landless southern farmers. The percentage of southern rural families receiving FERA help in 1933 was higher than in any other region. Moreover, while in other areas of the country FERA granted supplementary funds to local Emergency Relief Administrations, in the South the agency virtually underwrote the entire cost of relief. Likewise, the Civil Works Administration, designed to put the jobless to work on relief projects during the winter of 1933-1934, operated one of its largest programs in the South, a reflection of the region's great need.

Outside the plantation economy, southern farmers had been poor for generations. After the Civil War, matters worsened for almost all southern farmers, the incomes of many landowning farmers declining with each passing decade. But the primary victims of the rural South's chronic economic distress were the region's landless farmers, its tenants and sharecroppers; and their numbers grew. By 1930 tenants operated over 55 percent of all southern farms, or 1.8 million among 3.4 million farm operators. Both races were mired in the sorry situation. Two of every three tenants were white; and, while almost half of all white farm operators in the South were tenants, two-thirds of all black operators were. More than half of the black and a fourth of the white tenants were sharecroppers. Owning little farm equipment and with virtually no working capital, these hapless farm families numbered over five million whites and more than three million blacks, or about a fourth of the South's people. Into this South Harry Hopkins dispatched his correspondents. Their reports resembled the somewhat schizophrenic debate over the region's past and future as detailed by Cash, Vance, and Odum. For the most part the reporters despaired for both southern blacks and poor whites. They described southern agriculture as hopelessly outdated and the region's urban areas as facing an almost insurmountable social and economic crisis.

Yet, there was hope, too. In the midst of enormous human suffering, Hopkins's reporters glimpsed a special resolve in many southerners they met. Particularly, consistent with the progressive ethos, they saw such programs as agricultural diversification, resettlement, and the Tennessee Valley Authority (TVA) as a way of using federal bureaucracy and the application of science to pave the way for a better future for the South.

It was this intrusion of science and the federal government into the affairs of the South—New Deal paternalism—that would begin, many argue, the historic alteration of race relations in the South—despite the segregation patterns that persisted in the many New Deal programs discussed in previous chapters. In the end, southern critics of the New Deal insisted, Cash's "man at the center," the yeoman farmer, would be the loser. And while President Roosevelt would largely retain his considerable popularity among a majority of southerners, the so-called New Dealers and some of their legacy would not retain a similar reputation. A pattern of social, political, and racial relationships had been established in the post-Civil War Reconstruction era, and despite a push for Henry Grady's New South (Henry W. Grady, influential editor of *The Atlanta Constitution* in the 1880s, envisioned a modern South of capital investment and industrial expansion), that pattern had not been changed significantly even by the Industrial Revolution. However, southerners now beheld cataclysmic new social forces that presaged the postindustrial era. For better or for worse, then, the New Deal's largesse and good intentions were viewed by many as socially disruptive and the reporters that Hopkins sent South were seen as representing that force.

Hopkins sent Alan Johnstone to South Carolina, Florida, and Georgia in September of 1933 to aid state officials there in organizing the administration of New Deal relief. Johnstone told Hopkins that while the Georgia relief set-up was still in its infancy in many ways what he had "so far seen is sound and hitches up trained personnel of a character better than I thought possible to secure." Yet Johnstone correctly foresaw political troubles for an effective and adequate distribution of relief, particularly, as Hopkins reporters would later discover, from Georgia Governor Eugene Talmadge. Anti-New Deal almost from the start, Talmadge often characterized people on relief as "loafers" and "bums" and insisted that any family in Georgia "could live on five dollars a month!" To his chagrin, Johnstone also discovered that some county relief directors apparently shared Talmadge's views.[8]

A few months after Johnstone had gone into the South, Hopkins dispatched his ace reporter, Lorena Hickok, there. It was, she said later, the first time in her life she had ever been south of Charlottesville, Virginia. Like other first-time visitors to the South, Hickok would become both moved and disgusted, dismayed and fascinated, gloomy yet occasionally optimistic. Her initial assignment was to assess the impact of the CWA, and although she was prepared for the worst, to her surprise she initially found considerable enthusiasm for it. "As far as it's gone," Atlanta merchants told her, "it's a grand business." City officials informed her that the CWA was providing a million-dollar-a-month payroll for the city. At Rich's, Atlanta's largest department store, the credit manager reported that Christmas business in 1932 had been 40 percent cash and 60 percent credit; in 1933 the figures were exactly reversed.[9]

While Atlanta merchants were enjoying something of a business revival (and would not be hurt by prospective workers choosing to remain on CWA rolls rather than return to retail sales jobs) and thus applauded the CWA, Hickok was particularly surprised to find that most farm owners also supported the program. Before she ventured into the South, she had heard that Georgia farmers deeply resented the CWA wage rates because they believed that the rates would result in a farm labor shortage when spring arrived. However, after discussing the situation with large farmers who worked 200 or fewer acres, with others who operated hundreds more, and "with one big fellow" who farmed several thousand acres and worked between 150 and 200 plows, Hickok failed to find a single farmer who seemed worried about a possible labor shortage. In fact, the opposite seemed to be the case. Because CWA had not come close to eliminating the high unemployment rate, a Jackson County, Georgia, federal re-employment director, himself a farmer, told Hickok: "We could put a thousand more men to work on CWA and keep them there right straight through the summer and all next winter, and there'd still be no shortage of farm labor in this county." Alan Johnstone had reported the same thing the previous fall.

Significantly, Hickok observed, CWA was abetting the modernization of the South. A relic of the Old South's plantation economy, the New South's paternalistic system whereby landowners supported their tenants and sharecroppers had long hampered the region's economic development and had perpetuated hardships for both landlord and tenant alike. By hiring farm labor, the CWA reduced the number of sharecroppers and tenants that farmers would usually be obligated to support.

Nevertheless, small town bankers and businessmen who fashioned the tempo of life in the New South, just as planters had determined it in the Old, were critical of the CWA. Even as they admitted that the CWA had improved local economic conditions, business leaders insisted that the great majority of local projects were worthless. Most CWA work in the area was on highways, but critics complained to Hickok that most workers "were just shoveling mud out of the ditches and throwing it back onto the road." "Bourbons, heart and soul" (Hickok called them), they insisted that "it's charity, nothing else." One businessman thought that CWA workers should be paid 12½ cents an hour (rather than the 30 cents some CWA workers were receiving), a wage he said would satisfy most of them. Another remarked that since the projects were of a useless variety, the government should simply pay the lowest wages and allow the workers to sit around and "play checkers" all day.[10]

As Cash, historian U.B. Phillips, and other students of the South insisted, the old plantation paternalism, with all its faults, had been replaced by a harsh, cruel, and already outmoded industrialism. But to Georgia businessmen, who had operated their low-wage enterprises for decades, CWA, like the NRA codes, was the intruder from Washington who failed to understand the traditions of southern business. Clearly, as New Dealer Hickok saw it, modernization would necessitate disruptive, even traumatic social change. A fish canner in Savannah complained to her that because of CWA wage rates, he was experiencing great difficulty in obtaining labor, particularly black workers. Operating canneries and sheds along the Georgia-Florida coast, he employed both men and women to gather and process oysters, shrimp, and other coastal products. The canner told Hickok that eighty of his black workers in one plant had quit in a body to work for the CWA, and he was forced to close that plant. In another, 10 percent of his two hundred-man work force had quit, and he had stopped opening a third plant where he usually employed one hundred people because he was unable to get anyone to show up for work.

She heard complaints, too, about the system that allowed CWA wage rates to be higher than those set in NRA codes. A fertilizer producer told her that "as an employer and a taxpayer and a member of the code authority in my own industry, I can't see that it's right for the federal government to pay the same class of labor I employ more for relief work than I pay under the code."

Businessmen were also unhappy with the NRA code wages. The lumber code had set wages at 23 cents an hour, the laundry code at 14. Yet, businessmen grumbled unhappily to Alan Johnstone about the rates and a dry cleaner in Savannah who employed 185 men and women, about 70 percent of them black, complained to Hickok that since he had been operating under the code, his labor costs had increased 100 percent and he had lost $8,000. "I'm going along for a couple of months longer," he said, "but after that, if it doesn't get better, I reckon I'll have to quit, too." These businessmen, Hickok told Hopkins, insist that "Northerners dominate the scene in Washington" and simply "do not understand labor conditions in the South." [11]

The controversy over CWA and relief payments continued long after the New Deal terminated the agency in the spring of 1934. Martha Gellhorn heard the issue rehashed as she toured South Carolina in the fall of the year. CWA, she was told, like all relief, was little more than the "dole," and "pampering," and even worse. South Carolina businessmen complained that relief clients refused jobs in private industry for an obvious reason: it was difficult for local industries to match the 30-cents-an-hour work relief pay when private enterprise paid manual labor between 7½-cents to 10 cents an hour! This "high government pay," she reported to Hopkins, "is just bananas to the low class manual labor (principally Negro), which can now earn in two days what [it] formerly took a week to earn." In Charlotte, North Carolina, everyone in the relief administration criticized the high relief wages, and believed they were responsible for swelling the relief rolls "beyond reasonable limits" by making "relief too attractive." [12]

In addition to the wage crisis, local relief programs in the South suffered at the hands of businessmen who played fast and loose with NRA codes. The notorious "speed-up"—long a ploy of southern employers—endured despite the New Deal. In Savannah, a prominent businessman described by Hickok as "a very sound, level-headed sort," related a visit to his home by "a couple of White girls" who worked in a burlap bag factory in the city. The pair started work as learners with wages of $8.93 a week. After six weeks they were supposed to enter the skilled class at $12 a week. The number of bags they were required to produce each day had been increased until just before scheduled to earn the higher wage, they had to produce 1,800 bags each per day. "And now," one of the girls told him, "they tell us that beginning next week, we've got to turn out 2,500 a day. Mister, I've tried it. I've worked just as fast as I could all day, never taking my eyes off the machine, and the best I could do was 2,050."

Complaints came from all over and from all sides. A Florida waitress told Hickok that although "we're supposed to be under the code, I can't see as it's much different." The reporter uncovered little evidence that hotels had hired many more people, despite the seasonal business increases. "You're apt to see the same waitress in a hotel coffee shop," she wrote, "at 7 a.m. and 9 p.m." A Tampa relief administrator told her that because of the code, local department stores had realized their best

Christmas in years. Nevertheless, they resisted employing extra people, even temporary help. "It's a pretty picture, isn't it," wrote Hickok. "The government puts a lot of money in there and helps those buzzards out, and they won't cooperate by taking on more help to keep the ball rolling, but gleefully pocket all the profits themselves!"

In cotton mill towns such as Augusta, labor leaders complained that owners were flaunting the spirit of the codes. For skilled workers, they actually lowered hourly wage rates to the minimum; for others, they reduced hours so much that many workers earned no more than they had previously made. In addition, mill owners placed experienced men on the "learner basis" and paid them the minimum wage. Because many of the mills operated on shorter schedules, payrolls did not increase significantly, nor were that many new workers hired.[13]

While Hopkins's reporters considered these business practices as representing a corporate lack of social conscience as well as an understandable preoccupation with profit margins, they could not dismiss the terrible state of southern agriculture as social insularity or business greed. There was great trouble in the land. In countless conversations with the New Deal correspondents, farmers from all over the South echoed the call of regional planners and service intellectuals for a new diversification of southern agriculture. There simply was no future for southern agriculture, farm spokesmen insisted, unless southern farmers were willing to tread new paths. Cotton production, for instance, was doomed. Even ten-cent cotton could not compete with cotton grown elsewhere, where it could be produced for much lower costs per acre. A major problem, as in the wheat-producing states, was worn-out soil. And even in areas where the soil was adequate, fertilizer was a constant need, and it was the most expensive item in cotton production.

Much less expensive, or so it seemed to outsiders, was the cost of farm labor; here the numbers were great, the returns small. Depressed cotton prices, unsalable corn and pork, and outmoded agricultural production fueled rampant unemployment throughout the South. Yet, as elsewhere in the nation, southern businessmen persisted in claiming that New Deal projects were creating a labor shortage which they feared would undermine their businesses. Hickok believed that what these people actually feared was that they would never again be able to employ workers under their traditional system of wage peonage. As far as she could determine, most employers throughout the state had little difficulty in finding workers. In Macon, Georgia, the state reemployment director told her that he had over 200,000 people requesting employment and he had not been able to find a job for a single one. (This was particularly true in rural Georgia, where many had been unemployed for years.) A few months earlier he had sent out hundreds of letters, with self-addressed postcards enclosed, offering workers to farmers and other employers—in part to offset the complaint that New Deal programs were taking men and women out of private industry and off the farms—and did not receive a single reply! Because of this surplus, farmers were frequently merciless in their treatment of farm help, both black and white. Hopkins's reporters listened to endless stories of mistreatment. Farmers all over the state, Lorena Hickok was told, took advantage of the fact that their tenants and sharecroppers could neither read nor write; at the end of the season many got nothing for their crop because, being unable to read the agreement that the landlord had made with the New Deal, they failed to realize that they were to share the landlord's federal grant. Hickok lamented that most merely worked "for a house, a few sticks of wood to burn, a few grits, and a little pork, that's all." This condition, she observed, was largely due to the surplus of laborers, both black and white, "who are hardly more than beasts."

Probably not accustomed to seeing the likes of the working and living conditions she found in rural Georgia, Hickok entreated that by one means or another the people she encountered there "have got to be removed from the labor market." Then—and only then, she was told—would farm labor get a break in the state. "Then—and only then—will the situation [improve] where half-starved whites and blacks struggle in competition for less to eat then my dog gets at home, for the privilege of living in huts that are infinitely less comfortable than his kennel." [14]

As some of the farm planners surely realized, the New Deal's program of crop reduction further reduced job opportunities in southern agriculture. Many of the rural jobless were formerly farm workers; but many others were once mill hands, packing-house workers, highway workers, laborers for contractors, and young men who had had jobs in the north before the depression "and have drifted back to live with their families, who can't support them." Rather than refusing work, Hickok saw over and again these people begging for work at any price.

The flotsam of both tradition and change, these hapless rural people were caught between the paternalism of the Old South and the dynamism of the region's economic future. In northeastern Alabama, Hickok found such a "stranded population" in a county of 12,000 people, 10,000 of whom were on relief. A mountainous region with no industry, the area was not even suitable for farming. She reported that there were three doctors in the county: one of them was the health officer, another was practicing without a license, the third was an old man about to die. A week or so before Hickok arrived, the county relief director received word one evening that a woman was very ill out in the country. Along with a lady from the rehabilitation service, the director rushed to the scene where the two of them delivered a baby using the headlights of their automobile for light. Meanwhile, three hundred displaced tenant farmers sought sanctuary in an adjoining county. Every once in a while, one of them would beg the relief director: "Please buy us a tent, ma'am. We can't find no house." [15]

No single state could claim a monopoly on rural human degradation. One day Hickok drove from Wilson, North Carolina, into the country and visited three "squatter" families who had alighted on some farmer's land. In one "miserable hovel" she found "a family obviously very low grade mentally. Probably that man never would be able to make a living farming or any other way unless someone stood right over him and told him what to do." The house, she wrote, was about as weatherproof as an old-fashioned western corncrib. The week before, in wet and snowy weather, a relief official had tacked some tin sheeting to one side of the place to keep out the snow which before had blown in through cracks an inch wide. Sooner or later, when the farmer got tired of the squatters, they would end up in town.

The next family "was of better grade mentally." The house, although hardly more than a shed, was about as clean as possible given the circumstances. There were eight children, all well clothed, as the father had been working with the CWA all winter. But the place, even with the sun shining on this particular day and a fire in the stove inside, "was *cold*." It amounted to only a few old boards hanging together. "Some day," Hickok wrote, "the owner is going to tear it down—if it doesn't collapse—and *that* family will be in Wilson, too." Meanwhile, the landlord allowed them to stay, at 75 cents a week. "He's walked this county over," said the wife of her husband. "He can't git no place to crop."

A third family was living in a tobacco barn that the owner intended to move away in a few weeks. Since a tobacco barn has no windows, in order to get any air exept that which blew through the cracks, the family had to keep the door open. A "distinctly high grade" family, Hickok commented. The husband and father, a man of excellent reputation, had worked as a sharecropper since 1927, at which time he had moved to his father's farm. His father lost his property in 1932, and since then the son and his family had lived on the present land. But a new landlord had taken over, brought in his own tenants, and was allowing the present occupants of the tobacco barn to stay there only until they found another home. As yet they had found none, with only a few weeks to go before they would have to move on.

Yet, as the sixteen-year-old son in the above family told Hickok: "Seems like we just keep goin' lower and lower. He [his father] can't git no crop. He's been everywhere. All of us has bad colds ever since we moved into this place." Soon they would not even have that. The boy's sister was slight, "with fair hair and the kind of blue eyes that look right into your own." She wore a pair of frayed, but very clean overalls, over a thin dress.

The only ornament that adorned her simple clothing was a brooch pinned to her bosom: a campaign button from 1932—a profile of the president.[16]

If traditional agriculture in the South was doomed, and labor surpluses destined to increase, then what solutions could southern officials offer? One way out, an official whose opinions Hickok valued a great deal told her, would be the substitution of other farm products, such as fruits and vegetables, for cotton and the creation of improved distribution facilities for perishables so that truck gardening and fruit farming would be feasible. Lack of cold storage and other facilities for distribution had meant that widespread truck gardening and fruit raising were not that profitable in the South. Hickok's informant suggested, as an experiment, the creation of a few market centers with cold storage facilities, run by private business, with federal aid to start them. The point was that these companies would "advance money to truck gardeners and fruit growers on delivery of their produce at the market." Other ideas for crop diversification were suggested to Hickok, all from thoughtful people who insisted that "some sort of plan has got to be worked out for the agricultural South—a plan that will give them something to raise instead of cotton."

But the solution to the region's agricultural ills most frequently suggested by those with whom Hickok spoke was subsistence farming, a solution sought by many in other areas of the country as well. Supporters of such a program reasoned that the federal government, which already owned thousands of acres in the South, could provide the necessary land. Moreover, the government could take the money being spent for relief and invest it in subsistence programs. Thus, government would relieve itself of the relief business while providing a more permanent solution to the problem of surplus labor.

In Georgia, officials praised the subsistence homestead projects in Arthurdale, West Virginia, and elsewhere, but doubted that such expensive programs were necessary in their state. One such project had already been approved for the state, to be directed by University of Georgia officials. Hickok's confidants found it unnecessarily costly. Instead, state officials concluded that small-scale rural rehabilitation would be more effective. With the Georgia timber available, log cabins could be built for twenty-five or thirty dollars apiece, "a whole lot better than the cabin and tobacco [barn] houses in which many of these people are now living." Hickok felt that rural Georgians "would be perfectly suited" to such a program. Nor would they need much in material aid, for "anything would be better than what they have. They're so messed up with pellagra, and tuberculosis, and one thing and another that they simply haven't any morale to ruin at all. God, they're a wretched lot!"[17]

Hopkins's reporters were fascinated by the planned communities, subsistence homestead projects, and general rural rehabilitation projects they saw, which seemed to reflect the fierce determination of rural southerners to overcome awesome physical, economic, and social obstacles. Lorena Hickok seemed convinced that this type of program offered the best way out for people who had known economic deprivation for generations.

All over the South, Hickok witnessed considerable interest in subsistence farming projects. "You get them [public officials] started on that subject," she observed, "and they never want to stop. . . . There is a great deal of enthusiasm." Officials told her that emergency relief should be continued in industrial centers and cities; but as for rural areas, "instead of pouring in millions of dollars for emergency relief, we [should] start doing something that would contribute to a solution of the problem."

Southern officials even arrived at a strategy for rehabilitation. They urged that subsistence farming be substituted for emergency relief programs, and insisted that a compulsory education program for adults be a part of the system, "*not* to teach these people to read and write, but *how to live.*" To put it "boldly," one doctor told Hickok, "What these people need to be taught is how to build toilets."

Hickok was enthusiastic about this sort of rehabilitation, if not so convinced of the human potential of these pathetic people. Let the people do the work themselves, she advised Hopkins, possibly on some work relief basis. "*Let them* clear the land, build their own cabins, with a lot of supervision of course." A great need was for someone "to teach them how to raise vegetables and care for chickens and a cow and *see that they do it.*" These people needed doctors, dieticians, and nurses "to clean out the hookworm and pellagra. They tell me you would just have to stand right over them and *make* them do things." It was all very paternalistic, she realized, but "it's a grand chance to get hold of this situation and clean it up." It would not have to be permanent, she wrote. Clean out the disease, raise educational standards, and the next generation might be able to look after itself. But, she sadly concluded, "it looks as though we may have this generation on our hands for some time." [18]

Although most of the New Deal's rural rehabilitation programs were only in the planning stages at the time Hickok was in the South, she did observe several projects already underway. Firm in her belief that the present adult generation was beyond redemption, she nevertheless saw some hope for the future. In Tennessee that hope, according to Hickok, lay in "help[ing] the parents to get at least a fairly decent living now and do[ing] a bang-up job of public health and education on the children." Instead of relocating the families, the government should "try out orchards instead of corn on that [worn-out] table land" and make it clear that the children would not inherit the land but that government would take it and pay the heirs for it either with cash or land someplace else.

In Alabama, Hickok spent several April days touring the countryside

looking at rural rehabilitation programs. After speaking with businessmen, county agents, doctors, judges, large landowners, farmers, black and
white tenants, and relief officials, she reported that rural rehabilitation
"offers more hope than anything else these days." Indeed, for relief workers, "it's the only thing that cheers them up." [19]

In the South's urban centers, however, Hickok and the other reporters
found no such ray of hope. As a result of the Great Depression and the
New Deal's agricultural program—as well as long-term demographic
trends—southern cities, like those all over the nation, faced unprecedented immigration. City Fathers despaired at the enormity of the influx
and seriously doubted that their cities could accommodate the ever-
increasing numbers. The reporters were witnessing, of course, the conditions that would produce the massive World War II and postwar migration
of southern rural folk, particularly blacks, to Chicago, Philadelphia, Cleveland, and other cities "up North."

Southern mayors faced tremendous social and economic problems in
coping with the situation. The mayor of Savannah, Georgia, told Hopkins's people that his city was being invaded by thousands of blacks not
only from rural Georgia but from rural South Carolina as well. He complained to Lorena Hickok that because of the New Deal's work relief programs, Savannah, long a magnet for transients, was becoming a haven for
disinherited tenant farmers, particularly blacks. And he feared especially
that the city would have to support them long after the New Deal was gone.

A similar situation prevailed in South Carolina. Social workers found
that because there was so little work left on the farms, large numbers of
agricultural laborers were moving into Charleston and such textile centers
as Greenville, Anderson, and Spartanburg. Urban leaders told Hickok that
if the New Deal continued to spark urban migration, "all their Negroes
will be moving into town, hoping to get CWA jobs, unless we make those
jobs less attractive by working them longer hours for the same weekly pay."

Likewise in North Carolina, Hickok discovered thousands of displaced
farm workers moving into towns and cities. Once there, the migrants
promptly applied for relief. "The intake office in Wilson today," she
wrote Hopkins, "was so crowded you could hardly get into the place.
Every house, every abandoned shack, is filled with them. They even
break the locks off empty houses and move in."

City officials feared not only the economic crunch but equally the attending social upheaval. According to relief committees, clergymen, casework supervisors, and relief administrators, 75 percent of the displaced
families that had moved into Wilson were black. Most were illiterate,
Hickok was told, and most were afflicted with tuberculosis and the "social
diseases." Of the white families, many had pellagra and hookworm. "And
they are a dead weight on the community." [20]

Things were about the same in West Tennessee, where the migration of displaced white farm workers created an equal problem in Memphis. Alan Johnstone of the FERA staff wrote Hopkins that crop reductions had produced so many evictions of tenant families that the city faced a serious crisis in dealing with already overburdened relief rolls. For white transients, he observed, "Memphis is their refuge since the general present tendency is to prefer Negro families [as tenant farmers] to white."[21]

Transiency was only one manifestation of social dislocation caused by the Great Depression and the New Deal. Traditional norms and institutions were jarred loose and forced upholders of the status quo into a defensive posture. This was particularly true of the South's system of race relations. Despite the fact that the Agricultural Adjustment Administration (AAA), which attempted to raise farm prices, the Civilian Conservation Corps, which employed youth to plant trees and in other ways restore the broken land, and the Civil Works Administration and other relief programs were mostly segregated, the New Deal threatened to interpose itself between black and white and perhaps thus to unsettle the historic balance of southern white power. In fact, although Wilbur J. Cash observed that it all had little effect, many historians have argued that the New Deal posed the most serious challenge to the South's control of black/white labor and social relations since the Freedmen's Bureau of the 1860s.

As hardened as they were by what they had seen elsewhere in America, Hopkins's reporters Lorena Hickok, Martha Gellhorn, and Edward Webster as well as Alan Johnstone were stunned by the numbers of uprooted black sharecroppers rushing *en masse* to the promise of New Deal aid in southern cities and towns, swapping rural tenancy for urban relief. While Johnstone, Webster, and Gellhorn often described southern race relations in their reports to Hopkins, it was the most prominent female in the cast who seemed most pessimistic about Black America. Lorena Hickok, the most widely traveled of the Hopkins team, studied closely the ways whites reacted to the impact of the CWA in the South as they perceived its effect on blacks. Although she was born and raised in the Midwest, her over-reaction to racial conditions suggests that she had internalized social attitudes not entirely dissimilar to those of the South. According to her reports to Hopkins, most of the criticism of the CWA's impact issued not merely from historic white racism, but from a legitimate fear that the thousands of rural blacks who were moving into cities such as Savannah searching for CWA jobs created a critical social and economic problem, especially after CWA no longer functioned. Most white Savannians insisted that blacks did not need CWA jobs and that the wages were too high for Negroes, many of whom referred to CWA as "guv'ment easy money." White officials told her that blacks believed the "second coming of Christ had occurred." The more emotional and illiterate among them, she was told, went about saying "De Messiah hab come!"

In Savannah Hickok encountered a significantly large number of whites who seemed preoccupied with deep-rooted antiblack prejudices. "In fact," she wrote Hopkins, "if you compare it with the feeling down in Savannah, racial prejudice simply doesn't exist in Northern Georgia at all." Earlier, in Augusta, about a hundred miles north of Savannah, Hickok had reported that "these Southerners are being darned good sports" about the high wages that blacks were receiving for CWA work. "I guess it's the first time in the South that Negroes have ever received the same pay as white men for the same work," she wrote. "And I haven't heard a word of complaint." White people, she observed, "just smile when the subject is mentioned." Hickok found the tolerance surprising because "the race problem *is* a problem down here."

In time, she began to understand. While whites, she wrote, would never admit it, they seemed afraid of blacks, particularly in places like Savannah where the black population was so large. "More than half the population of the city is Negro—and *such* Negroes! Even their lips are black, and the whites of their eyes! They're almost as inarticulate as animals. They *are* animals. Many of them look and talk and act like creatures barely removed from the Ape. Some of them I talked with yesterday seemed to me hardly more intelligent than my police dog. . . ."

Before she left Savannah, Hickok hinted she might agree with some prejudices. "I'm not so sure these Southerners aren't right," she wrote Hopkins, that "while these illiterate creatures, whom they regard as animals, are getting more money than they ever had before, hundreds of white workmen are unable to get CWA jobs, and their families are hungry." On one occasion, when she accompanied an owner of a steam laundry through his business, she wrote: "It *was* different. I never saw so many Niggers in my life. . . . They were doing beautiful work, but, oh, how leisurely they were."

When CWA boosted hourly wage rates and reduced the hours of work, one businessman described to Hickok his view of the blacks' work ethic. "The reason why Niggers don't earn more," he told her, "is that they won't work more than two or three days a week. You all up North don't understand these Niggers. They don't want to work regularly." They work just enough to get by on, he insisted, and the new CWA rules "have given them just what they want. This is the Nigger's millennium, that's what it is."

Another businessman insisted that black workers had different attitudes toward work than whites. "Nigger labor's different, that's all," he told her. It was slower, less efficient than northern labor. He was used to it, knew how to handle it. "But we can't work with nigger labor and pay it high wages. My Niggers are good laundresses," he said, but while a laundry in the North would use four women "to put a shirt through the various processes of ironing, I use seven." He had tried to introduce "Northern methods of efficiency" in his business, he said; but "they just don't work with Niggers, that's all. It takes a lot more Niggers to do a job down here," he went on, "than it takes white people in the North. And that means a big payroll. Now, if I have to pay them too much—well, you can see what happens, can't you?" [22]

Relief officials tended to agree that blacks were making more money than they deserved, and they feared it might go on forever. "Any Nigger who gets over $8 a week is a spoiled Nigger," a federal reemployment director in Savannah told Hickok. A CWA official complained to her that blacks were being presented a distorted view of the future. "CWA can't go on forever, of course, but the Negroes don't see it that way," he said. "They regard the President as the Messiah, and they think that, if only they can get on CWA jobs, they'll all be getting $12 a week the rest of their lives." Relief officials also seemed to agree with business leaders that blacks should be paid less than whites. According to them, "the Negro diet is different, . . . their needs are simpler, . . . [and] what Negroes buy costs less money than the whites pay." Even when blacks had CWA jobs, she was told, they came around at Christmas time to get their customary hand-outs from their former employers, just as they always had. Old habits were hard to break, even with a New Deal.

Hickok's letters to Hopkins buzzed with antiblack overtones. In Augusta, a white Baptist minister—"And, believe me, in Georgia, the pastor of the First Baptist Church is an influential citizen"—told her that "he understood Negroes and loved them" as one "loves horses or dogs." He also suggested that "he still believed in slavery! He assured me that under the slave system the Negroes were much better off, economically and socially, than they are now."

In her search to understand the New Deal's effect on blacks, how they fared under the NRA codes, and their future in the American economic system, Hickok listened to a plethora of charges from black spokesmen "expressed as politely as their bitterness would permit." Hickok, who admitted that she would be bitter, too, in their place, nevertheless felt that this bitterness informed whatever they told her. They believed that a majority of the permanently unemployed would be blacks. They also insisted that most employers tended to discharge Negro workers and replace them with whites. About the only field of employment still left almost entirely to blacks, they told Hickok, was domestic service. And, they feared, "with a demand for higher wages all around, white people would invade that field, too." Black leaders insisted that an organization of white women in Atlanta openly promoted a movement to fire blacks and hire white people. "I don't doubt it's true," she wrote. "I've heard something of the same thing from white people." The attitude in the South, she believed "quite naturally," was that "if two men are hungry, a white man and a black man, and one of them must go on being hungry, it must be the black man, of course." [23]

Unless, perhaps, the white man was one of "Dixie's forgotten people," the poor whites of the South. Hickok's assessment of the South's poor rural whites was little better than her evaluation of southern blacks. If this was Cash's "man at the center," he had fallen considerably from grace, and was as worn out and decrepit as the soil beneath him. Yet, Hickok was often sympathetic, recommending large doses of paternalism as the cure. Admittedly, "they're lazy—I guess you'd be lazy, too, if you'd lived the way they have always, the way their fathers and their grandfathers lived before them—but their [sic] docile. Everybody seems to think they could be taught." And what a chance for teachers, social workers, doctors, and nurses, Hickok exclaimed. "There could be a compulsory education program for adults—you go to school so many hours a week, or you don't eat. *Not* reading and writing and that sort of thing, but education in *living*." They needed instruction in "the principles of sanitation and diet. Oh, Lord, they need it so!" [24]

In the minds of Hopkins's reporters, then, blacks were not alone among the South's "wretched of the earth." In East Tennessee, Hickok found great "bold patches" of rock-patterned mountainsides where timber had been cut to plant crops, but nothing grew. In West Tennessee, thin, soil-stunted crops, terrible housing, illiteracy, and evidence of prolonged undernourishment stamped a worn-out people. Worse, Hickok concluded, they had no knowledge of how to live decently or farm profitably even if they had decent land. All over the state she found "a wretched people," with living standards so low that once on relief "they are quite willing to stay there the rest of their lives. It's a mess." In West Tennessee Alan Johnstone found displaced rural peoples "helpless not only because of a lack of material resources—but what is worse—deficient in initiative and resourcefulness." [25]

In Florida, where incompetent relief administrators and petty politicians seemed to be little interested in improving the living conditions of the poor, Hickok was told there were between 80,000 and 90,000 cases of malaria in the state, and some 250,000 cases of hookworm. The latter malady, which drastically reduced a person's level of efficiency, doubtless affected "your 'poor white problem' down here." This was the South she had read and heard so much about. Perhaps the most doleful cries of despair over the southern "white trash" came from Martha Gellhorn. In South Carolina, thousands and thousands of sharecroppers, tenant farmers, and farmhands existed in tumbledown shacks rent-free, cluttering up farms and looking for jobs that did not exist. A gloomy Gellhorn reported that pellagra was rampant; she had seen it range from a diseased skin condition to insanity. She found anemia, rickets, worms, bronchitis, and other maladies, all mostly due to lowered resistance. The doctors with whom she spoke in South Carolina "speak feelingly about the future of the children." The dietary deficiency could not be blamed on relief programs; like Hickok, Gellhorn believed it was a lack of education more than anything else. "Even when there is some money in a family [mill workers] the diet continued to be a menace of dried beans, cornbread, sorghum, and meat." It was half poverty, half ignorance.

Gellhorn's portrait of South Carolina almost foreclosed the possibility of hope. Relief barely touched the problem; it was only a sort of hypodermic. The ailment was chronic and needed longtime, constructive planning to "re-train people, and re-establish them [in some other role or capacity] in society." Inadequate medical service for the poor, along with their ignorance, allowed syphilis to spread "like wild fire," a doctor told her. Again, Gellhorn attacked the lack of birth control. Of those on the relief rolls, she wrote, "it is an accepted fact that the more incapable and unequipped [physically, mentally, materially] the parents, the more offspring they produce." These offspring, she continued, "are in degeneration from their parents, and can merely swell the relief rolls, aiding neither themselves nor the community." She believed that clinics had to be built to care for and improve present health, as well as "to check the increase of unwanted, unprovided for, and unequipped children." [26]

While many southern Democratic politicians blatantly appealed to the racial prejudices of the region's poor whites, politics often worked against their economic betterment. Besides the regional traditions and federal failures that undermined the modernization of work patterns, industrial progress, and relief programs in the South, local and state politics sometimes aborted New Deal efforts to affect modernization in the South. "To many seasoned politicians," Hopkins's reporter Edward Webster told his boss, "the present situation is not an emergency; it is an opportunity which they are willing to exploit to the limit. Some of them want to control both the jobs and the granting of relief itself." [27]

While nearly all southern political leaders wanted some voice in the new federal programs, political interference varied from state to state. In Tennessee, where Alan Johnstone found the situation "difficult, but distinctly hopeful," and in Alabama and North Carolina, for instance, there seemed to be less political interference in the relief programs. And in Georgia, both Johnstone and Lorena Hickok observed that the anti-New Deal harangues of Governor Talmadge did not reflect popular opinion, regardless of socioeconomic class. The governor "was just hollerin'" about the CWA, said one small farmer, "because he couldn't run the show himself. I reckon he has a big followin' all right, but he won't be holdin' it, 'less he'll hush up."

Nevertheless, politics presented a problem to the Georgia relief set-up.

In Savannah, Hickok spoke with a prominent businessman whose judgments she valued. He insisted that before Hopkins ordered changes in Georgia's relief set-up a person could expect little help unless he knew the right people.

She found the relief situation in Greenville, South Carolina, "especially nasty" because of a "half-crazy guy who was fired from the job of administrator." When the state's congressmen demanded an investigation of the CWA, Hickok was assured that it was only "politics," a move intended to secure the reelection of certain members of the state's delegation.

But it was in Florida—perhaps more than in any other state—that Hickok found the CWA struggling almost desperately against politicians intent upon undermining modern work relief programs in order to further their own political interests. All over the state, from Miami in the south to Jacksonville in the north, she listened to scores of accounts of political interference by relief administrators who experienced great difficulties in fending off the politicians' demands.

For CWA officials determined to keep politics out of their business, a major problem was Florida's Governor David Scholz. Equally determined to use relief to serve his own purposes, Scholz fired the state relief administrator a few months before CWA was organized for not allowing him to run the show. From many directions, Hickok sensed "that anyone who has a pull with the Governor can go right over the heads of the local CWA and Reemployment people and get what he wants." The recently fired state relief administrator, now the Federal Reemployment director in Tampa, told her that despite the widely publicized row he had had with Scholz, people still came to him "looking for jobs armed with letters from the Governor demanding that they be put on."

Hickok found W. H. Green, the Dade County civil works and relief administrator, to be tough, efficient, and not at all "political minded." Green insisted to Hickok that the fault was with Governor Scholz. The local politicians, he told her, "wouldn't be so active if they didn't get encouragement from Tallahassee." He also recalled that "when FERA came in last summer, it took him two months to convince the local politicians that he wouldn't stand for any 'monkey business.'" When CWA began, he said, "they started right in again. They've 'quieted down a bit now,'" he told her, "but he still spends about 25 percent of his time trying to keep his administration out of politics." [28]

Although the social and economic condition of southern tenant farmers and other poor agricultural workers was desperate, Hopkins's reporters never regarded them as the grist for revolution. They believed that it was the middle class rather than the oppressed poor who were more likely to become militant and create social and political turmoil in the South. Lorena Hickok was impressed, for instance, by a comment she heard in

North Carolina: "It is these white collar people, when they get desperate, and not common labor, who start revolutions."

In any case, faithful to their charge, the reporters looked for signs of restlessness in the South, evidence of "reds" and "radicalism" and social disorder. According to their letters, they found little. At Carnesville, in northern Georgia, a few days before Hickok arrived in the state, a large crowd of about 1,800 people (mostly white) who had registered for employment but had been unable to obtain jobs, had threatened to riot, burn trucks, and sack the CWA office. Nothing of the sort occurred. Hickok heard about a rather "red" and "vociferous" labor element in the mill area around Charlotte, North Carolina, and of an "outlaw union" in Florida's citrus belt (apparently supported by many workers who had lost their jobs only days before Christmas). In addition, she wrote that a group called The Unemployed which had formed in Tampa was "continually raising Hell," probably with "a good deal of justification." Just about everything in Tampa was bad. [29]

Still, Edward Webster found organized labor in Louisiana, Oklahoma, Texas, and Arkansas "almost uniformly cooperative" with local relief administrators. There were, of course, "protest groups" in most of the cities he visited. He considered them to be "basically alike and undoubtedly under the guidance of a central body (perhaps the Southern Soviet Headquarters, 1010 Canal Street, New Orleans, La.)." However, he told Hopkins, "the leadership is very poor and membership is not at present increasing." And "it would seem to be the wrong policy," he advised his chief, "to become frightened about these groups or to make concessions to them as such." [30]

The reporters maintained a sense of equanimity. For example, Martha Gellhorn wrote Hopkins from South Carolina late in 1934 about an air of insecurity enveloping all social and economic classes. The "low-class relief cases" feared that the government would stop feeding them; the industrial worker lived "in a kind of feverish terror about his job"; and white-collar workers for the first time faced problems of adequate food and clothing. Yet, she found no protest groups. "There are no 'dangerous Reds.' If anything, these people are a sad grey, waiting, hoping, trusting. . . . There is no revolutionary talk." To Gellhorn the real problem was "not one of fighting off a 'Red menace' (those two goofy words make me mad every time I see them); but of fighting off hopelessness; despair; a dangerous feeling of helplessness and dependence." It would take "lean unrelieved years" of deprivation, she wrote, "before this part of the world will take to guns and pitch-forks." [31]

At times in the first year and a half of the New Deal, Hopkins's reporters in the South found reasons for hope. Observations of improvements in the business climate and from economic indicators in Birmingham, Atlanta, Charlotte, and in some rural areas punctuated their correspondence with Hopkins. But it was in Tennessee, on the final leg of her southern trip, that Lorena Hickok discovered real hope for the future: "A Promised Land," she wrote Hopkins, "bathed in golden sunlight, is rising out of the gray shadows of want and squalor and wretchedness down here in the Tennessee Valley these days." Ten thousand men were working on Tennessee Valley Authority projects, she reported, "building with timber and steel and concrete the New Deal's most magnificent project, creating an empire with potentialities so tremendous and so dazzling that they make one gasp." She had known little about the TVA when she went South, but, once there, she became "as excited as I used to get over adventure stories when I was a child. This *is* an adventure!"

The TVA, perhaps the New Deal's most daring project, was the ultimate in regional planning. As perceived by its creators, TVA was not merely to engage in the building of dams designed to control floods and produce electrical power; it was to engage in programs of social engineering as well. However it turned out, it was an immediate boon to the people of the Tennessee Valley. Serious economic and social problems persisted, of course, but people seemed less aware of them than before. In Knoxville, a cab driver told Hickok that he had not heard "anybody say anything about the Depression for three months." In Nashville, where the benefits from TVA were not so immediate and direct as in East Tennessee, people believed the benefits would come eventually. Reflecting this mood, Hickok's reports to Hopkins bubbled with enthusiasm. She eagerly described the attitudes of formerly depressed men now working, the clearing and building projects, the new "really *living* wage," the TVA's teaching programs in farming and trades, people "preparing themselves for the fuller lives they are to lead in that Promised Land."

One of Hickok's most pleasant stops in the South was in Tupelo, Mississippi, the first town to buy electric power from the TVA. "Everybody seems to be feeling grand," she wrote Hopkins, enthusiastically devoting half a report to Tupelo as she was en route from Memphis to Denver in June. Garment factories and textile mills were operating peacefully under the NRA code, and the local Chamber of Commerce was receiving inquiries from outside industries attracted to the area's low power rate.

Business had improved considerably since TVA power had begun. The operator of a thirty-eight-room hotel told Hickok that she now ran lights and fans in all the rooms, two vacuum cleaners, two electric irons, a refrigerator, and a radio—all for only twenty dollars a month. In Tupelo, there were six companies selling "electric equipment," Hickok wrote, including expensive models and less expensive designs produced by manufacturers in agreement with the TVA. She was told that in seventeen days, 137 refrigerators and 17 ranges were sold to eager customers anxious to devour the new electric power.

However, it was still too early to see how the new electric system was going to affect most townspeople and farmers in and around Tupelo and Corinth, just to the north. New wiring was just starting, ten miles of it in Tupelo. Nevertheless, appliance dealers were taking new orders from farmers every day. Helpfully, wiring a home was much less expensive than before; where it used to cost as much as fifty dollars to have an electric range installed in Tupelo, it now cost five.

As Hickok ended her southern odyssey in Mississippi and Tennessee, she exulted over the promise of TVA. In another decade, she wrote, "you wouldn't know this country. There's a chance to create a new kind of industrial life, with decent wages, decent housing. Gosh, what possibilities! You can't feel very sorry for Tennessee when you see that in the offing." [32]

It is hard to extrapolate from Hickok's writings or Webster's or Gellhorn's or Johnstone's a tidy statement to summarize their view of the South in 1934. Their observations of southern race relations seem to reflect Cash's gloomy conclusions about a South shackled to the past by warped tradition. Yet, beyond the pale of southern romanticism, beyond its poverty and despair, the reporters, on the whole, found the stirrings at least of a new world which had fired the imagination of Rupert Vance and Howard Odum. The construction work of CWA, the dams, the town and rural electrification projects, the subsistence homestead and education programs persuaded Hickok that the New Deal was slowly but surely transforming the South into a modern society. And no other section of the nation would change more in the following half-century.

8

Trouble in America's Eden

Hard Times in the West

■ God damn it, I think we ought to
let Japan have this state. Maybe they could straighten it out.
Lorena Hickok, from California

■ And if society . . . can't give a
man a job, then the Government, representing all the people, must do
it—a decent job at a living wage.

An Albuquerque lawyer

■ There's a lot about this that I
don't understand.
a Wyoming housewife

■ The West, the nation's newest
region, had the highest standard of living in the world. When Lorena
Hickok and other Hopkins correspondents made their way over deserts,
plains, and mountains in search of the American Eden during the fall of
1933 and the spring and summer of 1934, they found an almost inde-
scribably beautiful American empire. Yet, paradoxically they also found a
people struggling just as hard to survive the bludgeoning blows of economic hardship as any they had yet witnessed in their travels. In stark
contrast to a modern world of hydroelectric power, agribusiness, copper
mining, movie-making, and fragmented metropolises they discovered a

benighted world of filthy transient camps, scabrous Indian reservations, and gnawingly poor Mexican-American farms. Therefore, as elsewhere in America, so in the West their reports revealed the agonies attending the process of social and economic change.[1]

In late 1934, Lorena Hickok was rounding out her first year in Hopkins's employ. The West was her last stop. In many ways the year had been both dreary and hopeful for Hickok, and her experiences in the West would be no different. The frightening economic deprivation she had witnessed in the South was also starkly present in the West. In Wyoming, for example, while the worst effects of the depression were slower to be felt because of the state's overwhelmingly rural nature, the petroleum and coal industries were stagnant and the state endured declining agriculture prices and a high incidence of bank failures.

Likewise, Colorado suffered severe economic decline. The state's leading agricultural and mining industries neared bankruptcy. All maintenance and improvements on the state's extensive railroad system had been suspended and spokesmen for Colorado mining corporations grumbled about the nearly exhausted supply of prime-quality ore. With the severe decline in mining and agriculture the allied wholesale and retail trades in Denver suffered accordingly. It was much the same in Nevada, Utah, Arizona, and elsewhere in the West.

Even California—despite the glamour and romance of starlit Hollywood—felt the ravages of depression. In fact, California's losses were especially severe. On the one hand, much of the state's income was peculiarly sensitive to an overall national economic collapse—in such times, delicious fruits, motion pictures, and vacation opportunities were hardly regarded as necessities. On the other hand, the state's mild climate and economic opportunities drew thousands of migrants. When they arrived, too frequently packed in jalopies like John Steinbeck's Joad family in *The Grapes of Wrath*, they found conditions tragically similar to those they had fled. Small as well as large businesses failed by the thousands, leaving countless people unemployed in both industrial and agricultural areas. Turnover was particularly high among firms employing one, two, or three people. When these enterprises failed, the owner and his employees joined the ranks of the white-collar unemployed. Bank failures were frequent, as elsewhere, particularly among key institutions in San Francisco. When President Roosevelt ordered the "bank holiday" in March 1933, banks were in such a precarious state in California that Treasury officials only re-opened them "on the general principle that California had to have banks." During the bank holiday, Pasadena's elegant Huntington Hotel issued script negotiable within its confines for food, tips, cosmetics, newspapers, and the like.

Except for those wealthy enough to have rooms at the Huntington, family income for many people first declined and then disappeared. In Colorado between 1929 and 1933, per capita income plummetted 30 percent. While this was about the national average, only two western states fared better, Nevada at 25 percent and California at 29.

Many in the West were desperate. In Colorado in 1932, agricultural laborers were defined as "destitute" by the fact-finding State-Wide Unemployment Committee. According to New Mexico's director of Child Welfare Service, Rio Arriba County's people were on the verge of starvation; and a group of citizens in Lumberton petitioned the governor for aid, explaining that they had exhausted all possible resources of self-help. By the time of the New Deal, perhaps as many as one-third of all New Mexicans depended on others for subsistence. All over the West the indescribable distress begged for government aid.

And the New Deal responded. While the West may have had "an ideology of self help and a hostility to governmental interference," this "enduring tradition" did not prevent the area from accepting federal aid. Indeed, while the help may have been a little later in arriving than in other areas, the West benefited more from New Deal largesse than did any other section of the country—including the impoverished and Democratic South. In terms of the key New Deal programs such as FERA, CCC, CWA, and WPA, western states, including Utah, ranked among the top dozen in order of per-capita federal expenditure. In fact, the New Deal spent 60 percent more on the westerner than on the southerner. Sometimes even more: for example, while Nevada received $1,130 per capita and Wyoming $626, North Carolina got only $143 and the President's adopted state of Georgia received $171. The figures are similar when comparing the West to other sections of the country. For instance, Arizona received $597 per capita, while Pennsylvania netted only $189; New Mexico got $528 to New York's $205; Colorado $362 as opposed to Michigan's $184. In addition, the ratio of federal to state aid—an important consideration in the dispensation of work relief and relief—was greater in the mountain West than in any other area of the country except the South.[2]

Perhaps this generosity stemmed from the New Deal's hope of gaining political leverage in the traditionally Republican western states. As elsewhere the outlay of federal money also reflected the inability or the unwillingness of western states to raise adequate monies of their own. Further, many New Deal programs involving conservation, road construction, and farm relief adopted formulas that tended to benefit the very large but sparsely settled rural areas. Finally, the extent of natural and human suffering in the more isolated areas of these states was extensive and persistent.

It was to grasp the dimensions of need in the region that Hopkins dispatched Lorena Hickok, Pierce Williams, Clarence King, and Edward J. Webster to the West. They were to cover Texas, Colorado, Utah, Wyoming, Idaho, Arizona, New Mexico, Nevada, and California, states rich with oil, picturesque mountains, wealthy cattlemen, and ethnic and religious diversities such as the Mormons of Utah and the Spanish-Americans of the Southwest. The reporters were immediately struck by the drought the region was experiencing, which created the earlier-mentioned Dust Bowl. The millions of acres that blew away produced staggering economic losses; within two years, farm losses amounted to $25 million a day, while over two million Dust Bowl farmers were on relief.[3]

Hickok witnessed the greatest damage from the drought in northeastern New Mexico and eastern Colorado. Ironically, when she arrived in Colorado in June 1934, she had difficulty in motoring over the vast distances from place to place because it "rained so hard in the drought area that the roads were impassable." But before the cloudbursts arrived, the land was barren. The wheat grew only a few inches, if it came up at all, and then it burned brown. The soil was so dry that corn seed failed to germinate. Cattle searched endlessly between clumps of Russian thistle for bites of dry buffalo grass so short that they got mostly sand for their efforts.[4]

The rain might help the local livestock, but it could not help the local wheat farmers. In northern and eastern Colorado, farmers did not look for more than a 5-percent crop. In one county, a federal wheat inspector expected to see only about 300 bushels harvested from over 2,500 acres of land. Eastern Colorado was experiencing its fifth straight year of drought. It seemed "everybody is broke," with 85 percent of the cattle mortgaged; land values had dropped to less than a dollar an acre in some sections, and officials did not even bother with tax sales because the land was not worth it.

Later, in September, as Hickok made her way through Nevada across Utah and into Wyoming, drought conditions worsened. In western Wyoming, for instance, the sage brush was poorer and scanter than in Nevada, and as she drove east from Casper, she saw conditions she said approached those she had seen in the Dakotas almost a year before. Drought, grasshoppers, and a scorching sun had so ravaged the land that it looked like "it had been gone over with a safety razor."

Meanwhile, even in the more fertile and irrigated districts of the West such as farmland along the Arkansas River in Colorado and some of the upland country in Utah, Hickok found little water because the streams were dry and there was scarcely any snow in the mountains. At ten thousand feet the Tennessee Pass was virtually bare, and the largest tributaries in Colorado (including those out of the main drought area) had flows far below normal.

Even in California's rich San Joaquin Valley things were bad, particularly for the smaller farmers and fruit growers. One farmer with whom Hickok spoke sadly recalled better days: he once received about $150 a month out of his cows, now it was less than $60; he used to get 45 cents a pound for butter fat, now only 24 cents. The value of his property had declined to the point where he was unable to obtain a federal loan on his farm. "I'm probably going to lose it," he said.

Faced with the disastrous situation in the Dust Bowl and the economic decline in western farm and cattle counties, the New Deal had to contend with an almost impossible agricultural situation in the West. Although Texas cotton farmers were suffering from the general malaise, they were confused about the possible effects of the new quota system under the Bankhead Cotton Act. In Arizona and New Mexico, dry conditions and low prices for beef depressed stock-raising and farming, even in what was once "marvelously fertile land." The sheep industry in Nevada was in dire straits and cattle ranchers in Wyoming, where Hopkins's reporters heard less grumbling over conditions than elsewhere in the West, were faced with prices so depressed that the federal government was buying their livestock by lots in the stockyards at Rock Springs and elsewhere. The desperate cattlemen were appreciative. "I think we'd just pack up and move out and leave our stock to starve if the Government hadn't stepped in," a rancher told one reporter. "This gives us new hope to try again."[5]

Earlier, in Nevada, a state that received many more thousands of dollars of federal aid funds than it spent in state monies, Hickok encountered a quite different attitude. When ranchers and county agents, whose families were at least being adequately fed and clothed, complained to her about their plight, the much traveled and weary Hickok angrily told them about the children she had seen "running about with bare feet" in North Dakota in zero weather, and of South Dakota farmers "who were clawing mildewed Russian thistle out of the stacks they had cut for their cattle and making it into soup." She described cattle she had seen "so weak they could barely walk" and horses "that dropped dead from starvation when they tried to work them on the roads."[6]

The New Deal rescued western cattlemen and farmers. Besides the production-quota programs, federal loans, and the purchase of cattle and sheep, the New Deal helped western agriculturalists in other ways. For instance, in Elko, Humboldt, and other counties in Nevada, the federal government aided cattlemen by locating, digging, and maintaining water wells free of charge. Hickok regarded Nevada ranchers as among the greediest, grouchiest, and least appreciative of the people she encountered in her travels. The ranchers fought among themselves over the location of the wells (all on government property) and even their respective access to them. Nevertheless, "this is something [we] like," one of them told her. "All that CWA work was wasted, building parks and making skating rinks for kids."[7]

By the time Hickok reached the West, the CWA had been terminated, but according to Pierce Williams, both a Hopkins reporter and a federal official, the CWA had been a blessing in the West. "Generally speaking," he had written to Hopkins, "our situation . . . appears to be in reasonably satisfactory shape." Much more optimistic than the often angry Hickok, Williams pointed out that of course there were minor difficulties, "but these are such as would inevitably grow out of such a hasty organization as we have had to set up for civil works." Reporting from the state of Washington, Clarence King told Hopkins that "the effect of the CWA upon the morale of the people generally in these [western] states is remarkably encouraging."[8]

The CWA was short-lived. And perhaps because of the distance from Washington, it and other work relief programs were initiated later in the West than in areas closer to the nation's capital. Although this late start might have allowed the CWA to avoid the mistakes and delays in delivery of service that seemed to plague its programs east of the Mississippi, in fact, those in the West suffered from similar problems. As elsewhere, Hopkins's reporters found much to criticize, despite the financial generosity that characterized the New Deal in the West. Local and state politics had impeded the CWA's modernization of relief. Indeed, across the country from Texas to California and back to Texas, Hopkins's reporters complained that political interference had retarded the delivery of social programs. In Texas, "a Godawful mess," Hickok complained that it was politics "First, Last, and Always." In Arizona, where the minimum wage for work relief programs was 50 cents an hour, the jobs on state highways were dealt out as political patronage rather than on the basis of need and family size. In New Mexico, where available relief totaled $35,000 a month—for about 6,000 families!—Pierce Williams reported that he saw little possibility of the state legislature's appropriating additional revenues because Farm Holiday groups would block any new taxes and under the state constitution a popular referendum would be necessary to adopt such increases.[9]

Farther west in California in 1934, where anti-New Deal feeling was strong among corporate leaders and where the gubernatorial candidacy of leftist Democratic nominee Upton Sinclair perplexed party loyalists, relief programs were delayed because of constant indecision attributable to policial machinations. In late August, Hickok told Hopkins that relief allowances in Sacramento County—a pitiful four or five dollars for a family each month—were being allocated by county supervisors on a patronage/political basis. Even though these particular monies were state funds, their allocation reflected the general confusion and political preoccupation that afflicted the dispensing of relief funds over the state.[10]

In addition, Lorena Hickok recorded bad impressions of California's Emergency Relief Administration and work relief programs. Appalling inefficiency, genuine confusion over programs and purposes, and political interference hampered the relief effort to such an extent that she wondered "whether God himself [sic] could run this show out here and keep out of trouble." At the same time, California relief administrators continually fretted over Washington's lack of planning, the amount of money they would be receiving for a given period of time, and the general aura of uncertainty they saw enveloping the program.

One problem in particular was the dismal credit record of the State Emergency Relief Administration, or, as one California official put it, "our absolute indifference to our financial commitments." The problem stemmed from a lack of coordination among agency administrators. In San Bernardino and Riverside counties, grocery and rent orders went unpaid, partly due to confusion and indecision in Washington, partly traceable to local mismanagement. Relief standards all over the state remained "shamefully low." [11]

Hickok succumbed to "blue funk" over California's relief operation. Modernization of the state's services seemed light years away. In almost every county there were two set-ups, one county, one federal/state: two office staffs, two sets of caseworkers, two engineering supervisors, on down the line—"at each others' throats!" Officials in San Francisco required fifty-four papers to be signed before a client could be employed on a work relief project! While "some good things are being done," Hickok cried, "God damn it, I think we ought to let Japan have this state. Maybe they could straighten it out." [12]

In time, western states would blossom into models of competency in the delivery of public services. But in 1934, modernization remained only a distant prospect. Political interference, of course, posed an obstruction, but there were many others. For example, caseloads increased daily, particularly as the middle class's psychological resistance to relief broke down and as lower socioeconomic groups found greater security on the relief rolls. Escalating relief rolls threatened to demoralize large elements of American society, a situation compounded by the reluctance of relief officials to compel caseworkers to adequately scrutinize their relief rolls. The only way to reduce welfare loads equitably was to frequently investigate relief clients. Alas, few trained personnel existed. Hickok found that communities that utilized untrained volunteers to handle relief investigations usually serviced higher caseloads.

Even with trained caseworkers, unfortunate attitudes prevailed. Edward Webster insisted that caseworkers had to be "most carefully instructed concerning their own status and function." He was weary of "the stuffed-shirt Lady Bountiful, Lord Splurge attitude" of some, and annoyed by "the proprietary air and expansive verbal eroticism expressed so monotonously in the first person by others." As he concluded his December report to Hopkins, Webster also worried that caseworkers might be doing more—"perhaps by kindness, sometimes—to destroy the morale of the person receiving relief than all conceivable economic hardship could ever do." Webster also intimated that untrained relief workers were resurrecting the old prescientific dogmas that regarded poverty as attributable either to individual sin or to, in contemporary parlance, an orthogenetic defect. He fretted that too many "cases" were treated as if they were "psychopathic." Other reporters worried about the same thing.[13]

Relief administrators were less troubled, perhaps, but still annoyed by the inexperience and lack of maturity of some younger trained social workers. One official, while understanding that young people were apt to be immature, seriously questioned the wisdom of "turning these young sters, no matter how excellent their technical training, loose on these people." Lorena Hickok described for Hopkins "one of those college gals" in California who visited her clients "in a very elegant riding costume—breeches, top boots, crop, and all!" Her supervisor took the young lady aside and "suggested that a less sporty costume might be more appropriate."

While experience could transform "college gals" into social workers, it could not repair the egos of proud families hurt by relief. Hickok bemoaned the way relief clothing insulted middle-class relief families. A mother of two daughters in Texas asked her: "Why don't they give us materials and let us make our children's clothes ourselves, instead of making us take them from the sewing rooms? You've no idea how children hate wearing 'relief clothes.'" The material was striped and quite conspicuous, and at least one little boy in Texas "suffered hell" wearing relief trousers to school. "He says every kid in town whose family is on relief wears those pants," the boy's mother told Hickok. "That's how you know they're on relief."[14]

Both social workers and clients alike complained about confusing and inequitable relief eligibility rules, endless bureaucratic delays in delivery of services, poor administrative facilities, and a host of other irritations. However, the primary complaint Hickok, Webster, and Williams heard from western relief officials was the lack of administrative coordination, direction, and planning from Washington. "It seems to us," disgruntled California relief officials said, that "a big, comprehensive plan that takes in all the Governmental agencies" was in order. At the moment, the officials told Hickok, "there's no evidence of it that we can see. . . . There doesn't seem to be any plan at all." If the New Deal had such a plan, they pleaded, "then let us have it." Max Lewis, a field representative of the state relief administration, lamented to Hickok: "We haven't known—we still do not know—what Washington has in mind. We've never had, in the relief business, confidence of a stable program of any kind." When programs existed, others claimed, they were changed constantly, sometimes before local officials even knew it. "We have to keep revising our budgets all the time," one administrator said; "we've had to change them as often as twice a week." As much as they admired President Roosevelt, they felt "like sheep without a leader." In Fresno a group of "representative citizens" (county and city officials, among others) echoed the familiar refrain: "If only we could start out on a work program, know just how much money we are going to have and what we are going to do, and *stick to it*." [15]

These complaints about the inefficiency and lack of direction in New Deal relief programs were joined by a perhaps even more significant contention by local relief officials that such programs should discriminate between and among socioeconomic classes. Hopkins's reporters heartily endorsed the idea. In fact, they generally reflected a national preoccupation with racial and ethnic differences, stereotypical evaluations, and the pervasive gloom concerning minority groups and the American future. Wherever they traveled the reporters unsheathed their own white Protestant middle-class yardstick to measure the cultural and ethical values of local populations. And no matter whether the population they observed contained large blocks of French-Canadians (Maine), blacks (Detroit, the South), or Spanish-speaking Americans (the West), a deeply rooted ethnocentrism imbued their descriptions.

Consistent with this ethnocentrism the reporters displayed constant preoccupation with the travail of white-collar America, the architects, engineers, school teachers, the traditional success stories of the American Dream who, through no fault of their own, now found themselves beyond the pale of that dream and unable to do very much about it. "Damn it, it's the same old story," Lorena Hickok wrote from Arizona. "Two classes of people." Thousands of both classes were on relief, of course, but the feelings and reactions of the two classes were different; for example, whites, both blue and white collar, had "white" standards of living and for them "relief, as it now is, is anything but adequate. No jobs in sight. Growing restive." On the other hand, Mexicans [or, east of the Mississippi, Negroes], with much lower living standards, were described as finding relief not only adequate, but even attractive. They were, according to both Hickok and Webster, "perfectly contented." They were "willing to stay on relief the rest of their lives." Although many of these people were able to get work, wages were so low that they were probably better off on relief than working. Worse, there were so many Mexican and Negroes on relief that "with a limited amount of money, we are compelled to force the white man's standard of living down to that of the Mexican and Negroes." [16]

This was "the big relief problem today," Hickok contended as she made her way westward. The only way "to clean up this Negro-Mexican business," as she had always insisted, was to close the intake offices, turn the caseworkers loose for a thorough reinvestigation, and force every black and Mexican who could find work "at *whatever* wages, to take it and get off the relief rolls." Of course, employers would take advantage of the situation, she admitted, particularly farmers and housewives—"the two worst classes of employers in the country." Farmers continued to offer Spanish-Americans seven dollars a month to herd sheep, but had few takers from men who could get eight to ten dollars on relief. And housewives insisted that young girls of whatever ethnic background ought to be happy to work for merely their room and board.

But employers in Arizona also had legitimate problems, Hickok wrote. For one thing, the public works program paid fifty cents an hour minimum, a wage that very few workers and practically no Spanish-Americans in the state were being paid. Businessmen complained that they could not compete with the government's relief program. Then, there was the "Latin temperament," as Hickok called it. The half-Spanish, half-Indian, did not seem to "want" things badly enough. The easy-going, pleasure-seeking Spanish half would not "get out and hustle"; and "the Indian in them certainly wouldn't make them ambitious." Like the blacks Hickok found in the South, the Spanish-American of the West found the twenty-one dollars a month from the New Deal "just Heaven. He'd have a grand time on $10 or $12." And like the southern black, the Spanish-Americans' diet was cheaper, and probably better for them than what the whites were eating on subsistence rations.[17]

One solution to the problem was to develop separate standards of relief—an idea that Hickok admitted "will sound horrible in Washington." But they were already doing this in Tucson. Without much publicity, and with rare administrative skill, relief clients were divided into four categories, from the professionals at the top (engineers, teachers, lawyers, and the like) to the Mexicans, Spanish-Americans, and American Indians at the bottom. Each of the four "classes" had their own intake centers (there was "no mixing"). Relief grants were the most generous in Class A, declining down through the other three groups. Relief officials told Hickok it was the smoothest program they had operated thus far. Whenever Hickok found a local program such as this, she (like the New Deal strategists) could never make up her mind between imposing national standards of relief and, on the other hand, granting latitude and discretion to local authorities.

In New Mexico and West Texas the story was the same: perennially poor Mexicans, Spanish-Americans, and blacks perfectly content, even happy over relief. In El Paso, relief figured to less than nine dollars per family, adequate enough for the ethnics but not nearly so for the white families. About all the New Deal was doing for whites was to get them something to eat; there was no help in paying rent, and not enough done to clothe them. "I'm talking about white people now, people with pretty much the same ambitions and standards of living that you and I would expect to have." [18] Now they had become drifters, part of the army of wandering Americans crisscrossing the spacious regions of the West. Confused and desperate, this new American nomad was just as hell-bent on escaping an impossible present as he was upon discovering a better future. Mainly, this gypsy band just searched, constantly in motion.

From the Southwest to the Pacific Coast, back into Nevada and Colorado, and even up into Wyoming and the cattle country, Hopkins's reporters agonized over the plight of America's new displaced persons, the transients. Early in the New Deal, according to Pierce Williams, the federal government's transient service was working rather well. Reporting to Hopkins that there were stations in seven western states, Williams wrote that the camps "are proving a wonderful thing. I really believe we shall have something to show as a contribution to the solution of the problem of transiency by next summer." [19]

By the next summer, Lorena Hickok was in the West. Her reports to her chief in Washington were far less sanguine than those of Williams. In New Mexico, migrant war veterans and failed farmers from Oklahoma, Arkansas, and Texas—the legendary "Okies"—were drawing relief while trying to homestead on land too dry to do anything but blow away. While their chances for improvement were "pretty damned slim," ironically, conditions for some transients in Arizona were "too good." Near Phoenix, Hickok discovered a camp of transient families who were receiving far more adequate care than were local residents on relief. The camp represented "what we'd *like* to do for the great masses of our clients who live in these towns." Due to the absence of national standards, of course, unequal provisions for the needy prevailed all over. But in Arizona a federal official told Hickok that things for transients were presently so good, that "if we don't watch out, we're going to have the entire population of Oklahoma on the road." [20]

Ironically, in their search for a new life, the Okies traveled too far—to California, when Arizona might have been a better goal. Because Arizona's transient program operated solely on federal monies, local politicians did not obstruct it. In fact, as Hickok viewed it, the "great weakness in the transient show seems to be that it isn't stopping transiency." Arizona officials provided gasoline, even railroad tickets for transient families; perhaps this was their way of encouraging them to go home.

In Colorado, where officials were not encouraging transient turnover in the fashion of Arizona, Hickok found the problem "a bit overwhelming." Over 14,000 cases were served in May of 1934 and in Denver, 125 single men were registering every day at the city's "awful" transient station. For this reason, perhaps, the turnover was also great. "Too many of them just use the shelter as a free hotel," Hickok reported, "coming in on freights late at night and leaving early the following morning, immediately after breakfast." The place was terrible. No wonder they left. Yet, she also discovered in Colorado "some decidedly promising camps and their campsites are marvelous—about the best I've ever seen."

As with other relief programs, the success of transient operations in the West depended upon efficient administration; the official at one camp Hickok visited in Arizona was "running the best transient show I've seen" (except for the one in Florence, Alabama, where "they've got a genius in charge"). She once visited a transient camp for single women at Pacific Grove in California which, although a very small operation hampered by endless red tape, she found "Beautiful. Good staff. Fine plan." The twenty-five or so middle-aged women transients living there "had begun to show decided improvement in moral and physical health." [21]

But like almost all the recuperative programs over the country, the results were uneven, even when the programs were only a few miles apart. For instance, Hickok found the unattached male transient work camps in California a "flop." Officials couldn't "get any work out of them" because the transients believed they were supposed to receive more than five dollars a month in wages! Further, while the men found comfort and a measure of security in the camp, they felt isolated, and were anxious to get out and look for jobs. Overall, the transient business as a recuperative program seemed doomed to failure.

Two weeks later at a transient camp near Elko, Nevada, Hickok conceded defeat. "We're not solving this thing," she wrote Hopkins, "not that I think we could, as a matter of fact." The most the camp could possibly do, she lamented, was to offer "over-night free stops to them," and to herd some of them into camps "where we beg them to remain. The trains out here are so thick with them that you could pick 'em off like bedbugs." At the Elko camp, the director (who broke down and wept on her shoulder) labeled the unattached male transients "a lot of bums" who would not stay put but always returned. This particular director, "too young, too inexperienced, and too kind of sissified," in Hickok's view, was characteristic most of the officials in the West's transient program. [22]

As discussed earlier, the reporters mirrored the great national concern over the thousands of young men who swelled the transient rolls. But if these wandering and aimless youths perplexed reformers worried about the nation's future (the National Youth Administration of 1935 was specially designed to aid this group), Hickok's letters from the West in 1934 reflected an equal national concern for the plight of older Americans, equally disoriented and displaced by the ravages of the Great Depression. In describing the severe economic bind affecting the new superannuated man, made superfluous at an early age by the economy and by the practices of the corporations, Hickok envisioned an entire generation of jobless people. For instance, in Texas, the still fairly prosperous oil industry was not hiring anyone over thirty-five, though forty-five seemed to be the general age limit. Because of insurance costs and penurious pension programs, the oil companies deemed older workers too costly and bad risks. Another factor was the NRA's oil code; since the companies had to pay the code's minimum wage, they wanted younger workers better able to "earn" the new wage. Wherever Hickok went, from Texas to Wyoming, she heard the same refrain: "He's not going to get his job back. They're taking all younger men." [23]

It seemed to Hickok that

> before we get through with this business, we're going to have not only stranded populations, but *a whole stranded generation.* What's the answer? Why, damn it, a man of 45 has a halfgrown family! And a man of 35—in many cases he isn't even married yet! Add that whole generation to the list of people who aren't going to get their jobs back because of technological advances, and—well, you've got something! [24]

Because of their age and experience, many of the older jobless westerners joined self-help programs similar to the rehabilitation project Henry Francis had found in Belle Vernon, Pennsylvania, and other reporters saw in Richmond, Dayton, and Lansing, Michigan. For instance, in Bakersfield, California, the county supervisors had purchased a large warehouse for self-help sewing and mattress production. In and around Denver, there were a number of self-help projects in operation when Hickok was there in late June. While these were only stop-gap operations, they did help people in the short run. Some were nonprofit businesses of the unemployed, organized along the lines of any private business, with experienced but unemployed men in charge of the operation.

In the wide open spaces that characterized so much of the West, rural rehabilitation programs were common. While the short summer season made seed programs difficult in Wyoming, for instance, there were programs that transferred families from dry farming regions to more productive ones. In New Mexico there was a program run by the Rio Grande Conservancy that had room for 12,000 relief families. Its aim was to temporarily resettle Spanish-American farm workers, unemployed railroad workers, skilled carpenters, mechanics, migrant laborers, coal, copper, and silver miners, and stranded oil workers.

By the time these relief programs began operating, the country was preparing to pass judgment on the New Deal for the first time in the congressional elections of 1934. And whatever its successes or failures it was essential to Hopkins's reporters that the New Deal continue its search for the most appropriate ways of dealing with the agony of the American people. Consequently, as they moved over the West, they were always attentive to political opinions expressed about the president and his administration.

Over and over in the West as in the East, Pierce Williams, Clarence King, and Lorena Hickok found great trust in and affection for the president. "Everywhere among the rank and file of folk," King wrote Hopkins, "one sensed a feeling of sincere respect and confidence in the President." In Salt Lake City a caseworker supervisor told Hickok how people on relief "look toward the Federal Government somewhat as people do toward God. They may not expect justice from private employers but they do expect it from Washington." As exasperated as California relief officials were over the New Deal's indecision and uncertainty concerning the administration of relief, they all "believe[d] in the President. He has a hold on the people," one group told Hickok, "the like of which no other man ever had." As long as he continued to inspire the people as he had, they believed, he would receive their overwhelming support. Hickok once asked an official why he complained about the administration without casting any blame on the president; his response was brief but pregnant: "You don't like to pick flaws in your sweetheart."[25]

Hickok's effort to assess the political mood throughout the West during the late summer and early fall was hampered by the tendency of newspaper publishers to oppose Roosevelt while their working reporters were inclined toward respect, even affection, for him. "Why, they've joined the Newspaper Guild union," she exclaimed. "They seem to think the President will see to it that the publishers don't stand them up before a firing squad." Moreover, her tight schedule often forced Hickok to rely for opinion on former colleagues in the press—a young reporter in Los Angeles, a friend who covered labor for the Associated Press in San Francisco, and an acquaintance in Salt Lake City. These journalists were willing occasionally to write her "free for nuthin" the latest political news.[26]

But if Hickok's reporter friends supported Roosevelt, local newspaper publishers in the West just as strongly opposed him. She grumbled particularly about the press in Colorado and California. Of the *Denver Post* she wrote: "Lord, how I despise that newspaper! It is the filthiest rag. Even the *New York Evening Graphic* in its palmiest days, never had anything on the *Denver Post*." Hickok found the vilest anti-New Deal diatribes in California after the strikes by the San Francisco longshoremen and farm workers in the Imperial and San Joaquin valleys. Labor leaders, journalists, and state relief officials insisted that Harry Chandler of the *Los Angeles Times* and other newspaper executives were exploiting anti-Communist hysteria in the Imperial Valley to attack the Roosevelt administration. A California official of the Associated Press—himself anti-New Deal—told Hickok that in California, the Chamber of Commerce had unleashed a whispering campaign intended "to plant in the minds of the conservative, middle class of Californians the idea that all those about the President in Washington are Communist sympathizers, if not actually Communists." It was a bit different, Hickok noted, in the Imperial Valley—down there everybody in Washington was a Communist, "including the President himself." [27]

If the conservative press and the Chamber of Commerce were unhappy with the New Deal, so were the more militant labor leaders and the Communists. However, while the former yelled long and loud, the latter mainly pouted and planned ahead. As in other sections of the country, of course, the West had its few boisterous Communist groups, but Hickok, and later Edward Webster, found that the more revolutionary Communist activity was most conspicuous by its absence.

Although Hickok might have found ample reason for a worker's revolt, she decided that New Mexican laborers were too docile to do much of anything except to work their families at low wages and accept relief; and dispossessed workers in such small Arizona towns as Bisbee, Globe, and Miami were too drowsy from apathy and animated by hope to storm any barricades. Even in the ruthless environment of Colorado's sugar beet industry, there had been very little rebellion against going into the fields "under even the most unsatisfactory times. Those who are rebellious are making a lot of noise about it," she wrote Hopkins, "but for everyone who refuses to go into the fields probably a hundred have gone and under most unfavorable circumstances." [28]

In California, leftist labor leaders felt they had been betrayed by the New Deal in both the farm workers and longshoremen strikes of 1934. One of Hickok's "liberal" friends feared that non-Communist labor leaders who before had strongly supported the president were now very bitter toward him, and "are being forced more and more to the side of the Communists." The latter ("what few of them there actually are out here," as Hickok's AP friend put it) opposed the New Deal, at least for the moment. "They thought back in the late winter of 1932–33 [sic] that the revolution was right at hand," one reporter told her. "Now they say Roosevelt has postponed it for five or six years." [29]

Instead of anger or revolt, when Lorena Hickok moved among the populace in 1934 she found mostly a state of lingering shock, an almost desperate resignation, and widespread uncertainty. And so as they made their way eastward in 1934, finished with their tours as Hopkins's reporters from the West, Hickok, Webster, King, and Williams found the American people at midpassage between two eras that would affect profoundly their lives, those of their children, and of generations to come. It had been five years since the crash of 1929, and in five more years German and Russian armies would begin the rape of Poland, thus launching the horrors of World War II.

It was a much-traveled and now weary Lorena Hickok, Hopkins's premier reporter in the West, who listened to scary, foreboding, ominous, eerie, and strangely prescient observations on her return home. It was as if the people had some metaphysical knowledge of the profound social and economic changes to come, yet possessed little understanding of present time. From a Mormon newspaper editor in Utah:

> People are not so happy nor so hopeful as they were a year ago. They are wondering what is going to happen.

A wife and mother:

> Nobody seems to have any sense of security anymore. If your husband's got a job, you wonder how long he's going to keep it. People seem to worry so much more than they used to. Sometimes I look at my children—and I just wonder.

Over and over:

> Well, I guess things aren't ever going to be the same again.[30]

9

Conclusion

The Reporters' View of America

■ Lorena Hickok, Martha Gellhorn, Louisa Wilson, Robert Washburn, Lincoln Colcord, and the other writers and journalists selected by Hopkins to comb the nation for social data fashioned a unique and fascinating literary tapestry of life in Depression America. Hopkins demanded information about the most distraught segments of the country's jobless population. The reporters' mission took them from the heart of America's Farm Belt, made barren by drought and bitter with cold, into mill towns ravaged by plant closings, and through the scabrous urban slums of Philadelphia, Chicago, and New York City.

How much the observations of Hickok, Gellhorn, Francis, Webster, Colcord, and the others, whose 1933–1934 reports formed the tissue of this book, directly or indirectly influenced Hopkins's and the Roosevelt Administration's shaping of a national welfare system is at least speculative. As stated earlier, Hopkins read the reports; he commented on them and from time to time briefly alluded to them in other correspondence. The reports were retyped at the Federal Emergency Relief Administration offices in Washington, D.C., and presumably circulated. On at least one occasion a copy of one of the reports was forwarded to the President. Ultimately, however, like the mass of other FERA correspondence, these reports were filed away. Copies appear in both administrator Hopkins's papers as well as in FERA's records concerning particular states.

The content of reports must have at least strengthened Hopkins's conviction that extended joblessness vitiated the human spirit and that direct relief, assistance in money and kind, demoralized the recipient. Of greater importance, and as suggested in the first chapter, the reporters and their reporting represented a chapter in a broader national quest to discover American culture undertaken during the 1930s by writers, social scientists, artists, photographers, playwrights, and others. Like the Farm Security Administration photographers, some of whose vast work during the

1930s appears in this book, Hopkins's reporters sought to discover the diversity of the American people, to look at the life styles and beliefs of particular people, mill workers in Rhode Island, miners in Pennsylvania and West Virginia, Mexican-Americans in Arizona, and the many other peoples mentioned in this study. However, forced by their assignments to gather data about the harshest realities of the mass joblessness and social despair, some of Hopkins's reporters fashioned an essentially apocalyptic interpretation of the upheaval that stressed the end of industrialism and the tragic obsolesence of whole categories of humankind: black sharecroppers, southern and northern textile workers, bituminous coal miners, and countless others.

Their social philosophies shaped by the progressive ethos, the reporters believed that America was caught in the throes of a historic change from industrialism to a highly technological and modern postindustrialism. Tragically for the mass of unskilled urban and rural labor, the emerging modern society was characterized by a minimal demand for people with low technical skills. Contrary to the view popular in 1934, which considered depressions to be periodic economic troughs necessary to liquidate inefficient enterprise and rid society of artificial values, the reporters articulated the idea that the Great Depression was a stage in the nation's economic transformation that involved the cruel but inevitable purging from labor's ranks of superfluous workers not needed in the dawning postindustrial era. None of the writers viewed this winnowing of human chaff as a happy circumstance. Instead, they regarded the process as inexorable—even Darwinian. Indeed, it might be cataclysmic, rending society into hostile camps potentially ripe for social turmoil, even revolution. According to Hopkins's reporters, the strong, educated, and mainly white middle class—that is, the elect—were predestined to triumph over the weak. But unfortunately, the weak abounded. Hickok, Francis, and Gellhorn viewed entire populations in southwestern Pennsylvania, West Virginia, Kentucky, North Carolina, and New Hampshire, as stranded in technologically backward mill towns and isolated rural hollows.

If the writers expressed any compassion for these victims of modern times, they also revealed a certain callousness. Francis betrayed a hint of meanness in a description of settlement projects in West Virginia and Ohio, where his optimism for the human resiliency he saw displayed was sullied by his disparagement of the whole experiment as futile. In fact, an undercurrent of gloom infused many of the reporters' descriptions of relief projects, cooperative ventures, and other welfare experiments because of their overweening conviction that these efforts were piddling against the enormity of the social and technological transformation overtaking modern America.

Their frequent callousness comported with the belief that the denizens of slums, isolated mine patches, arid, unproductive farmland, and dying mill towns were an expendable segment of the population. These were the stranded, the permanently poor whose wretched dependency threatened to debase America's vulnerable, albeit venerable culture.

Sorting individuals according to their usefulness in a modern society, Hopkins's reporters often reflected deeply embedded racial and ethnic animosities. As evidenced in many chapters, ethnic stereotyping pervaded the reports.

Other mean and dark thoughts shrouded the thinking of Hopkins's well-educated, middle-class reporters, especially those like Martha Gellhorn who were strongly influenced by modern social scientific ideas about the possibilities for socially engineering a better world. Social engineering promised the use of the social, physical, and behavioral sciences as a means to reshape individuals and societies in conformity with prevailing cultural norms. In this vein, Gellhorn could ponder seriously the wisdom of allowing the hard-core poor the freedom to reproduce. She urged a campaign to disseminate birth control information to the poor. More subtly, sterilization of the defective was advocated, an idea that had widespread support in the 1930s. Several states enacted sterilization laws.

Others of a more compassionate bent proposed resettling America's stranded workers in cooperative communities or subsistence homesteads. The most conventional response to the problem—the one favored by Harry Hopkins—was government-sponsored work relief. Like birth control, sterilization, resettlement, and cooperative or subsistence farming, work relief assumed that the private marketplace could no longer provide jobs for all those seeking work. Martha Gellhorn seriously doubted that large numbers of America's able-bodied youth and middle-aged laborers would ever find useful employment. The thought conjured up a myriad of horrors.

This exhaustion of faith in the integrity of the American Dream infused the reporters' verdict on America. Nevertheless, while they fretfully portrayed the American scene in the mid 1930s in bleak hues, Hopkins's reporters refused to let the Great Depression completely overwhelm their liberal optimism. They observed frequently the faith that the most wretched of the jobless had in President Roosevelt. And like Hopkins, they trusted that work relief would shore up the eroding edifice of American values. Moreover, against the corruption and politicalization which they feared was immobilizing the administration of many state relief offices, they pointed to FERA, the model of efficiency and professionalization.

However, something vital was missing from the liberal rhetoric of Hopkins's reporters, something which earlier, at the turn of the century, had endowed progressivism with an unquenchable enthusiasm. True, scientifically the nation was becoming more sophisticated despite the Great Depression, and ultimately, technology and the institution of professional management, backed by the social and behavioral sciences, promised to restore the nation and middle-class culture to a firm foundation. Nevertheless, the crucial faith in the inevitability of progress no longer prevailed, and belief in the indomitableness of the human spirit had vanished.

After three years of massive unemployment and faced with the moldering ruins of the business management-dominated "New Era" of the 1920s, by 1934 Americans had abandoned the idea of human perfectibility. Here and there, individual psyches might be helped by intensive psychiatric casework or, *miribla dictu*, laboring on a work-relief project, but such incidents were not to be expected en masse. On the whole, few Americans in the 1930s, not even the reporters, believed that the bulk of the poor and jobless were salvageable, nor, alas, did they even fully subscribe to the notion that the nation's large ethnic and racial melting pot was assimilable into the body politic. For this reason, Americans, including many of the reporters, suspected that welfare programs, especially direct material and cash grants-in-aid to the poor, were excessively costly and wasteful. Likewise, in the 1930s, even public housing and work relief could be viewed by many as nothing more than boondoggles, or handouts to the unworthy poor.

Such a dim view of human worth and potential allowed free rein to suspicions about corruption and unscrupulousness both in relief clients and in administrators of public welfare and government in general. Yet, at the same time, people seemed resigned to the mushrooming of big government. Not so strangely, the 1930s proved to be not only an age of burgeoning federal bureaucracy, but in the world arena an era in which strong leaders, even dictators, enjoyed enormous power. It appears, then, that while in the eye of the Great Depression, Hopkins's reporters glimpsed an untoward side of the American character, a side of America rarely presented against the romance of Great Depression hardship and resilience, which, since the 1960s, has enticed the popular imagination.

Notes

■ The correspondence cited in these Notes is from three major sources: the Harry Hopkins Papers at the Franklin Delano Roosevelt Library, Hyde Park, New York; the Lorena Hickok Papers, also located at the FDR Library; and Record Group 69 of the Federal Emergency Relief Administration Papers at the National Archives, Washington, D.C. In the citations, these sources will be abbreviated as HP, LHP, and NA, respectively. Also, since all the correspondence to Hopkins was addressed to his Washington office, that place designation will be omitted in the notes.

The Dimensions of the Depression and the Quest for Data

1. Introductory chapter to a proposed book describing her travels, by Lorena Hickok; LHP.

2. See Arthur Schlesinger Jr.'s review of Doris Faber, *The Life of Lorena Hickok: E.R.'s Friend* (New York, N.Y., 1980) in *The New York Times Book Review*, February 17, 1980.

3. Warren I. Susman, *Culture As History: The Transformation of American Society in the Twentieth Century* (New York, N.Y., 1984); see also Arthur A. Ekirch, Jr., *Ideologies and Utopias: The Impact of the New Deal on American Thought* (Chicago, Ill., 1969).

4. *The Business Week*, November 18, 1932; *New Republic*, March 1, 1933.

5. William E. Leuchtenburg, *Franklin D. Roosevelt and the New Deal, 1932–1940* (New York, N.Y., 1963), pp. 1, 19; *New Republic*, March 8, 1933; *Scribner's Magazine*, March 1933.

6. Richard Kirkendall, "The New Deal and Agriculture," in John Braeman, Robert H. Bremner, and David Brody, eds., *The New Deal: The National Level*, vol. I (Columbus, Ohio, 1975), pp. 84–85; *Scribner's Magazine*, March 1933; Leuchtenburg, *Roosevelt and the New Deal*, pp. 23–24.

7. *Ibid.*; Edward Robb Ellis, *A Nation in Torment: The Great American Depression, 1929–1939* (New York, N.Y., 1970), p. 129.

8. *Scribner's Magazine*, March 1933; John Samuel Ezell, *The South Since 1865* (New York, N.Y., 1963), pp. 428–429.

9. Ezell, *The South Since 1865*, pp. 429–430; John Robert Moore, "The New Deal in Louisiana," in John Braeman, Robert H. Bremner, David Brody, eds., *The New Deal: The State and Local Levels*, vol. II (Columbus, Ohio, 1975), pp. 137–153.

10. Richard C. Keller, "Pennsylvania's Little New Deal," in Braeman, et. al., vol. II, pp. 51–52; David J. Maurer, "Relief Problems and Politics in Ohio," in *ibid.*, p. 78; *Nation*, February 15, March 1, 1933; *World Tomorrow*, March 1932; Caroline Bird, *The Invisible Scar* (New York, N.Y., 1966), pp. 26–27.

11. James F. Wickens, "Depression and the New Deal in Colorado," in Braeman, et. al., vol. II, pp. 270–272; William Pickens, "The New Deal in New Mexico," in *ibid.*, 318–319; Michael P. Malone, "The Montana New Dealers," in *ibid.*, p. 242; *The Forum*, March 1933; *New Republic*, March 8, 1933.

12. *Time*, March 20, 1933; *New Republic*, February 22, 1933; Leuchtenburg, *Roosevelt and the New Deal*, pp. 17, 38–39.

13. See Leah Hannah Feder, *Unemployment Relief in Periods of Depression: A Study of Measures Adopted in Certain American Cities, 1857–1922* (New York, N.Y., 1936); Roy Lubove, *The Professional Altruist: The Emergency of Social Work As a Career, 1880–1930* (Cambridge, Mass., 1965); Robert H. Bremner, *From the Depths: The Discovery of Poverty in the United States* (New York, N.Y., 1969); Robert H. Wiebe, *The Search for Order, 1877–1920* (New York, N.Y., 1967); Johanna C. Colcord, *Community Planning and Unemployment Emergencies: Recommendations Growing Out of Experience* (New York, N.Y., 1930).

14. See Lubove, *The Professional Altruist;* Josephine Brown, *Public Relief: 1929–1939* (New York, N.Y., 1940); John F. Bauman, "The City, The Depression and Relief: The Philadelphia Experiences, 1929–1939," Ph.D. dissertation, Rutgers University, 1969.

15. See Feder, *Unemployment Relief in Periods of Depression;* Bremner, *From the Depths;* T. A. Larson, "The New Deal in Wyoming," *Pacific Historical Review*, XXXVIII, 3 (August 1969), 253; Searle Charles, *Minister of Relief: Harry Hopkins and the Depression* (Syracuse, N.Y., 1963); Frank Friedel, *Franklin D. Roosevelt: The Triumph* (Boston, Mass., 1956), pp. 219–223.

16. On "pauperizing" the jobless, see James M. Williams, *Human Aspects of Unemployment and Relief* (Chapel Hill, N.C., 1933), pp. 123–125; Margaret E. Rich, *The Administration of Relief in Unemployment Emergencies* (New York, N.Y., 1930).

17. Clark A. Chambers, *Seedtime of Reform: American Social Services and Social Action, 1918–1933* (Ann Arbor, Mich., 1967), pp. 99–101; see also Albert U. Romasco, *The Poverty of Abundance: Hoover, The Nation, The Depression* (New York, N.Y., 1965).

18. See testimony of Karl deSchweinitz and Jacob Billikopf, Federal Cooperation in Unemployment Relief, *Hearings* before the Subcommittee of the Committee of Manufacturers, U.S. Senate, 72nd Cong., 1st Sess., S. 4592 (Washington, D.C., 1932).

19. On "Men and Women of Sympathy and Training," see Williams, *Human Aspects of Unemployment and Relief*, p. 150; see also, Harry Hopkins, *Spending to Save: The Complete Story of Relief* (New York, N.Y., 1936), and Gertrude Springer, "The New Deal and the Old Dole," *Survey Graphic*, XXII (1933), 348; see Charles, *Minister of Relief*, and Frank J. Raeder, "Harry L. Hopkins: The Ambitious Crusader: an Historical Analysis of the Major Influences on His Life," *Annals of Iowa*, 44 (Fall 1977).

20. Bauman, "The City, The Depression, and Relief," 180; On being "downhearted and brooding," see Williams, *Human Aspects of Unemployment and Relief*, pp. 72–74; on the atmosphere of violence, see chapter on "The Marching Jobless in Philadelphia," in Thomas H. Coode and John F. Bauman, *People, Poverty and Politics: Pennsylvanians During the Great Depression* (Lewisburg, Pa., 1981); also, see James F. Wickens, "New Deal in Colorado," *Pacific Historical Review*, XXXVIII, 3 (August 1965), 202–206.

21. William W. Bremer, "Along the American Way: The New Deal Work Relief Programs for the Unemployed," *The Journal of American History*, LXII, 3 (December 1975), 636.

22. *Ibid.*, 636–638; see also Charles, *Minister of Relief*, and Corrington Gill, *Wasted Manpower: The Challenge of Unemployment* (New York, N.Y., 1939). For a recent appraisal of Hopkins see George McJimsey *Harry Hopkins: Ally of the Poor and Defender of Democracy* (Cambridge, Mass., 1986).

The Reporters and the Reports

1. Harry L. Hopkins, *Spending to Save: The Complete Story of Relief* (New York, N.Y., 1936), pp. 100–104; see also Albert Romasco, *The Poverty of Abundance: Hoover, the Nation and the Great Depression* (New York, N.Y., 1965); Searle Charles, *Minister of Relief: Harry Hopkins and the Depression* (Syracuse, N.Y., 1963).

2. Report of Eva Hance, Regional Social Worker, July 27, 1934, Box 406, Field Reports, NA: Oregon; also Corrington Gill, September 19, 1933, Box 406, Field Reports; Illinois, NA.

3. Hopkins, *Spending to Save*, pp. 100–107.

4. William W. Bremer, "Along the 'American Way': The New Deal's Work Relief Programs for the Unemployed," *The Journal of American History*, LXII, 3 (December 1975), 636–652; Harry L. Hopkins, Washington, D.C., to Franklin D. Roosevelt, December 29, 1933, Box 95, HP; see also Richard Lowitt and Maurine Beasley, eds., *One Third of a Nation: Lorena Hickok Reports on The Great Depression* (Urbana, Ill., 1981).

5. Hopkins, Washington, D.C., to Eric Biddle, Harrisburg, Pennsylvania, July 28, 1933, Box 406, Field Representative Reports, State Files, Old Series, NA.

6. On the "State of the Nation Reports," see Hopkins to State Emergency Relief Administrators, March 20, 1934; also W. R. Dyess, State ERA, Arkansas, to Hopkins, April 6, 1934; and Hopkins to State Emergency Relief Administrators, October 22, 1934, Box 61, HP.

7. On Pierce Williams reports, see, for example, Pierce Williams, Field

Representative, FERA, "Report on Conditions and Prospects of Employment in the Lumber Industry," November 25, 1934, Box 62, HP; also Pierce Williams, "Regional Survey dealing with Economic Insecurity of Workers," October 23, 1936, Box 62, HP.

8. On the Committee on Economic Security, see Daniel Nelson, *Unemployment Insurance: The American Experience, 1915–1935* (Madison, Wis., 1969), pp. 204–213; also, see "Informal Report of the Special Advisory Committee to the President's Committee on Economic Security," November 24, 1934, WPA Miscellaneous, in Aubrey Williams Papers, Franklin Delano Roosevelt Library, Hyde Park, New York (hereafter cited as AWP). Also, see Harry L. Hopkins, "Engagement Calendar," 1934–1935, Box 102, HP; on Hickok's Associated Press acquaintances, see Lorena Hickok to Hopkins, circa., February 1934, Box 67, HP.

9. See "Cards Recording Distribution of Survey Reports," HP; also, Lowitt and Beasley *One Third of a Nation*, pp. xvii–xxxv; Hopkins's July 1933 charge to Hickok appeared in a letter from Hopkins to Eric Biddle, State Emergency Relief Board, Harrisburg, Pennsylvania, July 28, 1933, Box 10, Old Subject File, NA; Hopkins told Biddle that he had asked Hickok to "look over the situation in Pennsylvania. Miss Hickok is not acting as a field representative but she is, on my behalf, going to observe not only the status of relief work in the United States, but its effect on people and try to get a picture of how the ordinary citizen feels about relief; whether in his judgment it is adequate or inadequate, and so forth. She is going to explore those avenues which would not normally be approached by our field representatives. She expects for instance to interview ministers, labor leaders, manufacturers, and visit the families themselves. She is particularly anxious, as am I, that her visit not be considered in any way as an investigation of your relief machinery."

10. Lorena Hickok, Tallahassee, Fla., to Miss Van Meter, Washington, D.C., January 24, 1934, Box 406, Field Representatives Reports, Old Subject File, NA.

11. See Harry L. Hopkins, Administrator, to "Dear Missy [Le Hand]," December 10, 1934, Box 95, HP; also, Hopkins to FDR, December 12, 1933, Box 95; and Distribution of Survey Cards, Box 65, HP; in at least one case, reports that crossed Hoover's desk resulted in the dismissal of a key Hopkins reporter. Martha Gellhorn later recalled that she thought she knew why she had been fired. On assignment for Hopkins in Idaho, she found the unemployed there victimized by a crooked contractor. Gellhorn never understood the frequent queries from Washington about protest groups. "Washington," she wrote, "didn't realize that these people suffered from despair, not anger. By buying them beer and haranguing them," recollected Gellhorn, "I convinced a few hesitant men to break the windows of the FERA office at night. Afterward someone would surely come and look into their grievances. . . . Naturally the men told the FBI that the Relief Lady had suggested this good idea." The FBI investigated, the contractor was arrested, and Gellhorn was fired by the Bureau for being a "dangerous Communist," a "subversive and a menace." See Martha Gellhorn, *Granta*, 23 (Spring 1988), 88–102.

12. Distribution of Survey Cards, Box 65, HP; and Hopkins to Miss Marguerite Le Hand, December 22, 1934, Box 95, HP.

13. Henry W. Francis, Morgantown, West Virginia to Hopkins, November 20, 1934, Box 406, Field Reports: West Virginia, NA.

14. See "Informal Report of the Special Advisory Committee to the President's Committee on Economic Security," November 24, 1934, WPA Miscellaneous, AWP.

15. On the "progressive ethos," see Clyde Griffen, "The Progressive Ethos," in Stanley Coben and Lorman Ratner, eds. *The Development of an American Culture* (Englewood Cliffs, N.J., 1970), 120–149; and John C. Burnham's essay on progressivism in John D. Buenker, et al., eds., *Progressivism* (Cambridge, Mass., 1977), pp. 3–31.

16. On the diversity of progressives, see Robert Wiebe, *The Search for Order, 1877–1920* (New York, N.Y., 1967).

17. Griffen, "The Progressive Ethos," 120–149; Burnham in Buenker, et al., *Progressivism*, p. 6.

18. Burnham in Buenker, et al., *Progressivism*, pp. 8–10, 18; John F. Bauman, "Disinfecting the Industrial City: The Philadelphia Housing Commission and Scientific Efficiency, 1909–1916," in Michael H. Ebner and Eugene M. Tobin, eds., *The Age of Urban Reform* (Port Washington, N.Y., 1977), pp. 117–131.

19. See Arthur S. Link and Richard L. McCormick, *Progressivism* (Arlington Heights, Illinois, 1983), pp. 85–92; also Samuel Haber, *Efficiency and Uplife: Scientific Management in the Progressive Era, 1890–1920* (Chicago, Ill., 1964).

20. Roy Lubove, *The Professional Altruist: The Emergence of Social Work As a Career, 1880–1930* (Cambridge, Mass., 1965).

21. Distribution of Survey Cards, Box 65, HP; and Hopkins to "Dear Missy," December 10, 1934, Box 95, HP.

22. Ishbel Ross, *Ladies of the Press* (New York, N.Y., 1936), pp. 203–209; Lowitt and Beasley, eds., *One Third of a Nation*, pp. xxv–xxxiv; Bernard Sternsher, "Depression and New Deal in Ohio: Lorena Hickok's Reports to Harry Hopkins, 1934–1936," *Ohio History*, 86 (Autumn 1977); "Introductory Chapter" to a proposed book describing her travels, Lorena Hickok, LHP; See also Doris Faber, *The Life of Lorena Hickok, E. R.'s Friend* (New York, N.Y., 1980).

23. Ross, *Ladies of the Press*, p. 207; Eleanor Roosevelt, *This I Remember* (New York, N.Y., 1949), p. 70; Hickok (Ohio), to Hopkins, September 22, 1935, Box 12, LHP.

24. Lowitt and Beasley, eds., *One Third of a Nation*, pp. xxxiv–xxxv.

25. Ross, *Ladies of the Press*, pp. 171–174; biographical references and works-published information found on catalog cards, author Louisa Wilson, Library of Congress, Washington, D.C. (hereafter cited as Catalog Card Information, author, LC). Wilson took the trip to China in 1936 and upon returning wrote a novel about her experience entitled *Broken Journey.*

26. On Hazel Reavis, see *New York Times*, April 18, 1940; see also obituary of Smith Reavis, *New York Times*, February 25, 1940.

27. On Ernestine Ball, see copyright data for article series entitled "Aimee in the Temple," November 9, 1926, in Copyright Catalog, Copyright Office, Library of Congress, Washington, D.C.

28. Catalog Card Information, Thomas Steep, LC; *New York Times*, September 4, 1944; Thomas Steep, *Chinese Fantastics* (New York, N.Y., 1929).

29. Catalog Card Information, Wayne Parrish, LC; "Man on a Rocket," *Time,* October 15, 1956, 86–87; *Current Biography,* September 1958, 31.

30. Information on Julian Claff can be found in his obituary, *New York Times,* January 23, 1976; see also Faber, *E. R.'s Friend,* pp. 80–81, 265, 305.

31. On Francis, see copyright data for articles on "Germany Needs Supplies," May 25, 1920, and "France Presses Need for Cable Ship," June 9, 1920, all in Copyright Catalog, Copyright Office, Library of Congress, Washington, D.C.

32. *New York Times,* December 30, 1959; List of FERA Personnel, HP; Jane DeHart Matthews, *The Federal Theatre, 1935–1939: Plays, Relief, and Politics* (Princeton, N.J., 1967), p. 74.

33. For a list of Gellhorn's works, see Harry Redkey Warfel, ed., *American Novelists of Today* (New York, N.Y., 1951), pp. 172–173; *New York Times,* February 13, 1969.

34. See Stanley Jasspon Kunitz, ed., *Twentieth Century Authors* (New York, N.Y., 1942); Kunitz, ed., *Twentieth Century Authors* (New York, N.Y., 1973).

35. Martha Gellhorn, Bryn Mawr, Pennsylvania, to Lorena Hickok, Washington, D.C., January 8, 1935, Box 13, LHP; see also Gellhorn, *Granta.*

36. Gellhorn, Key West, Florida, to "Dear Mrs. Roosevelt," Washington, D.C., January 5, 1937, Box 13, LHP.

37. Gellhorn, Paris, France, to "Dearest Mrs. Roosevelt," Washington, D.C., November 12, 1938, Box 13, LHP.

38. Warfol, ed., *American Novelists of Today,* p. 173; telegram, Gellhorn, New York, New York, to Lorena Hickok, November 9, 1934, Box 13, LHP.

39. Catalog Card Information, Martha Bensley Bruere, LC; *Wilson Library Bulletin* (October 1950), 108; Martha Bensley Bruere, *Your Forests* (New York, N.Y., 1945); Martha Bruere and Mary Ritter Beard, *Laughing Their Way: Women's Humor in America* (New York, N.Y., 1934); Allen Davis, *Spearheads of Reform: The Social Settlements and the Progressive Movement, 1890–1914* (New York, N.Y., 1967), p. 237; Clark A. Chambers, *Seedtime of Reform: American Social Service and Social Action, 1918–1933* (Ann Arbor, Mich., 1967), p. 139.

40. Catalog Card Information, Robert Washburn, LC; Robert Collyer Washburn, *The Jury of Death: Twenty Against the Underworld* (Garden City, N.Y., 1930); Robert Collyer Washburn, *The Life and Times of Lydia C. Pinkham* (New York, N.Y., 1931).

41. Walter Muir Whitehill, *Analecta Biographica: A Handful of New England Portraits* (Brattleboro, Vt., 1969), pp. 44–45; Christopher Lasch, *The New Radicalism in America: The Intellectual As a Social Type, 1889–1963* (New York, N.Y., 1965), pp. 225–251.

42. Lasch, *The New Radicalism,* pp. 245–251.

43. Lincoln Colcord, Detroit, Michigan, to Hopkins, December 14, 1934, Box 65, HP.

44. Catalog Card Information, Lincoln Colcord, LC; Whitehill, *Analecta Biographica,* pp. 56–59; Lincoln Colcord, *The Game of Life and Death: Stories of the Sea* (New York, N.Y., 1914); Colcord, *An Instrument of the Gods and Other Stories of the Sea* (New York, N.Y., 1922).

45. Catalog Card Information, Pierce Williams, LC; *New York Times,* April 26, 1952; Pierce Williams, *The Purchase of Medical Care Through Fixed Period*

Payments (New York: N.Y., 1976 [c. 1932]), Dist. Cards, FERA Employment List, NA.

46. Aspects of David M. Maynard's life are revealed in the pages of the *New York Times;* see, for example, the news of Maynard's marriage to Willa Evans (later annulled), *New York Times*, June 23, 1926, and his comment on the devaluation of the yen, *New York Times*, November 23, 1949; see also, *New York Times*, December 23, 1951.

47. Gellhorn, London, England, to Thomas H. Coode, California, Pennsylvania, April 17, 1980.

48. Hickok, "Introductory Chapter," LHP; Hickok, "Expense Account," July 29, 1933–August 5, 1933, Box 12; Hickok to Eleanor Roosevelt, Washington, D.C., July 25, 1936, Box 12, LHP.

49. Gellhorn, "New Hampshire," to Hopkins, December 13, 1934, Box 66, HP.

50. Gellhorn, "Report on Massachusetts," to Hopkins, November 15–25, 1934, Box 66, HP; Thomas Steep, "Chicago Commons," to Hopkins, November 17, 1934, Box 66, HP.

51. Bruere, Schenectady, N.Y., to Hopkins, November 5, 1934, Box 65, HP.

52. Louisa Wilson, Detroit, Michigan to Hopkins, November 17, 1934, Box 65; Thomas Steep, "Chicago Commons," to Hopkins, November 17, 1934; Steep, Chicago, Illinois, to Hopkins, November 4, 1934, Box 66, HP.

53. Robert Collyer Washburn, New Haven, Connecticut, to Hopkins, December 2, 1934, Box 65, HP; Bruere, Olean, New York, to Hopkins, November 27, 1934, box 65; Wayne Parrish, New York City, to Hopkins, November 19, 1934, Box 65, HP.

54. Colcord, Mt. Vernon, New York, to Hopkins, December 14, 1934, Box 65, HP.

55. Edward J. Webster, Washington, D.C., to Hopkins, November 2, 1934, Box 67, HP.

56. Gellhorn, "Report on Massachusetts," to Hopkins, November 15–25, 1934.

57. Gellhorn, (town unspecified), New Hampshire, to Hopkins, December 13, 1934, Box 66, HP.

58. Parrish, New York City, to Hopkins, November 19, 1934, Box 65; Gellhorn, "Report on Rhode Island," to Hopkins, December 17, 1934, Box 66, HP.

City Streets and Slouching Men

1. There are few accounts of the Great Depression in American cities; for exceptions see, Charles H. Trout, *Boston: The Great Depression and the New Deal* (New York, N.Y., 1971); Sidney Fine, *Frank Murphy: The Detroit Years* (Ann Arbor, Mich., 1975); Raymond Koch, "Politics and Relief in Minneapolis During the 1930s," *Minnesota History*, 42, 2, (Winter 1968); Bonnie Fox Schwartz, "Unemployment Relief in Philadelphia, 1930–1932," *Pennsylvania Magazine of History* *and Biography*, 92, (January 1969) 86–108; see also Albert Romasco, *The Poverty of Abundance: Hoover, the Nation, the Depression* (New York, N.Y., 1965) and Clarke Chambers, *Seedtime of Reform: American Social Service and Social Action*, 1918–1933 (Ann Arbor, Mich., 1967).

2. See Mark I. Gelfand, *A Nation of Cities: The Federal Government and Urban America, 1933–1965* (New York, N.Y., 1975); John F. Bauman, "The City, The Depression, and Relief: The Philadelphia Experience, 1929–1939," Ph.D. dissertation, Rutgers University, 1969.

3. See Harry L. Hopkins, *Spending to Save: The Complete Story of Relief* (New York, N.Y., 1936).

4. Lorena Hickok, New York City, to Hopkins, November 7, 1934, Box 11, LHP; Wayne W. Parrish, New York City, to Hopkins, November 11, November 17, 1934, Box 65, HP.

5. Thomas Steep, Chicago, Illinois, to Hopkins, November 4, 1934, Box 65; Steep, Chicago, Illinois, to Hopkins, November 17, 1934, Box 66, HP.

6. Julian Claff, Philadelphia, Pennsylvania, to Hopkins, November 4, 1934, Box 65, HP; Martha Gellhorn, Camden, New Jersey, to Hopkins, April, 25 1935, Box 66, HP.

7. Lincoln Colcord, Detroit, Michigan, to Hopkins, November 4, 1934; Steep, Gary, Indiana, to Hopkins, November 24, 1934, Box 65, HP; Lorena Hickok, Birmingham, Alabama, to Hopkins, April 1, 1934, Box 11, LHP; Martha Bensley Bruere, Palisades, New York, to Hopkins, December 7, 1934, Box 65, HP.

8. David M. Maynard, Cleveland, Ohio, to Hopkins, November 25, 1934, Box 65, HP; Colcord, Cleveland Heights, Ohio, to Hopkins, December 10, 1934, Box 65, HP; Maynard, Columbus, Ohio, to Hopkins, November 1, 1934, Box 66, HP; Hickok, Washington, D.C., to Hopkins, December 6, 1934, Box 11, LHP.

9. Steep, Chicago, Illinois, to Hopkins, November 17, 1934, Box 66, HP; Claff, Scranton, Pennsylvania, to Hopkins, November 25, 1934, Box 65, HP; Hickok, "Report on Pennsylvania," to Hopkins, August (?), 1933, Box 11, LHP. Steep, Gary, Indiana, to Hopkins, November 24, 1934, HP.

10. See Albert U. Romasco, *The Poverty of Abundance: Hoover, the Nation, the Depression* (New York, N.Y., 1965) and Searle Charles, *Minister of Relief: Harry Hopkins and the Depression* (Syracuse, N.Y., 1963); Hickok, New York City, to Hopkins, November 18, 1934, Box 11, LHP.

11. Edward J. Webster, "Final Report of Observations in St. Louis, Kansas City, et al. . . ," to Hopkins, December 8, 1934, Box 67, HP.

12. Hickok, New York City, to Hopkins, November (?), 1934, Box 11, LHP; Robert Collyer Washburn, New Haven, Connecticut, to Hopkins, December 2, 1934, Box 65, HP; Louisa Wilson, Akron, Ohio, to Hopkins, December 6, 1934, Box 65, HP.

13. William W. Bremer, "Along the American Way: The New Deal's Work Relief Programs for the Unemployed," *The Journal of American History*, LXII, 3 (December 1975), 636–652; Steep, Chicago, Illinois, to Hopkins, November 17, 1934; Wilson, Detroit, to Hopkins, November 24, 1934, Box 65, HP; Maynard, Columbus, Ohio, to Hopkins, November 1, 1934.

14. See Josephine Brown, *Public Relief, 1929–1939* (New York, N.Y., 1940); and Charles, *Minister of Relief;* Wilson, Akron, Ohio, to Hopkins, December 6, 1934, Box 65, HP; Maynard, Cleveland, Ohio, to Hopkins, November 15, 1934, Box 65, HP; Colcord, Detroit, Michigan, to Hopkins, November 4, 1934, Box 65, HP.

15. Claff, Philadelphia, Pennsylvania, to Hopkins, November 17, 1934, Box 65, HP; Bruere, Buffalo, New York, to Hopkins, November 19, 1934, Box 65, HP.

16. Hickok, New York City, to Hopkins, November (date unspecified) 1934, Box 11, LHP.

17. See John Higham, *Send These to Me: Jews and Other Immigrants in Urban America* (New York, N.Y., 1975); Bruere, Buffalo, New York, to Hopkins, November 19, 1934; Washburn, Boston, Massachusetts, to Hopkins, November 3, 1934, Box 65, HP; Steep, "Chicago Commons," to Hopkins, November 17, 1934, Box 66. HP.

18. Claff, Philadelphia, Pennsylvania, to Hopkins, November 17, 1934; Wilson, Detroit, Michigan, to Hopkins, November 17, 1934, Box 65, HP; Hickok, Houston, Texas, to Hopkins, April 13, 1934, Box 11, LHP; Colcord, Detroit, Michigan, to Hopkins, November 18, 1934, Box 65, HP; Steep, Chicago, Illinois, to Hopkins, November 4, 1934, Box 66, HP.

19. See Bernard Karsh, "The Impact of the Political Left," in Milton Derber and Edwin Young, eds., *Labor and the New Deal* (Madison, Wis., 1961), and Daniel J. Leab, "United We Eat: The Creation and Organization of the Unemployed Councils in 1930," *Labor History* 8 (Fall 1967); Parrish, New York City, to Hopkins, November 11, 1934, Box 65, HP.

20. Hickok, Des Moines, Iowa, to Hopkins, November 25, 1933, Box 11, LHP.

21. Howard Meyers, Washington, D.C., to Mr. Padriac Merrick, Portland, Oregon, August 3, 1934, Box 406, NA.

22. Webster, "Final Report . . . ," to Hopkins, December 8, 1934; Gellhorn, Camden, New Jersey, to Hopkins, April 25, 1934; Steep, Gary, Indiana, to Hopkins, November 24, 1934; Claff, Philadelphia, Pennsylvania, to Hopkins, November 25, 1934, Box 65, HP; Maynard, Cleveland, Ohio, to Hopkins, November 25, 1934.

23. Washburn, Boston, Massachusetts, to Hopkins, November 3, 1934; Colcord, Detroit, Michigan, to Hopkins, November 4, 1934; Wilson, Detroit, Michigan, to Hopkins, November 24, 1934, Box 65, HP.

Beleaguered Households: The Agony of the American Family and the Unattached Person

1. In the past decade the history of the family has received considerable attention; see Peter Laslett, *Household and Family in Past Time* (Cambridge, England, 1972); Maris Vinovskis, "From Household Size to Life Course: Some Observations on Recent Trends in Family History," *American Behavioral Scientist* 21

(November 1977), 264; for contemporary accounts of how well, or how poorly the family was weathering the Great Depression, see Mirra Komarovsky, *The Unemployed Man and His Family: The Effect of Unemployment Upon the Status of the Man in Fifty-nine Families* (New York, N.Y., for the Institute of Social Research, 1940); see also Marion Elderton, ed., *Case Studies of Unemployment* (Philadelphia, Pa., 1931); on the bleak outlook for the reemployment of the jobless in the 1930s, see Joanna C. Colcord, "The Challenge of the Continuing Depression," *The Annals* 176 (November 1934), 21–23; and "Unemployment, 1937," *Fortune* 16 (July–December 1937), 188.

2. See Tamara K. Hareven, *Family Time and Industrial Time: The Relationship Between Family and Work in a New England Industrial Community* (Cambridge, Mass., 1982).

3. See Edward Shorter, *The Making of the Modern Family* (New York, N.Y., 1975); also Winifred D. Wandersee Bolin, "The Economics of Middle-Income Family Life: Working Women During the Great Depression," *The Journal of American History*, LXV, 1 (June 1978), 60–74.

4. William Graebner, "The Unstable World of Benjamin Spock: Social Engineering in a Democratic Culture, 1917–1950," *The Journal of American History* 67, 3 (December 1980), 612–630; Bolin, "The Economics of Middle-Income Family Life," 65–70.

5. Martha Gellhorn, "Report on Massachusetts, November 15–25," to Harry Hopkins, November 30, 1934, Box 66, HP; Gellhorn, Washington, D.C., ("I came in today from Gastonia,") to Hopkins, November 30, 1934, Box 65, HP.

6. Lorena Hickok, Phoenix, Arizona, to Hopkins, May 4, 1934, HP.

7. See Glen H. Elder, *Children of the Great Depression: Social Change in the Life Experience* (Chicago, Ill., 1974).

8. Edward J. Webster, "Final Report of Observations in St. Louis, Kansas City, et al. . . ," to Hopkins, December 8, 1934, HP.

9. Gellhorn, "Report on Massachusetts, November 15–25," to Hopkins, November 30, 1934, Box 66, HP.

10. Thomas Steep, Chicago, Illinois, to Hopkins, November 4, 1934, Box 66, HP.

11. Louisa Wilson, Detroit, Michigan, to Hopkins, November 24, 1934, Box 65, HP.

12. Steep, Chicago, Illinois, to Hopkins, November 4, November 17, 1934, Box 66, HP.

13. *Ibid.*

14. Martha Bensley Bruere, Olean, New York, to Hopkins, November 27, 1934, Box 65, HP.

15. Lea Howard, Great Falls, Montana, to Hopkins, March 14, 1935, Box 406, Field Reports: Montana, NA; Bruere, Buffalo, New York, to Hopkins, November 19, 1934, Box 65, HP.

16. Hickok, Houston, Texas, to Hopkins, April 13, 1934, Box 11, LHP.

17. Pierce Williams, Salt Lake City, Utah, to Hopkins, February 14, 1934, Box 406, Field Reports: Utah, NA.

18. See Herbert J. Gans, *The Urban Villagers: Group and Class in the Life of*

Italian-Americans (New York, N.Y., 1962); Humbert S. Nelli, *The Italians in Chicago, 1880–1930: A Study in Ethnic Mobility* (New York, N.Y., 1970); Stephan Thernstrom, *Poverty and Progress: Social Mobility in the Nineteenth-Century City* (Cambridge, Mass., 1964); Tamara K. Hareven, "Family Time and Industrial Time: Family and Work in a Planned Corporation Town, 1900–1924," *Journal of Urban History* 1 (May 1975); Caroline Golab, *Immigrant Destinations* (Philadelphia, Pa., 1972).

19. Steep, Chicago, Illinois, to Hopkins, November 4, 1934, Box 66, HP; Hickok, Montgomery, Alabama, to Hopkins, March 29, 1934, Box 11, LHP.

20. Wayne Parrish, New York City, to Hopkins, November 11, 1934, Box 65, HP.

21. Hickok, Montgomery, Alabama, to Hopkins, March 29, 1934, Box 11, LHP.

22. Hazel Reavis, Pittsburgh, Pennsylvania, to Hopkins, November 4, 1934, Box 66, HP.

23. Parrish, New York City, to Hopkins, November 11, 1934, Box 65, HP.

24. Gellhorn, "Report on Rhode Island," to Hopkins, December 17, 1934, Box 66, HP.

25. Wilson, Akron, Ohio, to Hopkins, December 6, 1934, Box 65; Wilson, Detroit, to Hopkins, November 17, 1934, Box 65, HP.

26. Gellhorn, "Report on Rhode Island," to Hopkins, December 17, 1934, Box 66, HP.

27. David M. Maynard, (location unspecified), to Hopkins, November 1, 1934, Box 66, HP.

28. Gellhorn, "Report on Massachusetts, November 15–25," to Hopkins, November 30, 1934, Box 66; Webster, "Final Report . . . ," to Hopkins, December 8, 1934, Box 67, HP.

29. Gellhorn, "Report on New Hampshire," to Hopkins, December 13, 1934, Box 66; Gellhorn, "Report to Mr. Hopkins on North Carolina," to Hopkins, November 30, 1934, Box 66, HP; also see Robert Dugdale, *The Jukes* (New York, N.Y., 1970 [c. 1910]).

30. See James H. Jones, *Bad Blood: The Tuskegee Syphilis Experiment* (New York, N.Y., 1981).

31. Hickok, Salt Lake City, Utah, to Hopkins, September 1, 1934, Box 11, LHP.

32. Hickok, En Route—Denver to Los Angeles, to Hopkins, June 23, 1934, Box 11, LHP.

33. Ernestine Ball, to Kathryn Godwin, October 29, 1934, Box 65, HP.

34. *Ibid.*; Bruere, Olean, New York, to Hopkins, November 27, 1934, Box 65, HP.

35. Robert Collyer Washburn, New Haven, Connecticut, to Hopkins, December 2, 1934, Box 65, HP.

36. Hickok, Phoenix, Arizona, to Hopkins, May 4, 1934, Box 11, HP.

37. Hickok, "Field Report, New York State, Outside of the Metropolitan Area," to Hopkins, September 12–19, 1933, Box 11, LHP.

Of Mill Towns, Mine Patches, and Stranded People

1. See U.S. Bureau of the Census, *Fifteenth Census of the U.S.: 1930* (Washington, D.C., 1930).
2. See Thomas H. Coode and John F. Bauman, *People, Poverty, and Politics: Pennsylvanians During the Great Depression* (Lewisburg, Pa., 1981); Muriel Early Sheppard, *Cloud By Day: The Story of Coal and Coke and People* (Chapel Hill, N.C., 1947); Irving Bernstein, *The Lean Years: A History of the American Worker, 1933–1941* (Boston, Mass., 1966); John F. Bauman, "Ethnic Adaptation in a Southwestern Pennsylvania Coal Patch, 1910–1940," *The Journal of Ethnic Studies*, 7 (Fall 1979).
3. See Sheppard, *Cloud By Day*, and Coode and Bauman, *People, Poverty, and Politics*.
4. Henry W. Francis, Clarksburg, West Virginia, to Hopkins, November 25, 1934, Box 65, HP; Francis, Morgantown, West Virginia, to Hopkins, November 18, 1934, Box 65, HP.
5. Francis, Clarksburg, West Virginia, to Hopkins, November 10, 1934, Box 65, HP.
6. Francis, Williamson, West Virginia, to Hopkins, December 7, 1934, Box 65, HP.
7. Lorena Hickok, "Report on Eastern Kentucky," to Hopkins, September 6, 1933, Box 11, LHP.
8. Hickok, "En Route to Washington, D.C.," to Hopkins, May 8, 1934, Box 11, LHP.
9. Hickok, San Antonio, Texas, to Hopkins, April 17, 1934, Box 11, LHP.
10. Hazel Reavis, Pittsburgh, Pennsylvania, to Hopkins, November 12, 1934, Box 66, HP.
11. Martha Gellhorn, Providence, Pawtucket, Woonsocket, Rhode Island, to Hopkins, December 17, 1934; Gellhorn, "Report on New Hampshire," to Hopkins, December 13, 1934, Box 66, HP.
12. Bauman, "Ethnic Adaptation," 15–17; Francis, Clarksburg, West Virginia, to Hopkins, November 25, 1934; Francis, Clarksburg, West Virginia, to Hopkins, December 1, 1934, Box 65, HP.
13. Francis, Uniontown, Pennsylvania, to Hopkins, December 1, 1934, Box 65, HP.
14. See Robert Coles, *Migrants, Sharecroppers, and Mountaineers* (Boston, 1971); Francis, Williamson, West Virginia, to Hopkins, December 7, 1934, Box 65, HP.
15. Hickok, "Report on West Virginia," to Hopkins, August 16–26, 1933, Box 11, LHP.
16. See Margaret Byington, *Homestead: The Households of a Mill Town* (New York, N.Y., 1910); Hazel Reavis, Pittsburgh, Pennsylvania, to Hopkins, November 12, 1934, Box 66, HP.
17. Gellhorn, "Report on Pennsylvania," to Hopkins, August 7–12, 1933, Box 11, LHP; Francis, Washington, Pennsylvania, to Hopkins, November 3, 1934, Box 66, HP; Francis, Morgantown, West Virginia, to Hopkins, November 18, 1934, Box 66, HP.

18. Hickok, "Report on Pennsylvania," to Hopkins, August 7–12, 1933, Box 11, LHP; Francis, Washington, Pennsylvania, to Hopkins, November 3, 1934; Francis, Morgantown, West Virginia, to Hopkins, November 18, 1934.

19. Francis, Clarksburg, West Virginia, to Hopkins, November 25, 1934; Francis, Uniontown, Pennsylvania, to Hopkins, November 10, 1934, Box 65, HP.

20. Reavis, Pittsburgh, Pennsylvania, to Hopkins, November 12, 1934; Gellhorn, "Report on Gastonia," to Hopkins, November 11, 1934, Box 66, HP.

21. See Roy Lubove, *The Professional Altruist: The Emergence of Social Work as a Career, 1880–1930* (Cambridge, Mass., 1965), and Albert Romasco, *The Poverty of Abundance: Hoover, the Nation, the Depression* (New York, N.Y., 1965); Hickok, "Field Report on Maine, September 21–29, 1933," to Hopkins, October 9, 1933; Hickok, "Report on Pennsylvania," to Hopkins, August 7–12, 1933, Box 11, LHP.

22. Francis, Washington, Pennsylvania, to Hopkins, November 3, 1934.

23. Hickok, "Report on Pennsylvania," to Hopkins, August 7–12, 1933; Francis, Uniontown, Pennsylvania, to Hopkins, December 1, 1934, Box 65, HP.

24. William W. Bremer, "Along the American Way: The New Deal Work Relief Programs for the Unemployed," *The Journal of American History*, LXII 3 (December 1975), 636–638.

25. Ernestine Ball, "FERA Survey Report," to Hopkins, December 19, 1934, Box 65, HP; Hickok, "Report on Pennsylvania," to Hopkins, August 7–12, 1933.

26. See Searle Charles, *Minister of Relief: Harry Hopkins and the Depression* (Syracuse, N.Y., 1963); Hickok, "Report on West Virginia," to Hopkins, August 16–26, 1933.

27. Francis, Uniontown, Pennsylvania, to Hopkins, November 10, 1934, Box 65, HP.

28. See Bernard Sternsher, *Rexford Tugwell and the New Deal* (New Brunswick, N.J., 1964); Joseph Arnold, *New Deal in the Suburbs: A History of the Greenbelt Towns Program. 1935–1954* (Columbus, Ohio, 1971); Paul Conkin, *Tomorrow a New World: The New Deal Community Program* (Ithaca, N.Y., 1959); Ball, "FERA Survey Report," to Hopkins, December 19, 1934.

29. Francis, Clarksburg, West Virginia, to Hopkins, November 25, 1934, Box 65, HP.

30. Ball, "FERA Survey Report," to Kathryn Godwin, Washington, D.C., October 29, 1934, Box 65, HP.

31. Francis, Williamson, West Virginia, to Hopkins, December 7, 1934.

32. Francis, Morgantown, West Virginia, to Hopkins, November 18, 1934.

Stricken Hamlets: Economic Hardship and Poverty in America's Agricultural Communities

1. For accounts of the agricultural distress, see, among others, John D. Hicks and Theodore Saloutos, *Agricultural Discontent in the Middle West* (Madison, Wis., 1951); Edward L. and Frederick H. Schapsmeier, *Henry A. Wallace of Iowa:*

The Agrarian Years 1910–1940 (Ames, Iowa, 1968); John L. Shover, *Cornbelt Rebellion* (Urbana, Ill., 1965); and Gilbert C. Fite, *George N. Peek and the Fight for Farm Parity* (Norman, Okla., 1954).

2.   Richard S. Kirkendall, *Social Scientists and Farm Politics in the Age of Roosevelt* (Columbia, Mo., 1966), pp. 255–261; Edmund deS. Brunner and J. H. Kolb, "Published Under the Direction of the President's Research Committee on Social Trends," *Rural Social Trends* (New York, N.Y., 1933), p. 60; Dwight Sanderson, *Rural Life in the Great Depression* (New York, N.Y., 1937), pp. 2–3; William H. Peterson, *The Great Farm Problem* (Chicago, Ill., 1959), p. xvi.

3.   Robert H. Wiebe, *The Search for Order, 1877–1920* (New York, N.Y., 1967), p. 122; Brunner and Kolb, *Rural Social Trends*, pp. 44–47, 60; Sanderson, *Rural Life*, p. 5.

4.   John L. Shover, "The Communist Party and The Midwest Farm Crisis of 1933," *Journal of American History*, LI, 2 (September 1964), 248–263.

5.   Memorandum, Mr. Tetreau to Corrington Gill and Mr. Mayers, April 2, 1934, Box 11, Old Subject File, NA.

6.   Lorena Hickok, "Field Report: New York State, Outside the Metropolitan Area, September 12–19 Inclusive," to Hopkins, Box 11, LHP.

7.   Hickok, "Field Report: Maine, September 21–29, 1933," to Hopkins, Box 11, LHP.

8.   Hickok, Dickinson, North Dakota, to Hopkins, October 30, 1933, Box 11, LHP; T. J. Edmonds, (town unspecified), Missouri, to Hopkins, November 25–27, 1933, Box 406, Field Reports: North Dakota, NA.

9.   Hickok, Minot, North Dakota, to Hopkins, November 1, 1933, Box 11, LHP.

10.   *Ibid.*; Pierce Atwater, (location unspecified), to Hopkins, January 10, 1935, Box 406, Field Reports: North Dakota, NA.

11.   Clarence King, (town unspecified), Montana, to Hopkins, March 12, 1934, Box 406, Field Reports: Montana, NA.

12.   Hickok, Bismarck, North Dakota, to Hopkins, November 3, 1933, Box 11, LHP; Hickok, Hibbing, Minnesota, to Hopkins, December 8, 1933, Box 11, LHP.

13.   Hickok, "Field Report: New York State, September 12–19, 1933," to Hopkins, Box 11, LHP.

14.   Hickok, "Field Report: Maine, September 21–29, 1933," to Hopkins, Box 11, LHP.

15.   Pierce Williams, (location unspecified), to Hopkins, April 9, April 16, 1934, Field Reports: Idaho, NA; Edmonds, Bismarck, North Dakota, to Aubrey Williams, Washington, July 23, 1934, Box 406, Field Reports: North Dakota, NA.

16.   Hickok, Minot, North Dakota, to Hopkins, November 1, 1933; Hickok, Sioux City, Iowa, to Hopkins, November 23, 1933, Box 11, LHP.

17.   Edmonds, (town unspecified), Missouri, to Hopkins, Washington, November 25–27, 1933, Box 406, Field Reports: North Dakota, NA.

18.   Hickok, Bismarck, North Dakota, to Hopkins, November 3, 1933.

19.   Hickok, Pierre, South Dakota, to Hopkins, November 9, 1933, Box 11, LHP.

20.   Hickok, Dickinson, North Dakota, to Hopkins, October 30, 1933; Hickok, Minot, North Dakota, to Hopkins, November 1, 1933, Box 11, LHP.

21. Edmonds, Bismarck, North Dakota, to Aubrey Williams, Washington, July 18, 1934, Box 406, Field Reports: North Dakota, NA.

22. Benjamin Glassberg, Helena, Montana, to Aubrey Williams, Washington, March 20, 1934, Field Reports: Montana, N.A.; Edmonds, Pocatello, Idaho, to Hopkins, December 30, 1934, Box 406, Field Reports: Idaho, NA.

23. Shover, *Cornbelt Rebellion*, p. 66.

24. Pierce Williams, Boise, Idaho, to Hopkins, December (?), 1933, Field Reports: Idaho, NA; J. C. Lindsey, Boise, Idaho, to John M. Carmody, Washington, April 18, 1934, Box 406, Field Reports: Idaho, NA.

25. Hickok, Sioux City, Iowa, to Hopkins, November 23, December 4, 1933; Hickok, Aberdeen, South Dakota, to Hopkins, November 7, 1933; Hickok, Winner, South Dakota, to Hopkins, November 10, 1933; Hickok, Brainerd, Minnesota, to Hopkins, December 7, 1933, Box 11, LHP.

26. Hickok, Sioux City, Iowa, to Hopkins, November 23, December 4, 1933; Hickok, Ortonville, Minnesota, to Hopkins, November 6, 1933, Box 11, LHP.

27. Hickok, "Field Report: New York State, Outside the Metropolitan Area, September 12–19 Inclusive," to Hopkins; Hickok, South Sioux City, Nebraska, to Hopkins, November (?), 1933, Box 11, LHP.

28. See Kirkendall, *Social Scientists and Farm Politics*, and Paul H. Johnstone, *Farmers in a Changing World, Yearbook of Agriculture*, 1940 (Washington, D.C., 1940).

The South: A Saga of Despair and Hope

1. Among many accounts of rural Southern poverty, see Paul E. Mertz, *New Deal Policy and Southern Rural Poverty* (Baton Rouge, La., 1978).

2. George B. Tindall, *The Emergence of the New South 1913–1945* (Baton Rouge, La., 1967), pp. 369–375.

3. Wilbur J. Cash, *The Mind of the South* (New York, N.Y., 1941); for an account of Cash's work, see Joseph L. Morrison, *W. J. Cash: Southern Prophet* (New York, N.Y., 1967).

4. See Rupert B. Vance, *Human Geography of the South* (Chapel Hill, N.C., 1932).

5. See Howard W. Odum, *Southern Regions of the United States* (Chapel Hill, N.C., 1936).

6. See Richard S. Kirkendall, *Social Scientists and Farm Politics in the Age of Roosevelt* (Columbia, Missouri, 1966).

7. Frank Freidel, *F.D.R. and the South* (Baton Rouge, La., 1965), pp. 2–10.

8. Alan Johnstone, Newberry, South Carolina, to Harry L. Hopkins, September 18, 1933, Box 406, NA.

9. Lorena Hickok, Athens, Georgia, to Hopkins, January 11, 1934, Box 11, LHP.

10. Hickok, Augusta, Georgia, to Hopkins, January 14, 1934, Box 11, LHP.

11. Hickok, Athens, Georgia, to Hopkins, January 11, 1934; Hickok,

Moultrie, Georgia, to Hopkins, January 23, 1934, Box 11, LHP; Johnstone, New-berry, South Carolina, to Hopkins, September 18, 1933.

12. Martha Gellhorn, Greenville, South Carolina, to Hopkins, November 18, 1934, Box 66, HP.

13. Hickok, Jesup, Georgia, to Hopkins, January 16, 1934, Box 11, LHP; Hickok, Daytona Beach, Florida, to Hopkins, January 31, 1934; Hickok, Augusta, Georgia, to Hopkins, January 14, 1934.

14. Hickok, Moultrie, Georgia, to Hopkins, January 23, 1934; Hickok, Athens, Georgia, to Hopkins, January 11, 1934.

15. Hickok, New Orleans, Louisiana, to Hopkins, April 7, 1934, Box 11, LHP.

16. Hickok, Raleigh, North Carolina, to Hopkins, February 14, 1934, Box 11, LHP.

17. Hickok, Moultrie, Georgia, to Hopkins, January 23, 1934; Hickok, Athens, Georgia, to Hopkins, January 11, 1934.

18. Hickok, Columbia, South Carolina, to Hopkins, February 5, 1934, Box 11, LHP.

19. Hickok, New Orleans, Louisiana, to Hopkins, April 7, 1934; Hickok, Raleigh, North Carolina, to Hopkins, February 14, 1934, Box 11, LHP.

20. Ibid.

21. Johnstone, Atlanta, Georgia, to Hopkins, June 21, 1934, Box 406, Field Reports: Tennessee, NA.

22. Hickok, Augusta, Georgia, to Hopkins, January 14, 1934; Hickok, Jesup, Georgia, to Hopkins, January 16, 1934.

23. Hickok, Charleston, South Carolina, to Hopkins, February 8, 1934; Hickok, Greensboro, North Carolina, to Hopkins, February 18, 1934, Box 11, LHP.

24. Hickok, Moultrie, Georgia, to Hopkins, January 23, 1934; Hickok, Tallahassee, Florida, to Hopkins, January 24, 1934, Box 11, LHP. For a discussion of these people, see J. Wayne Flint, *Dixie's Forgotten People: The South's Poor Whites* (Bloomington, Ill., 1979).

25. Johnstone, Atlanta, Georgia, to Hopkins, June 21, 1934.

26. Martha Gellhorn, Greenville, South Carolina, to Hopkins, November 18, 1934, Box 66, HP; Hickok, Miami, Florida, to Hopkins, January 29, 1934, LHP.

27. Edward J. Webster, "Final Report of Observations in St. Louis, Kansas City, et al. . . ," to Hopkins, December 8, 1934, Box 67, HP.

28. Hickok, Greenville, South Carolina, to Hopkins, February 7, 1934; Hickok, Miami, Florida, to Hopkins, January 28, January 29, 1934, Box 11, LHP; Johnstone, Atlanta, Georgia, to Hopkins, June 21, 1934.

29. Hickok, Miami, Florida, to Hopkins, January 29, 1934.

30. Webster, "Final Report . . . ," to Hopkins, December 8, 1934.

31. Gellhorn, Greenville, South Carolina, to Hopkins, November 18, 1934.

32. Hickok, Florence, Alabama, to Hopkins, June 6, 1934, Box 11, LHP. For an insider's version of the early TVA, see, among others, Arthur E. Morgan, *The Making of the TVA* (Buffalo, N.Y., 1974).

Trouble in America's Eden: Hard Times in the West

1. Howard W. Odum and Harry Estill Moore, *American Regionalism: A Cultural-Historical Approach to National Integration* (New York, N.Y., 1938), 550; for a recent work on the West during the Roosevelt Era, see Richard Lowitt, *The New Deal and the West* (Bloomington, Indiana, 1984).

2. For an account of the distress in the West, see, among others, John Braeman, Robert H. Bremner, and David Brody, eds., *The New Deal: The State and Local Levels*, vol. II (Columbus, Ohio, 1975); also see a series of articles, "The New Deal in The West," *Pacific Historical Review*, XXXVII, 3 (August 1969), 249–327.

3. Among books describing the Dust Bowl, see Donald Worster, *Dust Bowl: The Southern Plains in the 1930s* (New York, N.Y., 1979).

4. Lorena Hickok, Denver, Colorado, to Harry Hopkins, June 17, 1934, Box 11, LHP.

5. Hickok, Cheyenne, Wyoming, to Hopkins, September 9, 1934, Box 11, LHP.

6. Hickok, Winnemuca, Nevada, to Aubrey Williams, Washington, D.C., August 24, 1934, Box 11, LHP. (Hopkins spent the better part of July and August in Europe and while he was away, Williams served as acting administrator of FERA.)

7. Hickok, Salt Lake City, Utah, to Hopkins, September 2, 1934, Box 11, LHP.

8. Pierce Williams, Sacramento, California, to Hopkins, December (?), 1933, Box 406, NA.

9. Edward J. Webster, "Final Report of Observations in St. Louis, Kansas City, et al . . . ," to Hopkins, December 8, 1934, Box 67, HP; Hickok, San Antonio, Texas, to Hopkins, April 17, 1934, Box 11, LHP; Williams, Albuquerque, New Mexico, to Hopkins, (date unspecified), Box 406, NA.

10. Hickok, Salt Lake City, to Hopkins, September 1, 1934, Box 11, LHP.

11. Hickok, San Francisco, California, to Aubrey Williams, Washington, D.C., August 17, 1934, Box 11, LHP.

12. Hickok, Reno, Nevada, to Aubrey Williams, Washington, D.C., August 20, 1934, Box 11, LHP; Hickok, Los Angeles, California, to Hopkins, July 1, 1934, Box 11, LHP.

13. Webster, "Final Report . . . ," to Hopkins, December 8, 1934.

14. Hickok, San Antonio, Texas, to Hopkins, April 17, 1934; Hickok, Salt Lake City, Utah, to Hopkins, September 2, 1934.

15. Hickok, Los Angeles, California, to Hopkins, July 1, 1934, Box 11, LHP; Hickok, San Francisco, to Aubrey Williams, Washington, D.C., August 17, 1934, Box 11, LHP.

16. Hickok, Phoenix, Arizona, to Hopkins, May 4, 1934, Box 11, LHP; Webster, "Final Report . . . ," to Hopkins, December 8, 1934.

17. Hickok, Phoenix, Arizona, to Hopkins, May 4, 1934.

18. Hickok, Albuquerque, New Mexico, to Hopkins, April 25, 1934, Box 11, LHP.

19. Williams, Sacramento, California, to Hopkins, December (3), 1933, Box 406, NA.

20. Hickok, Phoenix, Arizona, to Hopkins, May 6, 11934, Box 11, LHP.

21. Hickok, Los Angeles, California, to Hopkins, June 25, 1934, LHP; Hickok, Reno, Nevada, to Aubrey Williams, Washington, August 20, 1934.

22. Hickok, Albuquerque, New Mexico, to Hopkins, April 25, 1934.

23. Ibid.

24. Hickok, San Antonio, Texas, to Hopkins, April 17, 1934.

25. Clarence King, (location unspecified), to Hopkins, March 12, 1934, Box 406, Field Reports: Montana and Washington, NA; Hickok, Los Angeles, California, to Hopkins, July 1, 1934.

26. Hickok, Rock Springs, Wyoming, to Hopkins, September 3, 1934, Box 11, LHP.

27. Hickok, Los Angeles, California, to Hopkins, June 25, 1934; Hickok, Bakersfield, California, to Aubrey Williams, Washington, D.C., August 15, 1934, Box 11, LHP; Hickok, Rock Springs, Wyoming, to Hopkins, September 3, 1934, Box 11, LHP.

28. Webster, "Final Report . . . ," to Hopkins, December 8, 1934; Hickok, "En Route to Washington," to Hopkins, May 8, 1934; Hickok, En Route to Los Angeles, California," to Hopkins, June 23, 1934, Box 11, LHP.

29. Hickok, Bakersfield, California, to Aubrey Williams, Washington, D.C., August 15, 1934.

30. Ibid.

Sources

■ Hopkins and his reporters, whose writings comprise the grist of this study, worked and wrote in the midst of the Great Depression. Several studies, some contemporaneous, were invaluable for understanding this context. The standard works on the Great Depression and the New Deal are well known; among them are Broadus Mitchell, *Depression Decade: From the New Era through the New Deal, 1929–1941* (New York, N.Y., 1966); William F. Leuchtenburg, *Franklin D. Roosevelt and the New Deal* (New York, N.Y., 1963); and Robert S. McElvaine, *The Great Depression: America, 1929–1941* (New York, N.Y., 1984). The monumental contributions to Great Depression and New Deal scholarship of Arthur Schlesinger Jr., Frank Freidel, and John Morton Blum have also been profitably consulted.

Graphic and poignant contemporary descriptions of the jobless and their plight can be found in James M. Williams, *Human Aspects of Unemployment and Relief* (Chapel Hill, N.C., 1933), and Ewan Clague and Webster Powell, *Ten Thousand Out of Work* (Philadelphia, Pa., 1933). Recent studies examine particular aspects of the Great Depression and relief. See Janet Poppendieck's *Breadlines Knee-Deep in Wheat: Food Assistance in the Great Depression* (New Brunswick, N.J., 1986), and Joan M. Crouse, *The Homeless Transient in the Great Depression: New York State, 1929–1941* (Buffalo, N.Y., 1986).

The jobless as well as the reporters dispatched by Hopkins to report on conditions in America lived in a nation whose values and norms were shaped by consumerism, a maturing industrialism, and an uncertainty about the place of the individual and individualism in a mass society. The late Warren I. Susman, in his *Culture As History: The Transformation of American Society in the Twentieth Century* (New York, N.Y., 1984), and Caroline Bird, in *The Invisible Scar* (New York, N.Y., 1966), afford keen, and sometimes brilliant insights into the culture of the 1930s. A recent collection of essays, Stephen W. Baskerville and Ralph Willet, eds., *Nothing Else to Fear: New Perspectives on America in the Thirties* (Manchester, England, 1985) contributes further to our understanding of the 1930s.

The evolution of public relief, a prominent theme in all the reports, and Hopkins's role in that development is described by a contemporary, Josephine Brown, in *Public Relief: 1929–1939* (New York, N.Y., 1940), as well as by William W. Bremer in "Along the American Way: The New Deal Work Relief Programs for the Unemployed," *The Journal of American History*, LXII, 3 (December 1975), and Irving Bernstein, in *The Caring Society: The New Deal, the Worker, and the Great Depression* (Boston, Mass., 1985). In her *The Civil Works Administration, 1933–1934: The Business of Emergency Employment in the New Deal* (Princeton, N.J., 1984), Bonnie Fox Schwartz provides a definitive study of the significance of the short-lived CWA, focusing on the conflicting ideas about work and relief held by engineers and social workers. Albert U. Romasco's *The Politics of Recovery: Roosevelt's New Deal* (New York, N.Y., 1983) is also largely devoted to relief programs in the early New Deal and claims that their objectives were almost totally political. A new study by Phoebe Cutler, *The Public Landscape of the New Deal* (New Haven, Conn., 1985), examines how New Deal work relief projects helped change the very appearance of America. On Hopkins, see Searle Charles, *Minister of Relief: Harry Hopkins and the Depression* (Syracuse, N.Y., 1976), and George McJimsey's new biography, *Harry Hopkins: Ally of the Poor and Defender of Democracy* (Cambridge, Mass., 1987).

Little biographical information exists for most of the reporters. Because several of Hopkins's reporters had authored or would later author books, some data on their lives appeared in cyclopedic volumes such as Stanley Jasspon Kunitz, ed., *Twentieth Century Authors* (New York, N.Y., 1942) and Harry Redkey Warfel, ed., *American Novelists of Today* (New York, N.Y., 1973). The biographical data on the catalog cards in the Library of Congress, Washington, D.C., proved extremely useful. Further information was obtained from a perusal of their often obscure written works.

Information was readily available on Lorena Hickok and Martha Gellhorn. Richard Lowitt and Maurine Beasley included biographical information on Hickok in *One Third of a Nation* (Urbana, Ill., 1981). Doris Faber's study *The Life of Lorena Hickok: E.R.'s Friend* (New York, N.Y., 1980) is illuminating. Ishbel Ross discussed Hickok in *Ladies of the Press* (New York, N.Y., 1936). Martha Gellhorn's life can be rather clearly glimpsed in Warfel's *American Novelists* and Kunitz's *Twentieth Century Authors*, in reviews of her books in the *New York Times*, and in biographies of her ex-husband, Ernest Hemingway, such as Carlos Baker's *Ernest Hemingway: A Life Story* (New York, N.Y., 1969). Considerable attention is also paid Gellhorn in Bernice Kert's *Hemingway Women* (New York, N.Y., 1983).

Until his papers are fully assembled in Maine, Lincoln Colcord's life must be pieced together from fragmentary evidence. Apparently, Colcord's papers say nothing about his tour of duty with Harry Hopkins. Nevertheless, a limited amount of biographical information on the author's life appears in Walter Muir Whitehill's *Analecta Biographica: A Handful of New England Portraits* (Brattleboro, Vermont, 1930), and Christopher Lasch, *The New Radicalism in America: The Intellectual As a Social Type, 1889–1963* (New York, N.Y., 1965).

Bits and pieces of information on the other reporters had to be gleaned from obituaries where they were available, and from the sparse information that Hopkins recorded on "Distribution of Survey Cards," found in the Hopkins Papers, Franklin D. Roosevelt Library, Hyde Park, New York.

Several historical works help erect a context to illuminate the reporters' foray into the depressed neighborhoods of urban America. Charles H. Trout's *Boston: The Great Depression and the New Deal* (New York, N.Y., 1971) describes the unemployment, housing evictions, hunger, and relief efforts in Boston. New York during the Great Depression is examined in William W. Bremer's *Depression Winters: New York Social Workers and the New Deal* (Philadelphia, Pa., 1984). For Philadelphia, see Bonnie Fox Schwartz, "Unemployment Relief in Philadelphia, 1930–1932," *Pennsylvania Magazine of History and Biography*, 92 (June 1969), and John F. Bauman, "The City, the Depression, and Relief: The Philadelphia Experience, 1929–1939," Ph.D. dissertation, Rutgers University, 1969. Raymond Koch looks at the Great Depression in Minneapolis in "Public Relief in Minneapolis During the 1930s," *Minneapolis History*, 42 (Winter 1968). For the Great Depression in a southern city, see Roger Biles, *Memphis in the Great Depression* (Knoxville, Tenn., 1986). Clark Chambers's *Seedtime of Reform: American Social Service and Social Action, 1918–1933* (Ann Arbor, Mich., 1967) also contains information on the severity of the depression in urban America. Some of the best portraits of the economic deprivation in American cities come from contemporary descriptions. See Mauritz A. Hallgren's *Seeds of Revolt: A Study of American Life and the Temper of the American People During the Depression* (New York, N.Y., 1933). *Survey Magazine*, the journal of the National Conference on Social Work, contained scores of case studies of the problem of joblessness and relief in urban America.

Labor militance and the organizations of the political left in American cities during the Great Depression are described in several works, including Bernard Karsh's "The Impact of the Political Left," in Milton Derber and Edwin Young, eds., *Labor and the New Deal* (Madison, Wis., 1961), and Daniel J. Leab, "United We Eat: The Creation and Organization of the Unemployed Councils in 1930," *Labor History*, 8 (Fall 1967). Irving Bernstein's *The Lean Years: A History of the American Worker, 1920–1933*

(Boston, Mass., 1960) and *Turbulent Years: A History of the American Worker, 1933–1941* (Boston, Mass., 1969) provide solid information on the role of labor and labor organizing during the 1930s.

Alarmed by the severity of the Great Depression and the effect of joblessness on family life, scholars have subjected the family to intense scrutiny. Among the most useful contemporary studies of the family and the Great Depression are Mirra Komorovsky, *The Unemployed Man and His Family: The Effect of Unemployment Upon the Status of the Man in Fifty-nine Families* (New York, N.Y., 1940); Marion Elderton, ed., *Case Studies of Unemployment* (Philadelphia, Pa., 1931); John M. Williams, *Human Aspects of Unemployment and Relief: With Special Reference to the Effects of the Depression on Children* (Chapel Hill, N.C., 1933); and, of course, Robert S. Lynd and Helen Merrell Lynd, *Middletown in Transition: A Study of Culture Conflicts* (New York, N.Y., 1937). Both Clinch Calkins in *Some Folks Won't Work* (New York, N.Y., 1930) and Ewan Clague and Webster Powell in *Ten Thousand Out of Work* (Philadelphia, Pa., 1933) discuss how joblessness affected family functioning. William Graebner in "The Unstable World of Benjamin Spock: Social Engineering in a Democratic Culture, 1917–1950," *Journal of American History*, 67 (December 1980), and Wandersee Bolin in "The Economics of Middle-Income Family Life: Working Women During the Great Depression," *Journal of American History*, 65 (June 1978), offer especially valuable insights into the changing nature of the American family in the 1930s.

Relatively little has been written about the Great Depression, joblessness, and relief in America's many small industrial towns. In fact, the FERA reports may be a significant source of social and economic data on the small-town dimension of the Great Depression. Thomas H. Coode and John F. Bauman's *People, Poverty and Politics: Pennsylvanians During the Great Depression* (Lewisburg, Pa., 1981) examines the Great Depression in small Pennsylvania agricultural and industrial communities. George T. Blakey's *Hard Times and the New Deal in Kentucky, 1929–1939* (Lexington, Ky., 1986) focuses on the achievements of the state and federal agencies, but also contains information on poverty and relief in Kentucky towns. Thomas H. Coode's *Bugdust and Blackdamp: Life and Work in the Old Coal Patch* (Rices Landing, Pa., 1986), examines depression hardships in small Pennsylvania mining communities.

Significantly, New Dealers such as Rexford Tugwell hoped to revitalize small-town life and engineer a reversal of the rural-to-urban trend that since the 1870s had been swelling city populations. The story of the New Deal Greenbelt and Resettlement Administration program which attempted to revive small-town living is told by Joseph Arnold in *New Deal in the Suburbs: A History of the Greenbelt Town Program, 1935–1954* (Columbus, Ohio, 1971) and Paul Conkin in *Tomorrow a New World: The New Deal*

Community Program (Ithaca, N.Y., 1959). See also Daniel Schaffer, *Garden Cities for America: The Radburn Experience* (Philadelphia, Pa., 1980).

Contemporary accounts of the long distress of the American farmer include Dwight Sanderson, *Rural Life in the Great Depression* (New York, N.Y., 1937), and Edmund deS. Brunner and J. H. Kolb's work published under the direction of the President's Research Committee on Social Trends, *Rural Social Trends* (New York, N.Y., 1933). Historians have not been remiss in describing the farmers' plight. The works of Edward L. and Frederick H. Schapsmeier's *Henry A. Wallace of Iowa: The Agrarian Years, 1910–1940* (Ames, Iowa, 1968), and Gilbert C. Fite's *George N. Peek and the Fight for Farm Parity* (Norman, Okla., 1954) provide interesting and useful profiles of farm leaders and New Deal agricultural programs. Richard S. Kirkendall's *Social Scientists and Farm Politics in the Age of Roosevelt* (Columbia, Mo., 1966) is essential. The books of John D. Hicks and Theodore Saloutos are well known; the final contribution of the latter, *The American Farmer and the New Deal* (Ames, Iowa, 1982) argues that despite administrative shortcomings and personal conflicts, farmers benefited significantly from Roosevelt's farm programs. For accounts of radical politics in rural America, see John L. Shover, *Cornbelt Rebellion* (Urbana, Ill., 1965), and Lowell K. Dyson, *Red Harvest: The Communist Party and American Farmers* (Lincoln, Neb., 1982), among others.

Besides the useful volumes on the South listed in the text notes to Chapter Seven, recent works on this topic include Michael O'Brien, *The Idea of the American South, 1920–1941* (Baltimore, Md., 1979), a discussion of Howard Odum and other southern regionalists; Richard H. King, *A Southern Renaissance: The Cultural Awakening of the American South, 1930–1955* (New York, N.Y., 1980), a psychoanalytical account of Odum, Wilbur J. Cash, and other southern writers; and James C. Cobb, *Industrialization and Southern Society, 1877–1984* (Lexington, Ky., 1984), which emphasizes industrial development in the New South. Peter Daniel's series of interpretative essays on continuity and change in the recent South, *Standing at the Crossroads: Southern Life Since 1900* (New York, N.Y., 1986), and Jack Temple Kirby's study of the rural-to-urban continuum in the South, *Rural Worlds Lost: The American South, 1920–1960* (Baton Rouge, La., 1987), are also quite useful for understanding the depression South.

Among the many histories of the Tennessee Valley Authority, see Michael T. McDonald and John Muldowny, *TVA and the Dispossessed: The Resettlement of Population in the Norris Dam Area* (Knoxville, Tenn., 1982), an account which argues that while the Authority's goals were commendable enough, its means and results were not always very pleasant.

There are, of course, many works on the New Deal and black Americans. Recent books include Harvard Sitkoff, *A New Deal for Blacks: The Emergence of Civil Rights as a National Issue*, vol. I: *The Depression Decade*

(New York, 1978); John B. Kirby, *Black Americans in the Roosevelt Era: Liberalism and Race* (Knoxville, Tenn., 1980); and Nancy J. Weiss, *Farewell to the Party of Lincoln: Black Politics in the Age of FDR* (Princeton, N.J., 1983).

On the West, Richard Lowitt's *The New Deal and the West* (Bloomington, Ind., 1984) is definitive. See also the scholarly articles in the *Pacific Historical Review* XXXVII, 3 (August, 1969), and John Braeman, Robert H. Bremner, and David Brody, eds., *The New Deal: The State and Local Levels*, vol. II (Columbus, Ohio, 1975). For an account of a western ethnic population and the Great Depression, see Thomas E. Sheridan, *Los Tusconenses: The Mexican Community in Tuscon, 1854–1941* (Tuscon, Ariz., 1986).

Index